Preparing socially responsible entrepreneurs through education.

Ronald J. Beasley

ABSTRACT

The research examines the state of social entrepreneurship curricula, that is,

programs that combine education for sustainable development and traditional business

entrepreneurialism instruction, at leading business school MBA programs in the United

States. The research seeks to contribute to understandings of how sustainable

development and entrepreneurial curriculum can be best integrated to enhance the

training of social, or sustainable development, entrepreneurs. The research shows how

sustainability leadership theories have become increasingly important to businesses and

their corporate strategies, and then focuses specifically on entrepreneurial ventures to

determine if any models of social enterprise education have been devised by experts in

the fields of business, entrepreneurship, or sustainability. This research then shows that

theories that incorporate sustainable development principles into basic business and

entrepreneurial theory do exist. The field research then examines the presence of these

social entrepreneurship-related training and resources in MBA curricula and shows that

there is still an absence of comprehensive curricula that incorporate sustainability

leadership into university-level coursework on entrepreneurship and business. The second part of the field research synthesizes the feedback of social enterprise practitioners, i.e.

individuals with an MBA from a top-rated school are involved in the creation and

running of social enterprise, on the efficacy of this training offered and at top-rated MBA

programs and on the effectiveness of the current social enterprise curricula and how to

further develop social enterprise training in these top-rated MBA programs and also in

other MBA programs.

TABLE OF CONTENTS

LIST OF TABLES

LIST OF FIGURES

Chapter 1: Introduction and Framework

Research Goals and Overview

The research examined the state of social entrepreneurship curricula, that is, programs that combine education for sustainable development (ESD) and traditional business entrepreneurialism instruction, at leading business school MBA programs in the United States. The research seeks to contribute to understandings of how sustainable development and entrepreneurial curriculum can be best integrated to enhance the training of social, or sustainable development, entrepreneurs. The goal of the research is to provide insight on how to combine insights from pedagogy relating to ESD, social enterprise, and entrepreneurship in order to create a new model curriculum for promoting social entrepreneurship at leading MBA programs. This could possibly assist MBA programs to better train social entrepreneurs to launch successful and impactful social enterprises.

The research first examined literature regarding aspects or resources deemed to be beneficial in training social entrepreneurs and then applied it to the current state of social entrepreneurship curricula in top-rated MBA programs in the United States. The literature review demonstrates the increasing demand for entrepreneurs to incorporate sustainable development concepts into their businesses models as consumers and other stakeholders are demanding higher levels of sustainability and social responsibility from the private sector.

Next, the first part of the field research examined the presence of social entrepreneurship-related training and resources in MBA curricula. This research shows that while certain business schools are embracing programs to support would-be social entrepreneurs to receive their initial comprehensive training on business creation and development, there is still an absence at many institutions in incorporating a comprehensive program of social entrepreneurship into MBA curricula. The second part of the field research synthesized the feedback of social enterprise practitioners on the usefulness of this current training on social enterprise curricula offered at top-rated MBA programs. The third part examined how these top-MBA programs can further develop social enterprise training. Conclusions from the third part of the research could also be applied to other MBA programs which wish to improve or develop social enterprise programs.

The remainder of this chapter will first define the key concepts associated with this research and then will highlight the basic structure of the research. The chapter will provide a context for the research, highlighting the rise of social entrepreneurship but the lag in training and curricula for social entrepreneurs. The chapter will also outline the three research questions and then provide a brief methodology on how each of the questions were addressed.

Research Context

The main focus of this research is the education of social entrepreneurs. The literature review demonstrates that there has been an increase in literature highlighting the importance of social entrepreneurs juxtaposed against a realization that the actual methods and models for training and mentoring these new social entrepreneurs are sparse and not fully developed by both the academic community and the business world. This research attempts to identify better methods to educate social entrepreneurs in order to advance the development of social enterprises designed to address issues related to sustainable development. Entrepreneurship and Social Entrepreneurship education can encompass many different means of instruction and occur in a wide range of settings. These methods can range from self-made individuals with little or no formal training anecdotally starting ventures in their garages to highly formalized incubator programs or multi-year degree granting courses at universities. This research focused on MBA programs in the United States, as my personal interests and experiences lie in this area, especially concerning social entrepreneurship.

Research Questions

The research questions sought to first document the prevalence of social entrepreneurship training in the curricula of top MBA programs and then add new research to the field of social entrepreneurship education by analyzing the perspectives of both social entrepreneurship practitioners, i.e., MBA alumni or current students who are currently involved in creating and running social enterprises.

Question 1.

Which resources associated with prominent academic theories regarding training social entrepreneurs do the top-rated MBA programs in the United States offer to their students?

This involved a literature review to identify relevant academic theories. This was followed by a comprehensive content analysis of wide aspects of curricula and resources at the highest-ranked MBA programs to catalog the presence of any resources identified in the literature concerning training social entrepreneurs.

Question 2.

From the perspectives of selected MBA alumni and current students involved in the creation and management of social enterprises, what is the relationship between the resources that top-rated MBA programs in the United States offer and the usefulness of these resources in reality?

To gather this information, field research was conducted, which involved interviewing a mixture of 34 MBA alumni and current students whom are all involved in social entrepreneurship ventures. Preliminary research found that nearly all of the top-MBA programs in some way highlight their school's involvement in training social entrepreneurs, or, at least, in training traditional entrepreneurs to be aware of broader issues related to sustainable development and social responsibility. The research for this question sought to collect the interviewees' perspectives on the actual depth and effectiveness of the curricula and resources promoted as social entrepreneurship or social enterprise at top-ranked MBA programs.

Question 3.

From the perspectives of selected MBA alumni and current students involved in the creation and management of social enterprises, what are ways MBA programs in the United States best train social entrepreneurs?

To gather this information, the same individuals as interviewed above were utilized. The research sought to collect first-hand accounts from social entrepreneurs on the effectiveness of their MBA educations in preparing them to lead social enterprises and any suggestions, gained from experience at school and as leaders in social enterprises, on what steps or actions these entrepreneurs believe business schools could take to better prepare MBAs for leading social ventures.

Methodological Approach: Brief Overview

This research is structured into four parts: 1) A literature/theory review on the current intersection in educational pedagogy concerning sustainable development and business and entrepreneurship curricula, specifically with the ultimate intent on identifying resources deemed to be beneficial to training social entrepreneurs, 2) an overview of the school-stated resources offered to social entrepreneurs in top-rated MBA programs, 3) an evaluation of these espoused resources by interviewing current MBA students and alumni with experience creating and running social enterprises in order to obtain their perspectives, and 4) based on academic literature coupled with the insights of the MBA students and alumni interviewed, an analysis of the strengths of current aspects of social enterprise education at certain universities and an identification of gaps and deficiencies that could be addressed to further integrate ESD and social enterprise principles into entrepreneurship training for social entrepreneurs.

In Part 1, academic literature was first used to outline current educational theories or frameworks for integrating sustainable development into entrepreneurship curricula and if any models of social entrepreneurship education have been devised by experts in the fields of business or sustainability. This involved a literature review to identify relevant academic theories.

Part 2 is a comprehensive content analysis of wide aspects of curricula and resources at the highest-ranked MBA programs to catalog the presence of any resources identified in the literature concerning training social entrepreneurs. This content analysis is designed to identify the current state of social entrepreneurship education initiatives at top-rated MBA programs, focusing on course offerings, the presence of formal training centers or incubators, and the integration of business and sustainability schools or faculties, amongst other aspects. Part 2 involved both quantitative and quantitative methods. Through the content analysis process of available materials on the curricula of top-rated MBA programs, the presence, or absence, of key tools for entrepreneurial development as identified in the literature review was documented. This data was then aggregated to present an overview of the prevalence of key characteristics in social enterprise that may be common across multiple MBA programs as well as to identify certain trends that may be on the rise. Using this information, understanding of the state of social entrepreneurship education was established, enabling suggested areas for improvement, through field research in Part 3.

Through research and networking, individuals involved in social enterprise who are willing to participate were identified, for Parts 3 and 4, conducted thirty four individual interviews with these people. These selected individuals are MBA alumni or current business school students who have launched, or are currently attempting to launch, social enterprises. The interviews were open-ended interviews with a uniform set of questions posed to each social entrepreneur. The questions were developed from theoretical best practices and identified valuable resources identified in the literature

6

review and curriculum assessment phases. The aim of these interviews was to compare what is said to be offered at business schools with the personal narratives of students and alumni at the schools. These social entrepreneurs are the individuals attempting to put theory into practice in order to create viable enterprises. These entrepreneurs' narratives were analyzed in relation to the empirical evidence gathered earlier to highlight both strengths and weaknesses in the theories surrounding social enterprise and the curricula designed to assist social entrepreneurs succeed.

By synthesizing the interviews conducted for Parts 3 and 4 and comparing them in relation to the leanings in Parts 1 and 2, I attempted to identify the best aspects of current ESD curricula for entrepreneurial education and also identify deficiencies or gaps in the curricula where ESD is not well integrated into entrepreneurial curricula. The conceptual framework presented above was developed using Maxwell (2013), Ravitch and Carl (2016), and Ravitch and Riggan (2017).

Chapter 2: Literature Review

Overview

The literature review lays the groundwork for the research by examining current educational theories or frameworks in use regarding integrating sustainable development into entrepreneurship curricula. This enquiry weaves together, under an umbrella of social entrepreneurship education, the theoretical framework of research that spans various fields and disciplines.

The literature review begins by tracing the growth of sustainable development theory from its origins in simple environmental stewardship and conservation to its transformation into a complex discipline that spans the realms of economic, social development, and environmental issues. The review then traces the evolution of sustainability in educational theories, again from early origins in teaching about environmental conservation into a topic that has now become embedded in all levels or education and across disciplines such as management, business leadership, and entrepreneurship.

Key Concepts and Terms Defined

Below is a brief synopses of key concepts and terms that are used throughout this research. These terms serve as the primary concepts throughout the literature review and each concept is detailed further in various sections of this chapter.

Sustainable Development.

The 1987 World Commission on Economic Development (WCED), known more commonly as The Brundtland Commission, released a report titled *Our Common Future* that provides the most widely accepted modern-day definition of sustainable development as "development that meets the needs of the present without compromising the ability of future generations to meet their own needs" (Brundtland, 1987, p. 41). While many may think simply of environmental concerns when sustainable development is mentioned, the Brundtland definition encompasses a broader range of social and economic issues. This wide-ranging concept, which connects the environment, societal well-being, and economic growth, is the notion envisioned when referring to sustainable development and sustainability throughout this paper.

Education for Sustainable Development.

The United Nations Educational, Scientific, and Cultural Association (UNESCO) (2017a) asserts that sustainable development cannot be achieved simply through political, economic, or technology solutions; rather people must change the way that they think and act about sustainability. This is accomplished through ESD, which enables people "to constructively and creatively address present and future global challenges and create more sustainable and resilient societies" (UNESCO, 2017a, website quote). ESD is both holistic in nature and transformational in design and addresses both learning content and outcomes, as well as pedagogy and the learning environment. ESD is designed to achieve its purpose by transforming society through altering how people perceive sustainable development and address sustainable social development in all aspects of their lives.

Sustainability Leadership.

Bendell and Little (2015) of the Institute for Leadership and Sustainability at the University of Cumbria offer this definition: "Sustainability leadership is any ethical behaviour that has the intention and effect of helping groups of people achieve environmental or social outcomes that one assesses as significant and that they would not have otherwise achieved" (p. 4). Further sections of this paper detail characteristics and traits associated with sustainability leadership and sustainability leaders.

Sustainable Development Entrepreneurship and/or Social Entrepreneurship.

The terms social entrepreneur and sustainable development entrepreneur can be used relatively interchangeably when discussing the literature since, as previously noted, sustainability refers to the interplay of environmental, economic, and social outcomes (Clifford and Dixon, 2006; Hockerts, 2006). For convenience, the term social entrepreneur is used, as later research in the paper will show that this is the most common term used by business schools to describe the discipline that integrates entrepreneurship with sustainable development.

Zahra et al. (2009) provide a comprehensive definition of social entrepreneurship as a discipline that "encompasses the activities and processes undertaken to discover, define, and exploit opportunities in order to enhance social wealth by creating new ventures or managing existing organizations in an innovative manner" (p. 519). Casasnovas (2013), drawing from Nicholas (2006), represents social entrepreneurship in the illustration below as the intersection of innovation, market orientation, and social mission.

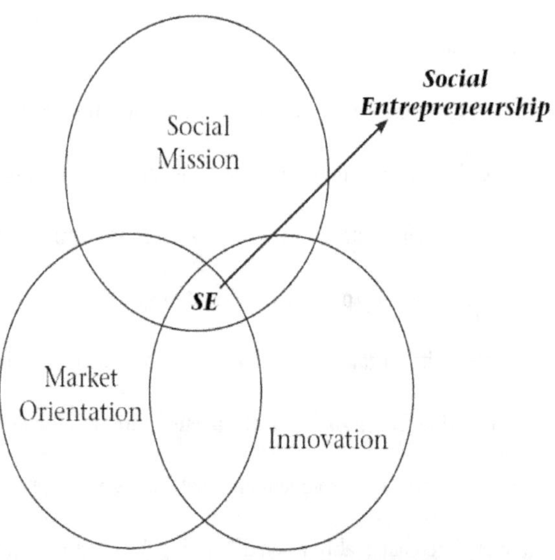

Figure 1: Social Entrepreneurship Venn diagram (Casasnovas, 2013)

The United Nations (UN) (2015) introduced the Sustainable Development Goals

(SDGs) as a roadmap to transform the world through a sustainable development agenda.

These SDGs will be addressed later in the literature review, but, for clarity of definition,

this paper will define a social enterprise as any private sector organization with a primary

focus on addressing any of these SDGs.

Outline of Topics Covered

The literature review begins with an overview of sustainable development theory,

from its roots in pure environmental conservation to its transformation into a cross-

disciplinary field. The review shows how sustainability became tied to education,

known as ESD theory. The review then traces how ESD has transformed from a purely

environmental focus into a type of leadership theory taught throughout various disciplines. The review then highlights ESD and sustainability leadership theories' roles in the growing trends in business and the private sector to adopt sustainability strategies in for-profit models instead of simply in public relations or corporate responsibility strategies. The analysis then highlights concepts associated with successful sustainability leadership, especially in the private sector. Next, the review links the successful sustainability leadership in business strategies to entrepreneurship theory as the main focus of the research will be centered on the education of social entrepreneurs. Finally, the review examines theories related to the best practices for the education of social entrepreneurs in MBA programs. There are emerging spaces in business for social entrepreneurs to thrive by implementing business models that incorporate sustainability as a driving force in a for-profit model; educating these individuals in the correct aspects of both sustainability and entrepreneurship is key to their chances for success.

In order, the major topics covered in the literature review are:

1. History of Sustainable Development and the Basics of its Principles, Objectives, and Goals

2. Origins of Education for Sustainable Development Theory

3. History and Characteristics of Sustainability Leadership Theory

4. Social Entrepreneurship: Emergence of sustainability in entrepreneurship theory

5. Definition of Social Enterprise and Social Entrepreneur Types

6. Role of the Social Entrepreneur in Promoting/Implementing Sustainable Development Strategies

7. Methods for Teaching Social Entrepreneurship Skills at Universities

8. Current State of Social Entrepreneurship Education at Universities

History of Sustainable Development and the Basics of its Principles, Objectives, and Goals

Sustainable development is a concept that has evolved from its origins in basic environmental stewardship to currently become a holistic, complex, and inter-disciplinary approach to societal and planetary wellbeing. Beynaghi et al. (2016) give a concise summary of the progression in three distinct stages:

1. Human environment: concerns for the natural environment and its conservation and preservation

2. Environment and development: concerns with human economic development that is harmful to the environment

3. Sustainable development [as we know it today]: an attempt to reconcile tensions between economic development and environmental preservation through integrating progress and de-conflicting issues related to the three dimensions of environment, economy, and society

The review below tracks how the above evolution of sustainable development principles evolved into the modern concept of sustainable development.

Concerns for the environment and humans' stewardship of the planet have existed from humankind's earliest writings, as this quotation from the Bible illustrates:

> And God blessed them, and God said unto them, Be fruitful, and multiply, and replenish the earth, and subdue it: and have dominion over the fish of the sea, and over the fowl of the air, and over every living thing that moveth upon the earth.

(Genesis 1:28, King James Version)

In more recent times, linking the environment and socioeconomic issues began to take

shape primarily in the late 20th century, driven by the supra-national organizations created

in the post- World War II era. The UN Conference on the Human Environment in

Stockholm in 1972 was one of the first forums to link the environment and

socioeconomic issues such as poverty and other development issues in the developing

world. UNESCO (2006), when highlighting the history of ESD, notes that "the concept

of sustainable development emerged in the 1980s in response to a growing realization of

the need to balance economic and social progress with concern for the environment and

the stewardship of natural resources" (pp. 12-13). The momentum then grew into the

aforementioned seminal Brundtland conference of 1987.

As stated in the introduction to the literature review, the description from

Brundtland (1987) is the most widely accepted definition of sustainable development as

"development that meets the needs of the present without compromising the ability of

future generations to meet their own needs" (p. 41). This definition is commonly utilized

by leading organizations in sustainable development such as the International Institute for

Sustainable Development (IISD) (2013), the World Bank (WB) (2001), and the UN

(Drexhage & Murphy, 2010). Some sustainable development scholars, such as Sneddon,

Howarth, and Norgaard (2005), even refer to Brundtland as the watershed moment in

sustainable development history, citing a pre-Brundtland vs. post-Brundtland world, akin

to B.C. vs. A.D. Research below shows that sustainable development moved from its

origins of a primary focus on environmental concerns to also incorporating massive world-wide initiatives surrounding basic human development, poverty reduction, economic prosperity, and health-related initiatives.

An early compact list of ultimate sustainability objectives was proposed by Robèrt et al. (2002, p. 199):

1. "Eliminate our contribution to systematic increases in concentrations of substances from the Earth's crust."

2. "Eliminate our contribution to systematic increases in concentrations of substances produced by society."

3. "Eliminate our contribution to the systematic physical degradation of nature through over-harvesting, introductions, and other forms of modification."

4. "Contribute as much as we can to the meeting of human needs in our society and worldwide, over and above all the substitution and dematerialization measures taken in meeting the first three objectives"

Although somewhat broad in nature and scope, these above objectives are also good summary of what will later be shown that many social entrepreneurship enterprises are trying to accomplish through their business models. The first three objectives seem mostly focused on the environment, but the fourth objective addresses broader social concerns for development and how to meet them in a way that does not harm society.

The UN's (2002) World Summit on Stainable Development in 2002 met and issued the Johannesburg Declaration on Sustainable Development. This declaration reaffirmed the UN's commitment to sustainability and codified the organization's commitment to what had previously been referred to as the Three Pillars of Sustainable

Development. The UNESCO (2004) further explained these pillars in their draft

manuscript for the Decade of Education for Sustainable Development (DESD). The

pillars entailed:

1. Society: how social institutions, such as governments, play a role in change

   and development

2. Environment: being aware of the fragile nature of natural resources and the

   physical environment and how it can affect human activity. Also includes a

   commitment to evaluate environmental concerns when making decisions on

   social and economic development

3. Economy: understanding that economic growth can have an impact on

   society and the environment and realizing that economic plans should be

   assessed against their societal and environmental impacts

The three pillars all are independent areas of interest but all three must be considered as

affecting each other when one is making choices or planning policies.

The UN's (2000) Millennium Development Goals (MDGs) were another set of

guidelines that governments, corporations, non-governmental organizations (NGOs),

activists, educators, and social entrepreneurs could follow in their quests promote and

achieve sustainable development outcomes. The UN stressed the importance of these

goals to address troubling factors around the world that were increasingly given more

prominence in academia and the media. Mainly, since the industrial revolution, the

standard of living and life expectancy in the developed world have increased dramatically

while the developing world was still mired in poverty and disease. This was coupled with the increasing arguments by many environmental scholars, that industrialization had

begun to leave serious, and possibly permanent, negative effects on the planet (Brown et.

al, 1995; Gottleib, 1996; Mebratu, 1998). The eight goals, adopted by the UN in 2000 at

the largest-ever gathering of world leaders, aimed to promote development, reduce

extreme poverty, foster equality, and cure diseases, amongst other targets. Below are the

actual goals:

> Goal 1: Eradicate Extreme Hunger and Poverty
>
> Goal 2: Achieve Universal Primary Education
>
> Goal 3: Promote Gender Equality and Empower Women
>
> Goal 4: Reduce Child Mortality
>
> Goal 5: Improve Maternal Health
>
> Goal 6: Combat HIV/AIDS, Malaria, and other diseases
>
> Goal 7: Ensure Environmental Sustainability
>
> Goal 8: Develop a Global Partnership for Development (UN Millennium
>
> Project,
>
> 2006)

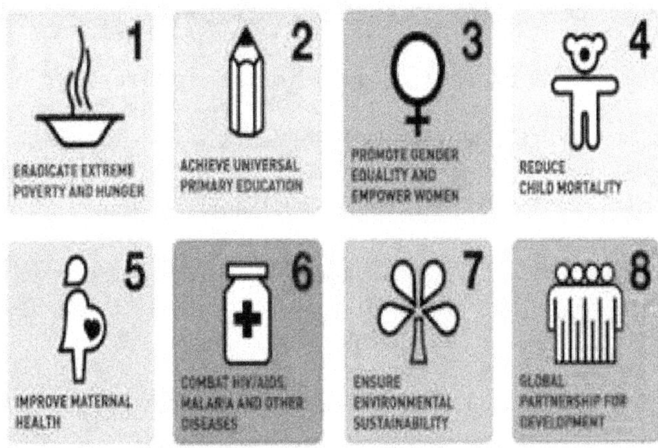

Figure 2: Millennium Development Goals (UN, 2000)

The MDG initiative was targeted to increase development and reduce poverty by

2015. As one may observe, the goals moved to address specific social issues as well as to

highlight environmental concerns, thus tying development and the environment under a

wider sustainable development umbrella. The final MDG report found that the initiative

was fairly successful over its life, reducing the number of people in extreme poverty

worldwide by 50%, increasing adult and child life expectancy, reducing diseases such as

HIV and malaria, and increasing environmental sustainability in areas such as ozone

layer protection, water safety, and sanitation, amongst others (UNDP, 2015a).

Upon completion of the MDG initiative, the UN (2015) instituted a follow-on

program titled "Transforming our word: the 2030 Agenda for Sustainable Development".

This agenda introduced seventeen Sustainable Development Goals (SDGs) to build on

and expand the MDGs over another fifteen-year period. These 17 SDGs, with 169

specific targets, have a more ambitious agenda than the MDGs, as the MDGs sought to

18

reduce poverty, while the SDGs seek to eliminate poverty entirely. The SDGs also
address concerns that were not in the MDGs, such as climate change, sustainable
consumption, and innovation (UNDP, 2015b).   A brief summary of each goal is below:

> Goal 1. End poverty in all its forms everywhere

> Goal 2. End hunger, achieve food security and improved nutrition and
> promote sustainable agriculture

> Goal 3. Ensure healthy lives and promote well-being for all at all ages

> Goal 4. Ensure inclusive and equitable quality education and promote
> lifelong learning opportunities for all

> Goal 5. Achieve gender equality and empower all women and girls

> Goal 6. Ensure availability and sustainable management of water and
> sanitation for all

> Goal 7 Ensure access to affordable, reliable, sustainable and modern
> energy for all

> Goal 8. Promote sustained, inclusive and sustainable economic growth,
> full and productive employment and decent work for all

> Goal 9. Build resilient infrastructure, promote inclusive and sustainable
> industrialization and foster innovation

> Goal 10. Reduce inequality within and among countries

> Goal 11. Make cities and human settlements inclusive, safe, resilient, and
> sustainable

> Goal 12. Ensure sustainable consumption and production patterns

Goal 13. Take urgent action to combat climate change and its impacts

Goal 14. Conserve and sustainably use the oceans, seas and marine

resources for sustainable development

Goal 15. Protect, restore and promote sustainable use of terrestrial

ecosystems, sustainably manage forests, combat desertification, and halt

and reverse land degradation and halt biodiversity loss

Goal 16. Promote peaceful and inclusive societies for sustainable

development, provide access to justice for all, and build effective,

accountable, and inclusive institutions at all levels

Goal 17. Strengthen the means of implementation and revitalize the

Global Partnership for Sustainable Development (UN, 2015).

Figure 3: Sustainable Development Goals (UN, 2015)

As noted earlier in the 'Key Terms' section, for this paper, these SDGs served as a

baseline for any organizations deemed social enterprises. A private sector organization

with a primary focus on addressing any of these SDGs is classified as a social enterprise.

Origins of Education for Sustainable Development Theory

While loosely present in the writings of some early environmental writers, ESD first came to prominence through development initiatives of the UN, especially after Brundtland, and then emerged as a unique category of academic educational theory. Unlike most significant movements in education, ESD was developed by people and organizations outside of the education community (McKeown et al., 2002). Some early environmental writers, like Schumacher (1974), who called education 'The Greatest Resource' to assist mankind in managing their natural resources in order to survive and prosper, did introduce concepts of teaching others about sustainable development; however, these concepts were tied more to economics than to education and leadership. ESD as an educational movement first began to show up in the writings of supra-national bodies, intergovernmental organizations, NGOs in relation to policy making and then developed as pedagogy in education soon afterwards with the assistance of The UN and other organizations. ESD emerged early in writings by the United Nations and other NGOs as it was a key priority for policy makers planning for economic growth amidst the backdrop of increasing worldwide sustainable development initiatives. The UN, led by UNESCO (2017a), holds that technology, political regulation, or financial instruments by themselves cannot achieve sustainable development goals. Rather, a robust education in sustainable development is required at all levels, and in in all social contexts, to produce tangible results in sustainable development.

In efforts to advance sustainable development after the 1987 Brundtland report, The UN held the 1992 Conference on Environment and Development. The conference published a guide for highlighting the role of education and training the public in sustainable development, which became known as Agenda 21. Chapter 36 of Agenda 21 listed education as critical in advancing the causes of sustainable development in order to assist people in addressing environmental and developmental issues. Agenda 21 stresses the need for ESD across all levels of schooling, from basic primary education to the highest level of university training. In the area of higher education level ESD, universities are recommended to include an environmentally-related management component in all applicable training activities and to incorporate cross-disciplinary courses into ESD. Agenda 21 also stresses the need for ESD at the post-graduate level in order to train decision makers in both the public and private sectors in sustainable development areas (UNSD, 1992).

UNESCO declared the years 2004-2015 to be the 'UN Decade of Education for Sustainable Development' (UN DESD). In its published framework for the UN DESD, UNESCO (2006) was clear to assert that ESD "should not be equated with environmental education. The latter is a well-established discipline, which focuses on humankind's relationship with the natural environment and on ways to conserve and preserve it and properly steward its resources" (p. 17). UNESCO continues to explain that ESD does encompass environmental education but is more concerned with the broader context of the three pillars of sustainable development, here now termed 'perspectives'. The three perspectives detailed in the framework are:

1. Sociocultural: to include human rights, peace and human security, gender equality, cultural diversity and intercultural understanding, health, HIV/AIDS,

and governance

2. Environmental: to include natural resources (water, energy, agriculture, biodiversity), climate change, rural development, sustainable urbanization, and disaster prevention and mitigation

3. Economic: to include poverty reduction, corporate responsibility and accountability, and market economy

Sustainable development is a complex interaction of all of the perspectives above and ESD must incorporate methods to teach the connections between all areas in order to teach a holistic curriculum on sustainable development.

The UNESCO (2006) framework stresses that ESD is designed for all peoples and all stages in life, emphasizing "lifelong learning, engaging all possible learning spaces, formal, non-formal and informal, from early childhood to adult life" (p. 5). The framework holds that ESD requires a re-examination of educational policy at all levels of education in order to develop the knowledge and skills needed to promote sustainability. ESD must be holistic and integrated into all curriculums, encompass shared values, be taught through a multi-method approach, and convey global principles that still have local relevance and cultural sensitivity. Everyone is identified as a stakeholder in ESD, from the international level actors down to local governments, as well as civil society and the private sector.

At the conclusion of the UN DESD, UNESCO (2014) released a Global Action Programme (GAP) on ESD in order to build on the achievements of ESD in the past decade and to provide a roadmap to better incorporate ESD into the priorities of non-governmental stakeholders such as higher academic institutions and the private sector. The roadmap notes that ESD must continue to move from the standalone teaching of simple environmental into a more holistic educational approach integrated throughout all curriculums. The roadmap highlights the benefits of ESD since it promotes leadership skills like "critical thinking, understanding complex systems, imagining future scenarios, and making decisions in a participatory and collaborative way" (p. 31). The UN then tasked UNESCO (2015) to highlight ESD as a driver of the SDGs and also mandated UNESCO (2017b) to lead the efforts to embed ESD into the UN's 'Global Education 2030 Agenda' (Education2030). UNESCO holds that ESD is one of the key instruments to achieve the SDGs as sustainable development begins with education since many individuals and organizations worldwide do not have the required knowledge to pair economic growth with sustainable and socially advantageous practices.

After the initial promotion of ESD by the UN and other intergovernmental organizations in the 1990s, academic writers began to incorporate sustainability concepts into educational pedagogy. ESD has evolved to become ingrained throughout most levels of educational curriculums, often supplanting the older concepts of environmental education (Dawe, Jucker, & Martin, 2005; Ferriera, Ryan, & Tilbury, 2007; Jicking & Wals, 2008). Vare and William (2007) write that "whether we view sustainable development as our greatest challenge or a subversive litany, every phase of education is now being urged to declare its support for ESD" (p. 3).

In the early 2000s, academic writers began to focus more on reforms in the education systems to better incorporate sustainability; at this time, research began to move away from earlier theories that were often centered mainly around a component of teaching students and educators on how to be better stewards for the environment to a more holistic approach to sustainable development that incorporated the three pillars of the environment, society, and the economy. Yencken and Wilkinson (2000) were early writers who expanded on a previous environmental-only focus by introducing four pillars of sustainable development: ecological, economic, equity, and political. Fien and Tilbury (2002) also make a distinction between purely environmental based education and education for sustainable leadership; the latter does include a focus on the environment but focuses on economic and social issues too. Nolet (2009) describes how ESD evolved to address the interconnectedness of the environment with both economic and social systems.

Hopkins and Mckeown (2002) wrote at length on how education is essential in moving society towards sustainability since people around the world are increasingly beginning to recognize that current trends in economic development are not sustainable. To the authors, ESD is therefore a key tool in moving society down a path to sustainability. Radu (2011) echoes the UN's call to integrate ESD into all aspects of life when he writes that ESD is "a lifelong learning perspective essential for the achievement of a sustainable society and is therefore desirable at all levels of formal education and training, as well as in non-formal and informal learning" (p. 253).

Several authors conducted extensive research into whether the UN DESD actually produced an increase in research integrating ESD into all aspects of education, especially higher education. The conclusions were that ESD research increased and began to become more integrated into higher education during the UN DESD. Barth and

Rieckmann (2013) conducted an extensive review of sustainability in international

literature, 110 journals in all, and found that research concerning ESD in higher

education began to increase steadily after 2008. Wals (2014), in evaluating the effectives

of the UN DESD, found that higher education institutions "are beginning to make more

systemic changes towards sustainability by re-orienting their education, research,

operations and community outreach activities all simultaneously" (p. 1). The author

found that, by analyzing articles in the International Journal of Sustainability in Higher

Education (IJSHE), a leading academic journal whose focus is revealed in its title, most

articles dealt with topics such as environmental management or reducing universities'

ecological footprints prior to 2010. Since 2010 however, many more articles are found

with topics such as pedagogy, learning, and instruction in sustainability. Beynaghi et al.

(2016), in evaluating ESD in a post UN DESD era, listed what they classified as distinct

phases of ESD in higher education and found that the UN DESD ushered in a new phase

where ESD, once taught as a one-dimensional environmental concept, is now a multi-

dimensional concept across disciplines and subjects. Even niche fields in higher

education saw increases in sustainability research after the UN DESD. Pipere, Veisson,

and Salite (2015) conducted a review of the Journal of Teacher Education for

Sustainability (JTEFS), a publication dealing mainly with research from the Baltics

regions, and found that the topics covered in the journal evolved and grew in similar

fashions as above during the DESD in relation to ESD, especially in higher education.

Colombo et al. (2015), when studying the field of industrial engineering education, found that ESD research increased dramatically in the field during the UN DESD and that the newer research stressed cross-disciplinary approaches and involved diverse learning methods. Brown and Sack (2015) contend that the UN DESD increased the demand for sustainability skills for Australian apprentices and trainees and therefore new research into ESD for those individuals and the specialized higher institutions that train then grew steadily during the UN DESD.

Burns, Diamond-Vaught, and Bauman (2015) tracked the evolution of sustainability education. The authors feel that the field is emerging as an interdisciplinary approach to help learners develop critical skills across many dimensions to solve the complex problem of sustainability. Similar to the skills described in the GAP roadmap mentioned above, the authors believe that ESD can create leaders who are creative problem solvers able to address the social, political, ecological, and economic issues associated with sustainability. This concept ties into the inclusion of sustainability principles into leadership theories discussed in the next section. Tilbury (2011) also found that as ESD evolves, especially in higher education institutions, the new research holds sustainability to be inter and multi-disciplinary that aims to focus on the need for social and structural change. Wals (2014) also noted that universities are introducing new learning techniques to promote ESD. These techniques recognize the complex nature of sustainability that transcends across multiple disciplines. Amongst these new learning techniques are

> many that require multi-stakeholder interaction, meaning making, negotiation,
>
> dealing with competing claims, handling diversity of perspectives (cultural,

disciplinary, socio-economic, etc.) and the resolving of real issues as they emerge in everyday life at home, in the university itself, in the community or in the work-place. (p. 5)

Sustainability Leadership

History of theory.

This section will show that ESD has slowly been integrated into leadership theory: first, in education, and then later into business and management fields, creating the sub-field of sustainability leadership. ESD, which began simply teaching about environmentalism and good environmental stewardship, eventually developed into sustainability leadership concepts with specific skill sets required to be a successful sustainability leader.

Sustainability leadership, as an actual term, is relatively new and began to surface in the beginning of the 21st century amongst North American educational researchers (Hopkins & McKeown, 2002; Hargreaves & Fink, 2003, 2004, 2005, and 2006; Fullan, 2005). The earliest origins of what can loosely be termed sustainability leadership principles evolved from purely environmental conservation concepts. Shriberg and MacDonald (2013) trace the origins of sustainability leadership from the writings of naturalists and intellectuals like Ralph Waldo Emerson and William Bartram in the 1700s and 1800s, through to the development of the modern-day environmental movement in the 1960s, and then to the current concept of an integrated realm of a combination of environmental, social, and economic issues postulated in ESD concepts.

Type of leadership traits.

Academic literature on sustainability leadership often portrays the topic as a concept or foundation of principles and not just as specific traits or characteristics associated with traditional leadership. Pepper and Wildy (2008) track how the concept of simply educating people about the environment transformed into the more complex realm of ESD, and then into sustainable leadership theories. The authors believe that the term sustainable leadership originated as theories of traditional leadership shifted to address the intense international pressure to promote sustainable development through education. The authors argue that while older, more traditional types of leadership emphasize personal strengths and characteristics, sustainability leadership theory is represented by theorists as "a concept and a strategy with foundational principles" (Pepper & Wildy, p. 616).

Bolden et al. (2003), in a comprehensive review of leadership theories over time, track the evolution of schools of thought from the "Great Man" and "Trait" theories, which focused on individuals and specific characteristics of born leaders, through to "Transactional" and "Transformational" schools, which focus on consensus leadership and interactions between leaders and followers. The authors find that, in the corporate world at least, sustainable leadership began to grow out of the transformational leadership models of corporate governance in the late 1990s as companies and organizations began to adopt more policies and programs related to corporate social responsibility and transparency. In an extensive review of university level programs designed to teach sustainability leadership, Shriberg and MacDonald (2013) found that almost all of the studied programs taught sustainability leadership as a type of transformational leadership.

Burns (2011, 2013) also found that transformational learning is the predominant

foundation for sustainable leadership pedagogical methods.

A Cambridge Institute for Sustainability Leadership (CISL) (2017) literature

review on leadership and leadership development, shown below in the table, also tracked

the evolution of leadership styles over time. Their analysis of sustainability leadership

also tied it closely to transformational leadership and stressed the complex and dynamic

nature of sustainability leadership based on the global pressures and challenges and

complex global socio-economic and environmental risks and opportunities faced by

sustainability leaders.

Theory/school	Description
Great Man or Trait school	Celebrates outstanding individual leaders (in the heroic tradition) and studies their traits or characteristics to understand their accomplishments as leaders.
Behavioural or Styles school	Describes leadership in terms of people- and task-orientation, suggesting that different combinations of these produce different styles of leadership.
Situational or Context school	Emphasises the importance of context in shaping leaders' responses to be more relationship or task motivated, or more authoritative or participative.
Contingency or Interactionist school	Proposes that leaders' influence is contingent on various factors (like positional power), which in turn determines appropriate leadership styles.
Transactional or Transformational school	Contrasts leadership as a negotiated cost-benefit exchange and as an appeal to self-transcendent values of pursuing shared goals for the common good.

Table 1: Leadership Theories (CISL, 2017)

Visser and Courtice (2011), also from CISL, write that sustainability leadership is

not a new kind of leadership, but rather is "a particular blend of leadership characteristics applied within a definitive context" (p. 4). The authors align it most with the "Contingency/Interactionist" school that is centered on the interaction between individual leaders and his/her framing context. Sustainability leadership models often stress an integration of numerous complex leadership qualities and types due to the complexity of the problem. The Akiyama, Li, and Onuki (2012) model, developed for educators on the skills that they need to teach their students, covers four quadrants of leadership: Intentional Leadership, Behavioral Leadership, Cultural Leadership, and Social or Systemic Leadership. The model lists essential knowledge, skills, and attitudes that students should develop in each of the four quadrants to become sustainability leaders both individually and collectively and on the interior and exterior. For instance, for the interior dimension, a student should have cultural and experiential knowledge and possess strong interpersonal skills while he/she should be well grounded in science and technology as well as project management and systems thinking for the exterior dimension. See Appendix 3 for details of the full model.

Austin, Stevenson, and Wei-Skillern (2006) analyzed the variables that sustainable development, or social entrepreneurs must address to lead successful ventures. Their model highlighted that these leaders must contend with other variables that traditional entrepreneurs do not necessarily consider. Below shows all of the variables that a sustainability leader must contend with to achieve positive Social Value Proposition (SVP) in his/her venture.

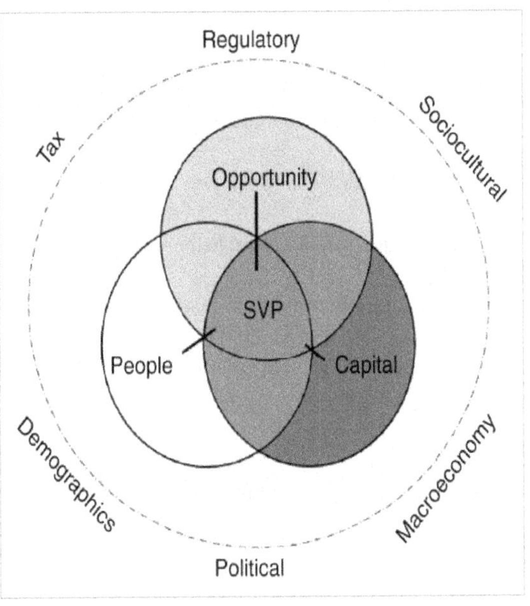

Figure 4: Variables to contend with to achieve Social Value Proposition (Austin, Stevenson, & Wei-Skillern, 2006)

Emergence in business leadership theory.

Sustainable leadership concepts began to surface in business and management theory around the late 20th century. In a speech to the Academy of Management as its President, Hambrick (1994) addressed many issues that he found with the organization and its ability to stay relevant in both the academic and corporate spheres. One goal he set was for the Academy to apply management theory to make a significant contribution to solving major problems facing society as a whole, since management theorists understand both the workings of complex organizations and the human behavior of individuals in these organizations.   Gladwin, Kenney, and Krause (1995), expanding on

32

Hambrick's speech, authored one of the earliest papers in a management journal, now

cited over 2000 times, that recognized the 'shifting paradigms for sustainable

development' and called the need to transform management theory and practice to

incorporate sustainable development principles "the greatest challenge facing the

Academy of Management" (p. 28). These authors believed that if management theorists

and their organizations were to continue to remain relevant and responsible, they needed

to promote sustainable development in order to make positive impacts on society through

business.

Just as the authors above were imploring academics to embrace sustainable

development, business leaders also began to realize its importance. Papagiannakis,

Voudouris, and Lioukas (2013) trace the process of corporate environmental strategy

over time and note that the 1990s were when managers also began to really realize how

important environmental decisions could be to a company's economic interests. The

authors recognize that as sustainable development theory and policies become more

commonplace in public discourse and government policies, companies' current

sustainable development strategies are driven by many more complex factors than simple

economic motives. DeSimone and Popoff (2000) make an early argument that there are

important economic incentives for leaders to ensure that their firms become sustainable.

The authors cite the experiences of large manufacturing companies in the 1970s, such as

Minnesota Mining & Manufacturing [now 3M] and Dow Chemical, in their efforts to cut

pollution and energy use. These companies, in addition to being seen by the public as

better corporate citizens, realized cost savings of hundreds of millions of dollars by reducing energy consumption and cutting clean-up expenses by reducing their output of pollution and toxic waste. Costs are saved through reducing materials used, energy consumed, and toxic waste created; extending product durability and enhancing the recyclability of materials produced; and maximizing the use of renewable resources. The authors termed this 'eco-efficiency' and characterized this as being able to create additional value by reducing the costs of environmental impacts while still being better able to meet customers' needs. Etzion (2007) also writes about the green success stories of such companies and how this influenced their future business practices to be more sustainable or environmentally conscious.

Metcalf and Benn (2013) discuss how authentic, ethical, and transformational leadership traits have all directly or indirectly been linked sustainability leadership as the theory for sustainability leadership grew out of corporate social responsibility (CSR) movements and theories of the later 20th century. Bansal (2005), when studying Canadian oil and gas, forestry, and mining firms, saw an early advent of CSR as these firms originally begin to integrate sustainable development into their business models first in the late 1980s due to attempts to address negative newspaper articles and other publicity related to their operations that were deemed to be harmful to the environment.

The CSR movement slowly grew and changed into the sustainable leadership principles of today. An example of the transformation can be seen by comparing the early research by Porter and van der Linde (1995a, 1995b), which made purely economic arguments that a corporation has monetary and competitive incentives to meet certain environmental goals, to the evolution of this theory that can be seen later in Porter and

Kramer's (2011) seminal work *Creating Shared Value* where the authors state that companies, not the government, must be the leaders who bring business and society back together. Kiron et al. (2015) note that corporate sustainability has moved from external public relations and addressing internal operational efficiencies to focusing on critical business issues that involve compound networks of stakeholders and undertakings. Business success can often depend on sustainability issues and therefore leaders must be well trained in this field. Zoeteman (2012) notes the transformational nature of sustainability leadership theory in the leadership traits of corporate culture.

Stiglitz, Sen, and Fitoussi (2010) note that the sustainability of the environment and its resources is closely connected to the sustainability of the business and economic cycles of growth. The overall ability to at least sustain, and possibly increase, the current level of social and economic welfare going forward is tied the ability to pass on resources, capital, and wealth to future generations. Future well-being depends on the quantity of the exhaustible resources and the quality of the renewable resources that can be passed to future generations.

Sriram, Ganes, and Madhumathi (2013) provide a detailed summary of the major characteristics of sustainable development principles in relation to business concepts. The authors noted these following seven points:

1. Businesses are complex systems with components, structures, and processes with numerous inputs and outputs, which in turn create waste. Sustainability factors into all of these areas

2. Sustainable development in business is a complex issue that can be

undertaken from the lowest to the highest levels of individual businesses to
the entire global business economy

3. Sustainable development planning horizons can be short term but extend all
the way out to several centuries

4. Sustainable development in business is affected by numerous market and
non-market related stakeholders

5. Business policy and strategy are key drivers in promoting the sustainable
development of business

6. There is both a business case and a moral case to support the promotion of
sustainable development in business

7. Business can enhance sustainable development through market, legal, and
CSR actions

When the UN began promoting its SDGs, it clearly noted the need for
businesses in the private sector, especially in the developed world, to participate. Private
sector resources are deemed as crucial partners to public sector investments in order to
promote growth, job creation, poverty eradication, and sustainability. An UNDP
discussion paper recently noted that the largest share of financing and resources to fund
the SDGs will come from the private sector (Riva & Neto, 2016). A UN Research
Institute for Social Development (UNRISD) report on promoting the SDGs notes that:

> private sector resources are crucial to complement public sector investments and
> to contribute to economic growth and job creation, as well as innovations in areas
> critical for sustainable development. Private sector actors, ranging from micro-
> enterprises to multinationals to financial sector actors, will all have an important

role to play in achieving sustainable development objectives. (Dugarova &
Gulasan, 2017, p. 68)

Social Business Model Canvas: Incorporating Social Practices into

Traditional Business Theories and Models.

The research for this study focuses on social entrepreneurs who have/will start

their own enterprises. All enterprises, whether large or small, or having been in existence

for hundreds of years or only a few days, have some sort of business model or plan.

While scholars may not agree on the specific definition of a business model, the concept

of the business model is recognized to be a key model in driving the success of a firm

(Morris, Schindehutte, & Allen, 2005; Zott, Amit, & Massa, 2011). Research later in this

paper will show that business plan development skills are seen as a key area for training

social entrepreneurs.

The "Business Model Canvas", created by Osterwalder and Pigneur (2010), is one

of the most cited recent works on the topic of business models. The authors define a

business model as describing "the rationale of how an organization creates, delivers, and

captures value" (p. 9) and stress that the concept of a business model "must be simple,

relevant, and intuitively understandable, while not oversimplifying the complexities of

how enterprises function" (p. 10). Osterwalder and Pigneur's (2010) business model

canvas look at nine "building blocks" that a business model can use "like a blueprint for a

strategy to be implemented through organizational structures, processes, and systems" (p.

10). The nine building blocks are: 1. Customer Segments, 2. Value Propositions, 3.

Channels, 4. Customer Relationships, 5. Revenue Streams, 6. Key Resources, 7. Key

Activities, 8. Key Partnerships, 9. Cost Structure. While the authors stress that their business model canvas can be used across a multitude of different organizational types and structures, there in not really any specific points that address social enterprises or sustainability focused organizations.

Scholars have recently begun to address business models that incorporate sustainability and social and economic welfare. The Center for Social Innovation at Stanford Graduate School of Business (n.d.) has taken the Business Model Canvas by Osterwalder and Pigneur (2010) mentioned above and customized it for social entrepreneurs. The Social Business Model Canvas pairs traditional market-based questions with questions related to social impact, e.g., "Who are the people who will buy your product/service?" with "Who are the people who will benefit?" Please see Appendix 4 for full details of the model.

Ludeke-Freund (2010) believes that business models that incorporate sustainability objectives can create competitive advantage in the new economic environment facing firms. Willard (2012) argues that the business case for sustainability is ever increasing and that business plans that incorporate sustainability into their strategies can see increased revenue and productivity as well as decreased risks and expenses. Schaltegger, Ludeke-Freund, and Hansen (2011) and Bocken et al. (2013) stress that a prerequisite for sustainable business models is that these models must first be economically sustainable to be viable. Bocken et al. (2013) postulate that "business model redesign may be a key to radically improve sustainable performance to create greater environmental and social value while delivering economic sustainability"

(p. 2). Joyce and Paquin (2016) build off of Osterwalder and Pigneur (2010) to develop a

"triple layered business model canvas [TLBMC]: a tool to design more sustainable

business models" (p. 1473). The "triple layers" refer to the concept of adding both and

environmental and social layers/considerations to the original business model canvas

orientated on economics. The "triple layers" also gives homage to Elkington (1997) who

coined the phrase "triple bottom-line" of people, planet, and profit to describe the trend of

ventures/companies developing strategies to address modern consumers' economic,

environmental, and social objectives. Joyce and Paquin's (2016) TLBMC develops and

integrates social and environmental layers throughout the standard business model

canvas. The authors believe that the TLBMC "has the potential to support those seeking

ways to transform organizations for sustainability" (p. 11). The TLBC could be

especially helpful to social entrepreneurs as it is designed for those individuals seeking

creative and novel approaches to innovate in the areas of sustainability and social

enterprise.

Social Entrepreneurship: Emergence of sustainability in entrepreneurship theory

The previous sections detail that sustainability began to show up in business and

management theory in the late 1990s and has since permeated through the topic. As these

principles began to flourish more in general business writings, sustainable concepts also

began to appear in the more specialized area of business entrepreneurship writings.

These next sections will address the development of the concept of an enterprise focused

predominantly or primarily on social good, and the types of entrepreneurs associated with

such organizations.

Definition of a social enterprise.

The previous section noted how CSR and sustainability concepts grew in large

traditional corporations to become important parts of business strategy. Most of these

traditional corporations still retained their original focus of offering a specific good or

service, but with an added CSR or sustainability component attached to their strategies.

In the business and academic worlds though, a newer concept of the social enterprise

began receiving more attention. The term social entrepreneurship first appeared in the

mid-1990s (Dees, 1994; Boschee, 1995; Haugh, 1995; Henton, Melville, & Walsh 1997).

Under this new discipline, social enterprises would operate generally as for-profit, or at

least hybrid, organizations, but their main good(s) or service(s) offered would be

designed to address a social or sustainability issue in society. Ebrahim, Batitilana, and

Mair (2014) concisely and accurately summarize this concept of a social enterprise when

they write:

> Social enterprises are neither typical charities nor typical businesses; rather they
> combine aspects of both. Their primary objective is to deliver social value to the
> beneficiaries of their social mission, and their primary revenue source is
> commercial, relying on markets instead of donations or grants to sustain
> themselves and to scale their operations. For these organizations, commercial
> activities are a means toward social ends. As such, social enterprises are hybrid
> organizations that combine aspects of both charity and business at their core. (p.
> 83)

Dees (1994), an early researcher on social entrepreneurship, defined social

enterprises as "private organizations dedicated to solving social problems, serving the

disadvantaged, and providing socially important goods that were not, in their judgement,

adequately provided by public agencies or private markets" (p. 4). The organizations use revenue generation and market penetration to achieve their goals. Haugh (1995)

describes social enterprises as business that trade for social purposes and whose outcomes

include both business achievements and social or sustainability goals. Isaak (1998), who

coined the term ecopreneur as "one who creates green-green businesses in order to

radically transform the economic sector in which he or she operates" (p. 81), later (2002)

wrote about the distinction between a 'green business', which is simply moving an

existing business to be environmentally friendly, and a 'green-green business', which is a

new entrepreneurial venture designed by an ecopreneur (social entrepreneur) to bring

about radical economic change in a certain sector, while still operating under free-market

principles. Stanford Graduate School of Business houses the Center for Social

Innovation. Phills, Deiglmeier, and Miller (2008), writing in the Center's journal

Stanford Social Innovation Review, highlight how social entrepreneurship had

traditionally been associated with government and non-profit initiatives but was

increasingly being tied to private sector companies and initiatives. Porter and Kramer

(2011) make a distinction between social enterprises and social programs often run by

NGOs or charities; they believe that social enterprises can scale up faster than social

programs and can have greater opportunities to create shared value. Porter and Kramer

note that the current state of social programs often prohibits growth and self-sustainment

whereas for profit ventures have better opportunities for success. The authors highlight

the role for social entrepreneurs in the new economy as social entrepreneurs are at the

forefront of creating enterprises that offer new products or services that meet social needs

but still are economically viable as a business model.

The Skoll Center for Social Entrepreneurship (2017) at Said Business School at Oxford, setup by Ebay co-founder Jeff Skoll as one of the first research centers for social entrepreneurship, defines social entrepreneurship as "practice of combining opportunity, innovation, and resourcefulness to address critical social and environmental challenges" (on website). Skoll's definition notes that social enterprise activity occurs across all fields and sectors in the modern economy. Alvord, Brown, and Letts (2004), one of the most cited earlier sources on social entrepreneurship, note that social enterprises are a catalyst for addressing development goals and societal transformation by using innovative solutions often linked to business principles.

Social Enterprise and Entrepreneur Types.

Kickul and Lyons (2016) note that finding a "uniformly accepted definition of social entrepreneurship" is problematic since academics and practitioners cannot even agree on a uniformly agreed definition of traditional entrepreneurship, thus "the latter impasse contributes to the former" (p. 16). Brock, Steinder, and Kim (2008) document thirteen different definitions of social entrepreneurship that they have observed in literature. Mair, Robinson, and Hockerts (2006) note that social entrepreneurship can encompass a fairly wide range of activities, to include:

> enterprising individuals devoted to making a difference; social purpose business ventures dedicated to adding for-profit motivations to the nonprofit sector; new types of philanthropists supporting venture capital-like 'investment' portfolios; and nonprofit organizations that are reinventing themselves by drawing on lessons learned from the business world. (p. 1)

Social entrepreneurism can be seen as growing out of the hesitancy or risk aversion of pure commercial ventures to address social problems not directly related to their business models as Hacking and Guthrie (2008) note that purely private sector proponents may "be reluctant to consider alternatives that lie outside their areas of business interest. In addition, developments by the private sector are not intended primarily to satisfy societal needs; although it is reasonable for societies to expect that they contribute to such needs" (p. 86). Casasnovas (2013) also notes a wide range of interpretations of social entrepreneurship used by researchers over the years, from one end of the spectrum, only non-profit organizations, to the other, of any for-profit organization with some sort of social mission.

Austin, Stevenson, and Wei-Skillern (2006) outline the main differences between social entrepreneurs and traditional, or 'commercial', entrepreneurs. The authors found four main areas of divergence between the two groups:

1. Market Failure: social entrepreneurs often arise when commercial entrepreneurs are unsuccessful in a market. This could be due to the fact that serving a market that is impoverished or developing is not seen to be commercially profitable through traditional means.

2. Mission: social enterprises' primary missions are to create social value whereas purely commercial enterprises' main goals are profits. This is somewhat simplified logic since commercial enterprises often do create societal benefits through their goods and services (medicine, education, safety, etc.), but the goal of commercial enterprises is primarily profit maximization.

3. Resource Mobilization: Although social enterprises can be for-profit ventures, their resource constraints, such as serving low-margin developed or

impoverished markets, means that social enterprises likely will have lower

profit margins than commercial enterprises. This will lead to issues such as

lower pay for social enterprise staff which can lead to issues in hiring the best

talent. Lower profits and margins also restrict capital markets financing

available to social enterprises.

4. Performance measurement: Since profit maximization is not the ultimate goal

of social entrepreneurs, the way that they measure their performance and

success is different from a commercial enterprise. Social entrepreneurs often

must answer to more non-financial stakeholders than commercial

entrepreneurs do.

Wry and York (2017) also address the differences between traditional and social

entrepreneurs, noting that social entrepreneurs possess a "plurality in … values and

goals" due to the need to balance both commercial logistics and social welfare promotion

(p. 3). Conger, York, and Wry (2012) note the differences in the goals that social versus

traditional entrepreneurs pursue when they write:

> Because social entrepreneurs hope to make a lasting impact and continue to
> address social and environmental problems over the long run, they should be
> more likely to pursue balanced goals than the typical commercial entrepreneur.
> This is because while a commercial enterprise can (arguably) persist over time
> without incorporating explicitly social or environmental goals, entrepreneurs
> seeking to address social or environmental issues through a new venture cannot
> survive without also pursuing economic sustainability. (p. 13)

Mort, Weerawardena, and Carnegie (2003) note the moral element of social

entrepreneurship when then describe it as

a multidimensional construct involving the expression of entrepreneurially virtuous behavior to achieve the social mission, a coherent unity of purpose and action in the face of moral complexity, the ability to recognize social value-creating opportunities and key decision-making characteristics of innovativeness, proactiveness, and risk-taking. (p. 76)

Based on the literature, social enterprises, broadly, can be split into two categories: non-profit ventures and for-profit ventures, although sometimes the two may overlap (Austin, Stevenson, & Wei-Skillern, 2006; Tracey & Phillips, 2007). The literature shows that early concepts of social entrepreneurship focused more on social good over profits, but later writings balance both goals to achieve a better state of equilibrium. Social entrepreneurship developed as an academic field as literature related to primarily to solving social issues began to appear prominently in the late 1990s with writers such as Boschee (1995, 1998), Emerson and Twerksy (1996), Leadbeater (1997), Thake and Zadek (1997), and Isaak (1998). Emerson and Twerksy (1996) wrote about combining commercial and social enterprises to achieve a social impact. Leadbeater (1997) focused his definition on entrepreneurial behavior that aim to meet social ends rather than for profit goals or ventures where profits from market related activities are used to benefit a disadvantaged group or cause. Thake and Zadek (1997) also wrote about entrepreneurs whose main drive was social justice over profit but noted that these entrepreneurs must seek to produce financially sustainable organizations in order to advance their solutions. Boschee (1998) initially defined social entrepreneurs as a new class of non-profit executives who utilize market forces to balance social mission and profit motives. Reis (1999) also narrowly classified social entrepreneurs as bringing business skills to non-profits. Thompson, Alvy, and Lees (2000), along with Mair and

Marit (2004), held social entrepreneurship as a broader category of individuals who gather together necessary resources to address unmet social issues. Mair and Marti (2004) produced one of the earliest studies of the social entrepreneurship field and cite organizations such as The Manchester Craftsman's Guild founded in 1968, The Grameen Bank founded in 1976, and Ashoka founded in 1980 as early non-profit ventures founded by entrepreneurs who attempted to integrate social and economic value.

Dees (1998) is one of the most often cited sources on the first category, non-profit or hybrid ventures, of social entrepreneurs. In his definition, the social entrepreneur is primarily focused on the social mission of his venture, not profit or wealth creation; these latter concepts are at best secondary, and often of little or no concern. The entrepreneur uses some fee related means to achieve his goal, but markets do not work well for social entrepreneurs since markets do not properly value intangible items such as social improvement or public goods. According to Dees, social entrepreneurs are just as likely to use methods such as donations, philanthropy, volunteers, grants, etc., rather than profits to operate, fund, and further their ventures. In this paper, this is not what is meant by social entrepreneur.

This research focuses on the second type of social entrepreneur: one who uses the profits or earned income of his/her venture to further their social and/or environmental cause(s). This type of social entrepreneur runs their venture like a for-profit entity and must look to exploit market opportunities when developing products and/or services that serve social ends (Boschee, 2001; Amin, Hudson, & Cameron, 2002; Oster, Massarsky, & Beinhacker, 2004). The purpose of the venture, however, is explicitly designed to further a specific social cause or multiple causes. This type of social entrepreneur, like an ordinary business executive, must utilize skills associated with operating in a free market to create, advance, and grow his/her social venture further. Zainol et al. (2014) summarize this type of social entrepreneurship very succinctly when they write "social entrepreneurship combines the passion of a social mission with an image of business-like discipline, innovation, and determination" (p. 184). When term social entrepreneur is used in this paper, it is in relation to this type of social entrepreneur.

Profit-seeking social enterprises face can face different issues from the purely non-profit ventures due to the former's reliance on the markets while still trying to deliver social benefits. Wry and Zhao (2018) discuss the tradeoffs associated between a hybrid social enterprise's financial and social goals, noting that for many enterprises, costs rise and revenues fall relative to the organization's increased focus on social benefits at the expense of market-based approaches. This can increase tension amongst the organization's stakeholders as some may prioritize social benefits over profits, and *vice versa*.

Ebrahim, Battilana, and Mair (2014) note that as social enterprises move further away from the non-profit model, there sometimes occurs a 'mission drift' towards revenue and a loss of emphasis on the organization's social mission as stakeholders become more focused on revenue and profits. There can be divergent interests between stakeholders as beneficiaries may seek further expanses in the social mission while investors or founders may seek to expand profits and returns on investment

Social Entrepreneur vs. Ecopreneur?

Earlier, it was stated that social entrepreneur and sustainable development entrepreneur, aka 'ecopreneur', can be used relatively interchangeably. Hockerts (2006) addressed whether these two terms are in fact, interchangeable. Hockerts notes that the two terms are quite similar, but that social entrepreneurship is a bit broader and traditionally covers both for-profit and non-profit type organizations, while ecopreneurship, as defined initially by Isaak (1998) and addressed by other authors (Larson, 2000; Shaltegger & Peterson, 2000; Walley & Taylor, 2002; Hockerts, 2003), often has more of a business or profit component to the organization. Hockets (2006) and Randjelovic, O'Rourke, and Orsato (2003) note that ecopreneurs may even go out of their way not to be perceived as too 'green' or 'ecological' in order to avoid deterring investors or customers; ecopreneurs have the ambition to be more like traditional business entrepreneurs than many non-profit social entrepreneurs do. Clifford and Dixon (2006), authors of several works on social and ecological entrepreneurship, also prefer the term social entrepreneur to ecopreneur, but for a different reason, as, to them, the latter seems too linguistically focused solely on environmental aspects instead of all sustainability-related issues. As the section above referenced that this paper will focus on the for-profit social entrepreneurs, it still is safe to use social entrepreneur, sustainable development entrepreneur, and ecopreneur interchangeably, as they all have basically the same goals and motivations.

Role of the Social Entrepreneur in Promoting/Implementing Sustainable Development

As the topic of this paper relates to how to better teach social entrepreneurs, it is important to address how social entrepreneurs can best promote sustainable development principles. The previous sections highlighted how ESD and sustainable development principles have developed over time to become engrained in business leadership and entrepreneurship theories. The next sections addresses the characteristics identified in literature that a sustainability leader needs to possess to be successful and how leaders can use these characteristics to promote sustainability within their organizations and to outside parties.

Individual characteristics and competencies of a successful sustainability leader.

This section highlights the concepts found in academic literature concerning the traits and characteristics that an individual must possess to become a successful sustainability leader. This review of sustainability leadership is not intended to be a comprehensive comparison and/or contrast between sustainably leadership and 'traditional' leadership, as one may see below that certain traits may overlap between the two fields. The literature presented earlier on social enterprises notes heavily that these enterprises share many similarities with traditional commercial enterprises, so one would assume that the leadership characteristics necessary to lead these two types of organizations overlap in some ways. This review, however, is designed to highlight the general traits recognized as important by literature focused on sustainability. Since sustainable development is a vast and complex field, a successful sustainability leader

must possess both strong personal leadership characteristics coupled with diverse skills

necessary to navigate intricate and often difficult environments, especially skills that

allow the leader to motivate, not compel, others to work towards a common sustainability

goal. Future sections will link these characteristics further to successful social

entrepreneurship ventures.

Visser and Courtice (2011) offer this "simple definition" of a sustainability leader

as "someone who inspires and supports action towards a better world" (p. 3). Their CISL

Model details numerous characteristics embodied by successful sustainability leaders.

The characteristics are broken down into traits, styles, skills, and types of knowledge

possessed, and while no one sustainability leader likely possesses all of the

characteristics, successful ones embody a majority of them. In addition, effective

sustainability leaders will also seek to instill and develop these qualities in others in order

to spread the sustainability message. See Appendix 1a for a full list of characteristics in

the model.

CISL (2018) released an updated leadership model in 2018, called the Cambridge

Impact Leadership Model. The model was devised because:

> Around the world, business innovation is leading to rapid and transformational
> changes in technology, consumption patterns and lifestyle aspirations. At the
> same time, societies are looking to businesses to lead change in response to urgent
> and systemic social and environmental challenges. These issues pose fundamental
> risks to the stability and wellbeing of societies, but also opportunities for
> adaptation. (p. 4)

This model incorporates sustainability leadership as a crucial area of overall business

leadership because business as usual is changing, as companies are now required by society to provide solutions to social and environmental challenges. These solutions however can provide new areas for business growth though. Because of the above changes to society's demands on business, business leaders and leadership theory must also adapt. The CISL (2018) model is one that specially notes that sustainability leadership is quite different from other leadership theories and that "traditional leadership frameworks and approaches do not yet acknowledge global challenges and do not equip leaders to navigate them" (p. 7). The model goes on to suggest that "in a significant number of businesses, Board members and management teams were most out of touch with the new context" (p.10). The model highlights the need to incorporate sustainably leadership principles throughout the organization in both its structure and goals and to be able to collaborate across the organization and with external stakeholders to promote and implement these goas and strategies. See Appendix 1b for a full list of characteristics in the model.

Burns et al. (2015) refer to sustainability leaders as "committed change agents, involved in work that reflects an emerging way of being that is rooted in interconnectedness, relationships, and mindfulness" (p. 133). Sustainability leaders take action and conduct their lives based on their values. Missimer and Connell (2012) conducted an extensive review of sustainability development leadership skills found in academic writings and also valued by international organizations and mapped the prevalence of these skills across numerous models. Skills such as systems thinking, teamwork, communication, motivating others, and practical problem solving were found in a majority of the models of successful sustainability leadership. See Appendix 2 for a full list of characteristics in the model.

Ferdig (2007) notes that sustainability leadership is a concerted effort by leaders to hold themselves as well as their organizations accountable for their impact on the planet, society, and the wellbeing of the local and global economies. She sees sustainability leadership as an effort to challenge entrenched human behaviors that for so long tended to ignore the harmful impacts of human habits. Ferdig suggests that sustainability leadership is a more nuanced concept than leadership in relatively stable environments since it must occur in a constantly dynamic and unpredictable environment. She notes the sustainability leaders may not be able to provide all of the answers to a problem but their best qualities may be the ability to "create opportunities for people to come together and generate their own answers" (p. 7). Ferdig feels that sustainability leadership empowers inherent leadership traits that can be found in almost all people and she believes that "anyone who takes responsibility for understanding and acting upon complex sustainability challenges qualifies as a 'sustainability leader' whether or not they hold formal leadership position or acknowledged political and social-economic influence" (p. 8). People do not have formal positions of leadership or power in society to be a successful sustainability leader.

Pepper and Wildy (2008) note that sustainable leadership principles are based on one wanting to achieve more than just personal goals, but goals that also matter to others and goals that can create a permanent or lasting legacy. The leader can use these goals to motivate others to work to achieve the end state. Newman-Storen (2014) argues that sustainability is predominately a path towards change and therefore leadership is key to sustainability since change requires strong and complex leadership. She believes that sustainability leaders are creative leaders who look at problems as a greater system, instead of just as individual elements, in order to find new or creative ways to solve pressing issues. Benn and Metcalf (2012) state that sustainability leadership "requires leaders of extraordinary abilities. These are likely to be leaders who can read and predict through complexity, can think through complex problems, engage groups in dynamic adaptive organisational change and can manage emotion appropriately" (p. 381). Dartey-Baah (2014) lists as key attributes of a leader for sustainability, not only the ability to control people and manage tasks efficiently, but more importantly an ability to be visionary and see problems as a complex combination of related issues instead of individually.

Timmer, Buckler, and Creech (2008) hold that many young people acquire some understanding of sustainability issues through the modern education system; in addition, though, successful sustainability leaders must also strengthen specific skills and values in order to be true leaders. Critical skills include communication, conflict resolution, creating complex networks, managing diverse teams, and acquiring a capacity of innovation and a global mindset. Juarez-Najera Dieleman and Turpin-Marion (2006) note that sustainability leadership requires new ways of assessing problems away from the logical and analytical reasoning commonly taught in the standard higher education system. The authors list skills such as "collaboration skills, communication skills, self-management skills, self-awareness skills, and critical thinking skills" as the skills that will allow leaders to become an agent of change for sustainability (p. 1037).

UNESCO (2017b) highlights how social entrepreneurs can help to solve several of the SDGs, especially ones that involve combining decent work and economic growth with sustainability principles. UNESCO describes sustainability as a highly complex discipline with competencies that cannot simply be taught, but need to be developed by the leaders themselves through action and reflecting on the experiences of this action. UNESCO lists several key competencies of sustainability leadership that are "transversal, multifunctional and context-independent. They do not replace specific competencies necessary for successful action in certain situations and contexts, but they encompass these and are more broadly focused" (p. 14). The UNESCO (2017b) key competencies for sustainability leadership are:

1. Systems thinking – recognize and understanding relationships, analyzing complex systems, and dealing with uncertainty

2. Anticipatory – understand and evaluate multiple scenarios (possible, probable, desirable), assess consequences of proposed actions, handle risks and changes

3. Normative – understand norms that drive peoples' actions, negotiate principles, targets, and goals in the context of uncertainty, contradictions, conflicts, and trade-offs

4. Strategic – implementing innovative actions to promote sustainability at all levels

5. Collaboration – learning from others, empathizing with needs of others, address conflicts in a group, facilitate collaboration

6. Critical Thinking – questioning norms and practices

7. Self-awareness – understanding one's own role in society, understanding how one's feelings and values motive one's actions

8. Integrated problem-solving – being able to apply different problem-solving frameworks to complex sustainability issues in order to develop viable, inclusive, and integrated sustainable development initiatives

Theories of successful sustainability leadership strategies.

The previous section detailed individual characteristics associated with successful sustainability leaders. This section will highlight literature concerning how leaders can successfully implement sustainability strategies in their organizations. Future sections will also link these strategies further to successful social entrepreneurship ventures.

This section primarily examines how a leader can implement sustainability strategies internally. The previous sections provided a synopsis of the business case for sustainable development, which highlights the rationale for having a firm with external sustainability principles. As the primary research question for the paper addresses social entrepreneurs, it should be safe to assume that any venture with an outward focus on sustainability as the major part of its business model should first have successfully implemented internal policies designed to have sustainability principles engrained in the corporate culture and business model. The summary of the below literature shows that numerous authors suggest that successful sustainability leadership strategies often include leaders who drive sustainability strategies from the top down and who make it a point to embed sustainability principles throughout their organizations and into their employees' ways of life and ways of thinking about the organization.

Top down, leadership-driven approach.

As mentioned previously when discussing the historical emergence of sustainability leadership, the theory emerged from transformational leadership theories that have elements that focus on interactions between leaders and followers. Much of the literature centers on the theory that leaders must drive their organizations' sustainability leadership cultures. Newman-Storen (2014) believes that transformational leadership styles can bridge creative attributes with sustainability issues. Stoughton and Ludema (2012) believe that the senior leaders of an organization integrates sustainability into the corporate culture by ensuring that sustainability strategies are aligned with the purposes of the business and then driving the top sustainability priorities throughout the organization. Mirvss and Menga (2010) highlight a top-down approach to a sustainability strategy that is coordinated by senior leaders to build momentum to drive the agenda down the corporate chain. This model can be successful with strong leaders but only if the leaders are committed to enacting the strategy and actually able to guide the program and impress their commitment on to those lower down the corporate ladder. Zoeteman (2012) feels that the CEO and all of his/her key leaders must be committed to sustainable development and also possess the correct knowledge in order to be able to guide their subordinates in implementing a sustainable development strategy.

Galpin, Whittington, and Bell (2015) feel that leaders must drive sustainability strategies by creating an infrastructure that promotes sustainability as this will lead to positive employee feelings towards the topic and thus also positive performance regarding sustainability. The authors believe that this framework can be applied across all industries and company sizes and will offer similar positive results in promoting sustainable cultures. Lacy, Arnott, and Lowitt, (2009) believe that the quality of leadership around promoting sustainability efforts is now more important than ever because even the best ideas for promoting sustainability will fail unless the leader can ensure that the greater workforce puts these ideas into practice and action. Visser (2011) feels that sustainability leaders must have the abilities to communicate a compelling narrative on how, through pursing sustainable initiatives, their corporations can assist to create a better society. If leaders can make a strong and convincing case for their strategies around sustainability, they will be better able to drive the implementation. Peterlin, Dimovski, and Penger (2013) conducted an extensive study of sustainability experts and found that an organization's commitment to sustainable development comes from the leader establishing and continually promoting a strong sustainability narrative.

Scholars addressing sustainability leadership organizations, especially private firms, cite the importance of leaders' abilities to engage their workforces in adopting sustainability as part of one's personal values. These values then help shape corporate strategy and goals. Galpin and Whittington (2012) believe that an engaged workforce is the core of a successfully sustainability leadership model. Once employees feel committed to a firm's sustainability mission, leaders should then incorporate sustainability leadership into their organizations' values, goals, strategy, and value chain. Ferdig (2007) notes two stages of developing one's own sustainability leadership skills. Initially the individual must first become self-aware of behaviors that can have negative effects on the planet's social, ecological, and economic systems. Next, the individual should use their leadership traits to make a greater impact by expanding their awareness to others so that the issue can be better addressed through joint action.

Lacy et al. (2009) cite employee's positive engagement as a major factor in the proactive execution of a sustainability leadership strategy. Employees must be engaged and trained in sustainability strategies and their implementation. Hargett and Williams (2009) believe that a values-based approach to leadership is paramount, as corporate leaders must actively work to embed sustainability leadership principles into their firms' cultures. If this is successful, then employees will embrace sustainable practices in many aspects of their jobs. Aborgast and Thorton (2012) note that implementing a successful sustainability requires "an extreme focus on metrics and communication" and that distilling sustainability concepts into "clear, actionable, and measurable initiatives" amongst the workforce is a key to success (p. 137). Grant (2012) suggests that leaders must develop and share a broad dialogue with others in order to drive sustainability initiatives.

Embedding sustainability principles throughout the organization.

De Souza Freitas et al. (2012) in studying sustainable corporate culture in Brazil, noted that management's imbedding of sustainability principles in human resources strategies help to build employee morale and engagement around sustainability strategies.

McPhee (2014) cites the need for leaders to cultivate their people as an ongoing source of value in order to drive sustainability agendas. Kiron et al. (2015) cite the importance of sustainability strategies as a top management agenda since this can lead to an increase in collaborative efforts throughout the company and with outside organizations. Sustainability leaders need to create deep trust within partnerships within their organizations in order to drive initiative and embed collaborative principles throughout the organizations.

Baumgartner (2009) noted that leaders at the highest levels must shape their organizational culture to value sustainable development if they want the strategies to succeed. This includes integrating sustainable development values into the corporation's values and also linking performance measures, such as pay and promotion, to the successful achievement of sustainable development measures. Silveira and Brandao (2012) noted that adopting sustainability strategies "has implications on strategic planning at all levels of the organization, and therefore allows the dissemination of the concept and its applications as comprehensively as possible" (p. 3701). The authors suggested that ESD must be implemented in all strategic planning in order to cement the sustainability concept into corporate culture.

Linnenluecke and Griffiths (2010) studied how organizational culture can drive sustainability initiatives. The authors found that top leaders could drive sustainability by incorporating its practices into the organization's context. Methods include integrating sustainability indicators directly into employee evaluations and employee training, which can promote a tangible context for change in the beliefs, values, and core assumptions of individuals. This helps to shape for employees understand the greater scheme of corporate sustainability. Martensson and Westerberg (2014) note that, in the past, companies' environmental policies were often disconnected from the traditional operations. The authors find that this led to ineffective policies and strategies. In order to better address environmental and sustainability goals, sustainability must be incorporated into all aspects of operations and strategy planning.

Promoting Sustainability: Importance of Social Entrepreneurs vs Lack of Educational Programs for Social Entrepreneurs

The above section highlighted how sustainability leadership is advancing in the private sector overall and how sustainability principles can be integrated into private sector organizations. This section details how social entrepreneurs can be at the forefront of promoting sustainability initiatives across the world. The section also shows that, although there has been an increase in literature highlighting the importance of social entrepreneurs, this is juxtaposed against a realization that the actual methods and models for training and mentoring these new social entrepreneurs are sparse and not well understood by both the academic community and the business world. This gap has led to a lack of entrepreneurial education curriculums specifically at business schools.

When the UN launched its framework for the DESD, it stressed that all levels of educational institutions, community based organizations, corporations, as well as the multitude of informal learning networks needed to incorporate ESD into their learning activities. Universities of higher education, however, were identified as having 'a particular role to play' in ESD. Universities are often the driving forces for shaping broader educational, policy, and business theories and practices. By educating students

in ESD, especially entrepreneurs and policy makers, universities have the ability to drive

the sustainable development agenda at the highest levels (UNESCO, 2006). Arbuthnott's

(2009) research on the effectiveness of ESD also confirms the aforementioned strategy of

UNESCO. She found that "directing ESD efforts to decision makers who can change

institutional infrastructures, regulations, and incentives such as financial benefits or social

approval will have the greatest impact on sustainable behavior" (p. 162). The author

identifies universities as a 'primary source of knowledge generation' for these individuals

with the greatest opportunities and abilities to promote and implement sustainability

strategies.

The UN (2016) resolution that adopted the SDGs calls for a partnership "bringing

together Governments, the private sector, civil society, the United Nations system, and

other

actors and mobilizing all available resources" (p. 10). Governments and international

organizations will set agendas, non-profits and NGOs will assist in outreach and charity,

individuals will do their parts in daily living, and the private sector will work hand-in-

hand with all of these other actors to bring their resources to bear to solve the pressing

goals of global society. The UNRISD report on promoting the SDGs notes that many

private sector investors are well-suited to make investments in sustainable development

related objectives based on the risk appetite and investment strategies of these firms and

investment funds (Dugarova & Gulasan, 2017). Entrepreneurs will especially be helpful

in areas where the traditional private sector corporations may not yet have robust operations. Areas like these include innovative financing mechanisms or technological innovations in areas such as food, water security, climate change, education, and health. It is as part of the private sector that this paper will address where social entrepreneurs can best assist in promoting sustainable development, as the social enterprises covered in this work are the ones that operate as for-profit ventures.

As previously mentioned, Elkington (1997) coined the phrase 'triple bottom-line' and was one of the first to write about traditional businesses addressing societal and environmental goals and/or concerns. Choi and Gray (2008) expand on this concept to study how social entrepreneurs use their skills to build profitable firms that solve social or environmental problems or objectives. However, the authors find that very little research has been conducted on the topic of sustainable entrepreneurship, especially outside the non-profit and public sector areas. Cohen and Winn (2007) note that social entrepreneurship can be utilized to combat market imperfections that have led to environmental degradation. Innovative entrepreneurs likely will be the ones who can identify market opportunities to address social or environment challenges while earning appropriate entrepreneurial rents for their goods or services.

Zahra et al. (2009) comment on the importance of social entrepreneurs in combatting adverse social conditions, especially in areas where governments, NGOs, and the private sector contributions have failed or been limited. Many not-for-profits or NGOs have seen government funding cut drastically during a global movement to privatize economies; these organizations must now increasingly rely on raising their own funds an operating a business model that is at least break even. This phenomenon requires that these organizations now employ entrepreneurial skills when operating and growing their organizations. Kirkwood and Walton (2014) note that importance of educating social entrepreneurs since "ecopreneurs may offer a win-win scenario for the economy and the environment" (p. 37). Hall et al. (2010) write "entrepreneurship is increasingly being recognized as a significant conduit for bringing about a transformation to sustainable products and processes, with numerous high-profile thinkers advocating entrepreneurship as a panacea for many social and environmental concerns" (p. 439). The authors follow this statement though with an assertion that "despite the promise entrepreneurship holds for fostering sustainable development, there remains considerable uncertainty regarding the nature of entrepreneurship's role in the area, and the academic discourse on sustainable development within the mainstream entrepreneurship literature has to date been sparse" (p. 439).

Kuckertz and Wagner (2010) also cite the positive aspects of entrepreneurial education to promote sustainable business growth. The authors note that unlike traditionally trained entrepreneurs who seek only to maximize profit, social entrepreneurs must be able not only to recognize profit but also be able to determine the value of intangible benefits related to sustainable outcomes. Therefore, programs that foster social entrepreneurism, in addition to basic entrepreneurism, are critical. Lourenco (2013) also notes that entrepreneurship can be used to promote sustainable development and that this curriculum can change multiple aspects of business and management school models of education. Achar (2008) examines the topic in terms of women worldwide and notes that women's entrepreneurship development results in both bringing women out of poverty but also aids the overall social and economic development in the country, especially in areas of the developing world.

Tsai (2013) examines ESD at business schools as proposes a model for better integrating the concept into curriculums. Tsai notes the need for ESD in business schools as more for-profit social enterprise firms appear in the modern economy. Tsai introduces a four-part model for integrating ESD in business schools. The model consists of:

1. Staying at the forefront of social enterprise innovation by conducting research and adjusting class design and curriculums

2. Implementing a 'Green Schools' concept by constructing and operating an environmentally efficient campus, thus fostering an organizational culture with an emphasis on sustainability

3. Building a social culture that encourages students, staff, and alumni, as well as the public and enterprises, to work together toward sustainability goals in school but also in greater society

4. Building an alliance between the government and business to extend models of sustainability throughout society

The third tenet of the model above, which involves social culture, notes that ESD is an interdisciplinary subject that needs to be integrated into numerous curriculums, to include entrepreneurial education and business economics.

In addition to academic research, survey studies have shown that students themselves are asking for more training regarding sustainable development. The Higher Education Academy (HEA), the UK's national body for enhancing learning and teaching in higher education, conducted a survey over the past five years of over 15,000 UK

university students and found that over 80% of the students felt that sustainable

development should be actively promoted in university courses. Most students felt that

ESD should be incorporated into all courses instead of simply adding additional

sustainability related courses (Drayson et al., 2014).

Methods for Developing Social Entrepreneurship Skills at Business Schools

This research is not intended to determine whether an MBA program is the best

method to educate social entrepreneurs compared to other approaches such as simply

founding a business and learning through trial and error or entering the business into a

longer-term accelerator program. This topic is a much larger subject to cover; although,

later analysis in the Chapter 4 results section will show why some prospective social

entrepreneurs did choose MBA programs over other methods designed to develop social

enterprises. The research assumes that an MBA program though is one viable method to

develop social enterprise skills, thus the research was designed to identify how MBA

programs can better train social entrepreneurs who choose to attend these programs.

The literature review section above noted that academics are addressing methods

for social enterprise education at universities. I could not find any detailed models

though of how exactly what resources should be offered in business schools. Tsai (2013),

quoted earlier, does note that both curricula and resources must be retooled to promote

social enterprise education, but does not go into that much detail on the resource part of

that suggestion. To identify key social enterprise resources that could be included in

MBA programs, I drew on social enterprise literature that addressed individual resources viewed as valuable and also reverse engineered a list of resources by examining both entrepreneurial literature and the actual social entrepreneurial resource offerings that business schools are advertising to the outside world in order to present a model of how business schools can further a holistic social entrepreneurship education.

Social Enterprise Specific Classes.

A main component of instruction in an MBA program is, of course, the classes that students undertake. Basic classes help impart core financial, business, leadership, operations, and management knowledge on the students. In addition to core curriculum, elective classes offer students teachings on many of the concepts mentioned earlier that cover sustainability, entrepreneurship, and social entrepreneurship in more detail. The literature on social enterprise classes generally finds these classes as decent way to educate social entrepreneurs, especially around the basic tenets of social entrepreneurship and sustainable development (Tracey and Phillips, 2007; Solomon, 2007; Miller, Wesley, & Williams, 2012; Welsh & Krueger, 2012)

(Social) Entrepreneurship Centers.

Business Schools and universities often house centers or institutes related to a specific topic or subject, e.g. politics, government, entrepreneurship, etc. The growth of university housed entrepreneurship centers has progressed quickly over the past decade. Finkle, Kuratko, and Goldsby (2006) trace the first entrepreneurship courses to the early 1970s. By 2006, when the authors conducted a study, the National Consortium of Entrepreneurship Centers noted that 146 U.S. based schools had full-fledged entrepreneurship centers. By 2017, the now-titled Global Consortium of

Entrepreneurship Centers (GCEC) (2017) list 200 member institutions and an earlier

Finkle et al. (2012) study lists 249 university based entrepreneurship centers, including

those who are not members of GCEC. Some schools even have multiple, independent

entrepreneurship centers, e.g. Babson College's (2017) Arthur M. Blank Center for

Entrepreneurship and the separate Center for Women's Entrepreneurial Leadership.

Finkle, Kuratko, and Goldsby (2006), later updated with Finkle et al. (2012), found that

entrepreneurship centers offer student entrepreneurs assistance in several different ways

with their prospective ventures. These benefits include internal outreach such as the

aforementioned BPCs and start-up labs, as well as internships, student clubs, internal

venture capital funding, access to entrepreneurial faculty members, and technology

transfers among student entrepreneurs. The external benefits included the

aforementioned mentoring from successful entrepreneurs as well as seminars/workshops,

guest speakers, and access to external venture capital funds and/or grants/seed money.

A similar search for research specific to social enterprise or social

entrepreneurship centers at universities does not turn up similar studies on their numbers

or effectiveness. Proprietary research conducted for this paper though does show that

such centers do exist at several of the top business schools though. As earlier in the

literature reviewed showed that social entrepreneurship is closely tied to normal

entrepreneurship principles, later analysis will attempt to examine the presence, or lack

thereof, of the Finkle et al. (2012) characteristics associated with successful

entrepreneurship centers with regards to the social entrepreneurship centers at the top

business schools.

In addition to classes, MBA programs offer many other opportunities and resources to potential social entrepreneurs. Key identified examples of these resources are detailed below.

Business Plan Competitions.

Business Plan Competitions (BPCs) are formal contests, usually sponsored by or sponsored jointly between an institution of higher education, a corporation, a non-profit, or a social or governmental organization, that are used to develop business plans through real-world learning (Cooper and McGowan, 2008). Honig (2004) describes a business plan as a written document that describes the current state and the presupposed future of an organization. Russell, Atchison, and Brooks (2008) summarize BPCs as being established to:

> provide a stimulus for new venture creation and for capturing the ideas, talents, and potential in the community, especially that of tertiary education students. Many of the competitions not only provide the opportunity to win seed money to start new ventures but also provide a means of developing the skills and contacts required for these new ventures to be successful. (p. 124)

The University of Texas (2015) is generally credited with starting the first BPC in an effort to assist MBA students through the conceptual process of conceiving an idea for a business, developing the idea, and presenting their findings for evaluation to a panel of experts. BPCs are designed to teach participants the skills required to plan multiple aspects of a company that are key to being a successful enterprise, such as budgeting, marketing, product design, operations; how to pitch these aspects to those who may invest in the company;

and how to continue to grow, develop, and further plan for these key aspects

going forward as the company becomes more successful.

BPCs have numerous different formats, target entrants, geographic focuses, and

other specific criteria, but they also share certain core similarities. Biz Plan Competitions

(2016), a website billing itself as the premier listing of BPCs, lists 260 active BPCs in the

U.S. and another 122 worldwide, as of December 2016, with combined prize money of

nearly $50 million. The site classifies BPCs into different categories also, such as

Undergraduate, Graduate, Business, Technology, Minority/Women, among others. BPCs

vary in certain ways, but most of the larger competitions share certain characteristics.

These characteristics include sponsorship by a larger entity; prize money; business

related 'prizes' such as incubation; access to expertise or other services; and access to

other tangible and intangible experiences such as networking opportunities, mentorship,

and education (Russell et al., 2008).

To enter a BPC, an individual first creates a business plan and then submits it to

the competition, typically online. Judges, usually experts in their fields, evaluate the

business plans and choose entrants to further explore. Some BPCs are conducted solely

online, but most of the more established and prestigious competitions—those that often

offer the highest prize money—conduct in person pitch sessions for those entrants

deemed to be worthy of further exploration. This often involves the entrants pitching the

business plan to the judges and then answering questions and, generally, receiving direct

feedback. Winners of BPCs are often granted cash prizes as well as some of the other

incentives mentioned above (Goodman, 2012; istart, 2015).

Skills learned in BPCs.

BPCs help participants learn or advance independent or entrepreneurial

was of thinking about challenges; expand networks; and develop problem solving

skills that are beneficial when dealing with uncertain or dynamic issues or

situations. These skills are further developed and refined by the assistance

provided by mentors and experts who can add highly specific and tightly targeted

advice designed to tackle problems that cannot solely be solved via independent

research or discovery by the participant learner.

As previously mentioned, all BPCs are not the same, but through research

conducted for this paper, most of the prominent BPCs seem to share many

similarities in structure and design. Russell, et al. (2008) find that BPCs "provide

a range of benefits to participants, the most important being the development of

entrepreneurial skills" as well as "increased self-confidence and risk-taking

propensity" (p. 132). The authors believe that BPCs help participants to develop

innovative attitudes to problem solving. Participants can manage how they learn

through the variety of choices of learning experiences offered in BPCs.

Participants involved in BPCs develop real-world skills through the immersive

properties of the diverse learning environment (Russell et al, 2008). Thomas,

Gudmundson, Turner, and Suhr (2014) describe the nature of BPCs as "designed

to bring people together for the purpose of creating a context in which an idea

might be developed and tested in a supportive and non-threatening environment"

(p. 35). Cooper and McGowan (2008) note that BPCs offer learning methods in which participants gain experience through conducting research, formulating ideas, and receiving feedback from judges and mentors. Participants also learn independently through observing other competing teams.

Start-up Labs (Incubators or Accelerators).

Another resource frequently associated with the development and growth of entrepreneurial ventures is the concept of start-up laboratories, often referred to as either incubators or accelerators. The terms incubator and accelerator, in certain broad terms, often are thought to represent a fairly similar concept of being an entity that provides aid to startups in the form of services such as training, mentoring, networking; possible funding; and, usually, a place to work that offers a co-location of multiple startup ventures, allowing for knowledge transfers (Casasnovas, 2013; Forrest, 2014; Stargars, 2014; Pauwels et al., 2016). Some authors do note differences between incubators and accelerators (Bosma & Stam, 2012; Cohen 2013; Isabelle, 2013; Lall, Bowles, & Baird, 2014). Incubators are sometimes considered to be organizations that assist enterprises in the earliest stages by shielding vulnerable business from market forces, thus helping them grown before they become independent; accelerators assist slightly more mature ventures to scale up quickly by accelerating market interactions after the initial incubation stage. Incubators are often associated with non-profits or educational institutions while accelerators may also be for-profit. Accelerators are often for a limed duration (3 to 6 months for many of the larger ones) while incubators can be more open-ended in duration. For the sake of this research though, the presence of an incubator, accelerator, or any other similarly-goaled body at a business school or university affiliated entity that provides aid, funding, mentoring, and workspaces to social enterprises is considered in the same category of a broader start-up laboratory.

Lall et al. (2014) specifically address the need for accelerators and incubators in promoting social enterprise as there is a lack of capital across the social enterprise sector. Start-ups labs offer "(a) business development support (e.g., consulting, technology assistance); (b) infrastructure support (e.g., access to office space, shared back office services); (c) network support (e.g., access to potential customers, investors, mentors); and (d) financial support (in the form of grants/investments)" (p. 2). The authors also note four major stages of development for start-up labs:

1. Idea Stage – "idea on paper" where there is only a basic plan but no prototype or product

2. Prototype Stage – most common area where there is a minimum model or prototype of the good or service but no revenue

3. Post-revenue stage – the venture has customers and a product/service on the market but is not yet to scale or profitable and probably has not raised much capital

4. Growth stage – venture is operating to scale and is typically profitable and/or has raised major sources of outside funding

Most university associated startup labs cater to student-led ventures that are in stage 1 or stage 2.

Access to Venture Capital.

Research has found that venture capital (VC) plays a leading role in start-up financing since start-ups often do not have access to traditional funding such as bank loans, due to the risk of new ventures. Also, start-ups with VC financing often grow faster over time then companies who have to rely on other sources of funding (Bates & Bradford, 1992; Sorenson & Stuart, 2001; Davila, Foster, & Gupta, 2003; Baum & Silverman, 2004). Many business schools, through centers/institutes, and through other means such as providing direct access to a pipeline of VC investors, offer fledgling start-ups opportunities for access to VC financing that other ventures may not have. Most of the VC research is centered on traditional start-up enterprises though. Wry and Haugh (2018) note that while research concerning the external funding of social enterprises is quite limited, scholars are beginning to study this more, including how social entrepreneurs can best pitch their business concepts to investors.

Mentors.

As is detailed below, research into entrepreneurial learning methods has shown the importance of mentors. Mentors can be present in BPCs, start-up labs, or simply for one-on-one situations with student social entrepreneurs. Mentors offer their services both in practical and emotional support for a venture and also offer access to social and business networks of senior decision makers to whom student entrepreneurs would not ordinarily have access (Center for Entrepreneurship, 2015). Vincent and Seymour (1994) describe mentoring as:

Derived from Greek mythology, mentoring implies a relationship between a young adult and an older, more experienced adult that helps the younger individual learn to navigate in the adult world and the world of work. Specifically, mentoring is the process of people (mentors) helping others (protégés) increase their chances of success by advising, guiding, and encouraging them.

Mentors function as teachers and coaches to create learning opportunities and to challenge the protégé to develop to full potential. Protégés participate in a relationship of willingness to accept advice, guidance, and encouragement to enhance success. (p. 15)

Mentors are valuable as they can provide role modelling functions, help protégés overcome barriers that are unfamiliar, and introduce protégés to powerful and productive networks that the protégés would otherwise not have access to on their own. Linehan and Walsh (1999) find that mentors provide mentees with key advice, training, career direction, guidance, and an introduction to unfamiliar networks, thus assisting the mentees to grow and develop their careers independently. Boud (2001) highlights the role that mentors play in entrepreneurial learning as mentors and coaches provide enhanced learning perspectives to the students and can challenge the participants beyond how they are normally accustomed to learning, which the author describes as learning primarily from performing one's normal work duties or from obtain qualifications through higher education.

Sullivan (2000) writes about mentors working to transfer their entrepreneurial experience to their mentees in order to assist the mentees in solving unfamiliar problems: "The role of the mentor is to enable the entrepreneur to reflect on actions and, perhaps, to modify future actions as a result; it is about enabling behavioural and attitudinal change" (p. 3). The entrepreneurs must use their skills to navigate their own way through the learning experience, but mentors can be valuable guides who can bridge gaps for the entrepreneurial learners when they are unable to complete certain tasks or solve certain problems on their own; this also incorporates social cognitivist aspects. Sullivan (2000) highlights that mentors must help their mentees through the process but not simply dictate how something must be accomplished: "Effective interventions to assist entrepreneurs to grow and develop must help them to learn rather than simply impose prescribed solutions as is the case through the provision of 'expert' consultancy" (p. 5). Jonassen and Rohrer-Murphy (1999) highlight the joint nature of entrepreneurial learning process between the educator/mentor and participant, placing entrepreneurial learning in the constructivist framework. Atkinson (2001) conducted a study of entrepreneurs and found the significance of mentoring as a key theme for success in achieving both personal and professional/business development as the mentors offer the mentees advice, guidance, and access to resources that the mentees would not have experience on their own. Edwards and Muir (2005) note that mentors are a key aspect of this discovery method, though, since the mentors can guide the students down their learning paths. Gimmon (2004) notes the importance of mentors in BPCs as a way to help increase participants' personal entrepreneurial skills.

In addition to the academic literature above, the role of the mentor is also a recurring theme in university BPC and star-up lab videos and websites. Mentors provide both feedback based on their own personal business experiences and access to greater networks of other successful entrepreneurs and resources ordinarily unavailable to students. The Rice BPC considers mentors to be "a powerful and sustaining thread in the program," as mentors are needed to help participants address issues that may be out of the knowledge realm of the participants (RBCP, 2015). In the George Washington University New Venture Competition, a survey of the team indicated that "mentors provide the most valuable input they receive from any outside source" (GW New Venture, 2015). The McCloskey BPC at the Mendoza College of Business at Notre Dame lists access to mentors and entrepreneurs-in-residence as critical in providing advice and networking opportunities otherwise unavailable to the participants. The individuals are able to facilitate interactions between the BPC participants and outside connections such as other established or aspiring entrepreneurs or experts in areas where the BPC participant has no connections, such as legal, intellectual property, or funding (Mendoza, 2015). The MIT-China Innovation and Entrepreneurship Forum (MIT-CHIEF) rewards its top teams with an exclusive mentorship program to help these business plans to move to the next level of development. Mentors serve as resources of personal experience for the BPC participants and also as links to other resources that participants may require (MIT-CHIEF, 2015).

In interviews posted to the Harvard Business School New Venture Competition website, winners discuss the most valuable aspects of BPCs. Julia Kurnik (2015) of Focus Foods states that the exposure to, and feedback from, the platform of experts in the competition at Harvard is a tremendous advantage of BPCs. Alex Santana (2015) lists the mentors, alumni network, and professors working with the BPC as helping his venture team understand many aspects of his venture and its related industry that his team would not have understood otherwise since his team was "a group of computer nerds that had so much to learn when [they] started this." Similarly, in interviews conducted with winners of the George Washington 2015 BPC, the participants mentioned the advice of mentors and feedback from judges as extremely important assistance in navigating difficult questions that arose in the competition. Teams also commented that BPCs taught the participants to take knowledge learned in classes and find a way to apply it to complex problems in BPCs (GW Office of Entrepreneurship, 2015).

Research on the Current State of Social Entrepreneurship Curriculum at Top Business Schools

This section highlights academic research on the state of social entrepreneurship curriculums in top business schools. Researchers on social entrepreneurship at top business schools seem to have mixed findings, as will be shown below; some studies find hardly any schools with sustainability curriculums and other studies find that many top schools are well on their way to training sustainability leaders. From an initial examination of the progression of the literature over the past decade or so, the theme does seem to show that overall, there still is a relative dearth of programs that integrate ESD into standard entrepreneurial curriculums throughout leading universities, but also that universities are beginning to see the merits of social entrepreneurship and thus are increasingly incorporating its principles into their curriculums.

Tracey, Phillips, and Haugh (2005) found that there has been a rise in social entrepreneurs attending business schools with entrepreneurship curriculums, but that most of these students had to attend regular entrepreneurship programs since programs in social entrepreneurship were not available. Christensen et al. (2007) surveyed the top-50 business schools in the Financial Times Rankings and did find that most, at least in name only, do have some requirement to incorporate sustainability into their curriculums and

that their students also are in favor of this. The research did not go further into the actual

content of these courses. Wu et al. (2010) expanded on this study to include 575

accredited business schools and found that only 6% actually had courses related to

sustainable development. The authors found that, overall, US based business schools

were less likely to teach ESD compared to their counterparts in Europe or Asia. This

research also did not delve further into the actual courses to evaluate the content to screen

for ESD and business strategy or entrepreneurism related topics.

Benn and Martin (2010) found that ESD has not been truly integrated into

business and management curriculums at institutions of higher education. These findings

are in spite of the authors' research that finds that sustainable development and ESD is a

concept that has received increasing levels of official support for both governments and

business throughout the world. Advocacy for ESD is important but it does not

automatically lead to the transfer of this urgency for ESD into actual institutions of higher

learning. Lourenco et al. (2012) cite ten other scholarly articles noting the lack of

sustainability related courses in business curriculums at academic institutions.

Audenbrand (2010) believes that integrating sustainability theory into business and

management strategy education has moved from the margins to the forefront recently, but

that much still needs to be done to create a lasting change in the mindset of business

school students. Rusinko (2010) cites multiple recent studies on how to better incorporate

ESD in business school curriculums and has devised a new matrix of her own to provide

a framework to address how to both incorporate ESD into existing structures and to develop new methods for instruction. She briefly mentions options for sustainable

entrepreneurship training but does not focus thoroughly on the concept.   Starik et al.

(2010) write that most business schools address environmental and social issues in as

legal or ethical concerns or cost factors instead of as factors that should be included in

strategic, management, economic, or operating decisions. There is no real marrying of

sustainable development and business strategies.

The Aspen Institute (2012), an international non-profit dedicated to leadership

and fostering open-minded dialogue, had published biannual reports ranking business

schools on the innovation and impact of their social and environmental curriculums. The

last report in 2012, titled *Beyond Grey Pinstripes* (BGP) found that 8 of the top 10, and

18 of the top 20 business schools in this area were located in the United States. The

research required business schools to respond to a comprehensive survey; 149 responded.

In the sample schools, the report found that there had been a 38% increase between 2009

and 2012 in the number of required courses in finance departments that had some sort of

social context and the number of schools that require students to take a course dedicated

to business and society has increased from 34% in 2001 to 79% in 2011. The survey

does not delve specifically into entrepreneurship classes but does note that 30% of classes

in the schools that responded have an emphasis on the intersection of social impact and

for-profit enterprises. Curiously though, the Aspen Institute discontinued the report, with

the last one being published in 2012. Bloomberg News reported that Aspen discontinued

the rankings after 2012 because a number of leading business schools declined to

participate in the survey. Top schools like Harvard, Tuck, MIT, and Chicago reportedly questioned the validity of the rankings because the survey only considered classes and not extracurricular activities and resources, institutes, and specializations. The article postulates that the report may have lost validity since the rankings were originated when business schools were not all "jam-packed with sustainability classes, cases, and clubs", implying that sustainability programs at business schools are routine now and not the exception (Di Meglio, 2012, online article quote). Wu et al. (2013) conducted a deeper analysis of the curriculums of the schools involved in the BGP 2009-2010 report to focus specifically on social entrepreneurship. Of the 100 schools in the BGP report, 17 specifically taught social entrepreneurship education while 68 taught a blend of traditional and social entrepreneurship; only 21 only taught traditional entrepreneurship education. Also, 61 schools had specific social entrepreneurship related centers/institutes. In examining the method of instruction, the authors noted that the social entrepreneurship programs were slightly less likely to rely on lecture as the main form of instruction and more likely to include speakers, case studies, conferences, and discussions than the traditional entrepreneurship programs. The authors found that the business schools with the most developed social entrepreneurship programs "followed the principle of learning by doing, not only enabled the students to balance theory and practice, but also supported the students in creating social enterprises" (p. 329).

Chapter 3: Research Methods

Overview

This section describes in detail the methodology for conducting this study.
Overall, it can be classified as a blend of summative and formative evaluation as the
intent was to evaluate the current state of how MBA programs train their social
entrepreneurs and, if there are discovered deficiencies, suggest ways to improve this
pedagogy going forward (Patton, 2002).

The literature review traced the development of sustainable development
principles from early concepts associated solely with environment protection through to
its modern-day incorporation into numerous aspects of society. In the realm of business
and management, sustainable development has taken hold in entrepreneurship disciplines,
creating a unique field of social entrepreneurship. As the private sector continues to react
to the demands or customers, governments, and other stakeholders, the literature showed
that there is an increasing demand for innovative solutions to sustainability related
problems. This is an area where social entrepreneurs can have direct, and marked, effects
in advancing the sustainability agenda.

The literature review also presented sustainable development as a complex
discipline that spans economic, social, and environmental realms. Leaders in the
sustainability space must   possess both strong personal leadership characteristics coupled
with diverse skills necessary to navigate intricate and often difficult environments,
especially skills that allow the leader to motivate, not compel, others to work towards a
common sustainability goal. In addition to those listed skills, social entrepreneurs must

also possess business and entrepreneurship skills associated with creating, growing, and sustaining an organization. Skills like these are not easily acquired without a combination of education, training, and experience. This research centers on one area where a social entrepreneur could hope to gain such education, training, and experience, MBA programs at top-rated business schools in the United States. The literature indicates that while both students are showing an increased interest in social entrepreneurship studies and business schools are attempting to incorporate ESD and social entrepreneurship into their MBA programs, the number of comprehensive social entrepreneurship programs are limited in both scope and number across MBA programs.

I believe that there is an opportunity to research and document critical skills and resources that MBA programs currently offer and then evaluate these against the first-hand experience of actual social entrepreneurs in order assess the effectiveness of these MBA programs and suggest modifications or additions to the curricula. Although there is most likely not a single group of skills that guarantee success for a would-be social entrepreneur, this research attempts to offer recommendations that MBA programs can implement to better develop their students to one day becomes leaders in promoting and leading sustainable development for-profit ventures.

The following sections describe the methodology used to collect the data to answer the three research questions that I addressed in my study:

Question 1:

Which resources associated with prominent academic theories regarding training social

entrepreneurs do the top-rated MBA programs in the United States offer to their

students?

Question 2:

From the perspectives of selected MBA alumni and current students involved in

the creation and management of social enterprises, what is the relationship

between the resources that top-rated MBA programs in the United States offer

and the usefulness of these resources in reality?

Question 3:

From the perspectives of selected MBA alumni and current students involved in

the creation and management of social enterprises, what are ways MBA programs

in the United States best train social entrepreneurs?

Participant Selection

In this study, business schools to analyze for Question 1 were selected first and

then individuals to interview for Questions 2 and 3.

Question 1.

This portion of the study was designed to evaluate how 'top' business schools are

integrating various resources that have been identified in academic theory as beneficial to

social entrepreneurs into their MBA programs. To document this, the list of top-ranked

business schools needed to be defined. To accomplish this, I devised a methodology to

introduce a bit more clarity around the term "top" business schools. While a simple

internet search produces numerous lists that rank the merits of business schools, there are a few rankings that stand out to most students who have ever undertaken an MBA. Some

researchers have also ranked the rankings (Gioia & Corley, 2002; Siemens et al, 2005;

Bradshaw, 2007; Peters, 2007). Utilizing this research; personal knowledge learned from

applying to and studying for an MBA and subsequently a decade of experience recruiting

MBAs afterwards; and observed rankings mentioned on business school websites, I

narrowed the criteria down to four separate rankings tables plus one specialty subset of

one of the four rankings, for a total of five separate rankings tables. The rankings tables

included are the 2016 editions of The Economist, The Financial Times (FT), Bloomberg

Businessweek, and the 2017 editions of U.S. News & World Reports Overall and U.S.

News and World Reports Entrepreneurship business school rankings. Below are brief

descriptions of the different rankings systems. For more detailed information on

methodology please see the References section for the links to methodology.

Individual survey rankings methodologies.

Survey	Schools Ranked	Input
The Financial Times Global MBA Ranking	100 fulltime programs worldwide	Alumni (59%), School (31%), Research (10%)
The Bloomberg Businessweek MBA Ranking	87 US programs and 31 non-US programs	Employers (35%), Alumni (31%), Students (15%), Job Placement (10%), Starting Salary (10%)
The Economist MBA Ranking	100 fulltime programs worldwide	School (80%), Students and Recent Alumni (20%)
The U.S. News Graduate School Ranking	131 US programs	Graduates (35%), School (25%), Deans and Directors (25%), Corporate Recruiters (15%)

Table 2: Individual survey ranking methodologies [Compiled from Graf (2017)]

Financial Times.

The FT (2016a) ranks the top 100 full-time programs worldwide based on data from recruiters, alumni, and recently graduating students.

Bloomberg Businessweek.

The Bloomberg Businessweek (2016) survey ranks the top 100 full-time U.S. based MBA programs based on data from recruiters, alumni, and recently graduating students.

Economist.

The Economist (2016a) ranks the top 100 full-time programs worldwide. Both the business schools and their alumni are surveyed on numerous different criteria.

U.S. New & World Reports.

The U.S. News & World Report (2017a) study ranks the top 100 (131 in actuality, since they allow for ties) of the 470 accredited MBA programs in the United States. Criteria are based on recruiter scores, salary, selectivity, peer assessment, and other weightings. The survey also ranks MBA programs based on certain specialties of excellence as recognized by deans of other business schools. Entrepreneurship is one of these specialties and this rankings table for the top-10 schools will be included in the methodology for this research. Both U.S. News & World Reports rankings allow for ties in the rankings table.

Overall 'top' school rankings methodology.

In order to create a large and diverse list of MBA programs to analyze in this study, I adopted a methodology to include all U.S. business schools showing up in the top-20 of at least one of the above ranking tables, plus all showing up in the top-10 of the

U.S. News & World Reports specialty entrepreneurship ranking table. While many of the

top programs appear in all four of the major rankings tables, others in appear in only one

ranking table. By simply aggregating the five ranking tables mentioned above, and

listing all business schools that show up in at least one of the rankings, the list of 'top'

business schools shows 26 U.S. based MBA programs. Below exhibits the MBA

programs on the list of top business school whose curriculums will be assessed for social

entrepreneurship.

University Name	Business School Name
Babson College	The F.W. Olin Graduate School
Carnegie Mellon	Tepper School of Business
Columbia University	Columbia Business School
Cornell University	SC Johnson College of Business
Dartmouth College	Tuck School of Business
Duke University	Fuqua School of Business
Emory University	Goizueta Business School
Harvard University	Harvard Business School
Indiana University	Kelley School of Business
Massachusetts Institute of Technology	Sloan School of Management

New York University	Leonard N. Stern School of Business
Northwestern University	Kellogg School of Management
Rice University	Jones Graduate School of Business
Stanford University	Graduate School of Business
Texas A&M	Mays Business School
University of California at Berkeley	Haas School of Business
University of California at Los Angeles	Anderson School of Management
University of Chicago	Booth School of Business
University of Michigan at Ann Arbor	Ross School of Business
University of North Carolina at Chapel Hill	Kenan-Flagler
University of Pennsylvania	Wharton School
University of Southern California	Marshall School of Business
University of Texas at Austin	McCombs School of Business
University of Virginia	Darden School of Business
University of Washington	Foster School of Business
Yale University	Yale School of Management

Table 3: Top-ranked MBA programs used in this study

Questions 2 and 3.

The study was designed to validate or supplement certain research conducted on resources and skills that are deemed as beneficial to developing social entrepreneur MBA students into successful social entrepreneurs. The literature review listed several of these attributes and the reasoning behind, and skills developed, in each one. In order to evaluate the effectiveness of these offerings at MBA schools, I purposely targeted a certain group of individuals whom I believed could best provide insight into this research (Creswell, 2009). The group of individuals whom I believed could best critique social enterprise pedagogy at top-MBA programs were active social entrepreneurs who founded or on the senior management team of a social enterprise and hold an MBA from, or were currently enrolled in, one of the top-rated MBA programs described in my research.

All individuals interviewed hold an MBA from, or were currently completing their MBA at, one of the top-rated business schools listed above in the research that have social enterprise centers or similarly-themed resources to train students. Since resources, faculty, future success of alumni, peer assessments, and course offerings factor into the MBA rankings, this study assumed that the top-ranked MBA programs are able to offer their students more than non-ranked programs and therefore these MBA students and alumni being interviewed were better able to comment on the actual effectiveness of many of the resources offered to social entrepreneurs at these top schools. The primary purpose of the interview questions was to evaluate the usefulness of the resources offered to social entrepreneurs; it was therefore logical to target students from schools that are documented, at least in theory, to offer specific social enterprise themed resources to their students.

Through the research conducted for this study, as noted in the literature review, the scope of social enterprise education, and methods used to teach it and resources for promoting it, has increased significantly over the past decade. Before I began to conduct the formal interviews with the social entrepreneurs, I spoke informally with a few social entrepreneurs with MBAs and found that all who graduated earlier, especially those prior to 2010, stated that few classes and resources related to specifically to social enterprise were offered while they were in business school. Therefore, I did not believe that interviewing these types of individuals will contribute much to my research as most of the questions would be inapplicable to their experiences. Due to these findings, I felt that it was more prudent to target social entrepreneurs who have completed their MBA programs within the current decade.

All individuals interviewed in the study met the broader definition of social entrepreneur utilized in this paper; that is, they are involved in a venture that involves a mission or business plan that is primarily centered on addressing a social or sustainable development related issue. This type of social entrepreneur must look to exploit market opportunities when developing products and/or services that serve social ends (Boschee, 2001; Amin, Hudson, & Cameron, 2002; Oster, Massarsky, & Beinhacker, 2004). In a hypothetical world of unlimited interview subjects, my preference would have been to interview only social entrepreneurs who have started purely for-profit ventures, but after much research in identifying and contacting these types of individuals, it became clear that this population would not lead to a sufficiently large sample size for this study as the population, combined with their receptiveness to be interviewed, is limited. I therefore decided to also include social entrepreneurs who have started non-profits that still are market-focused and revenue-generating enterprises, enterprises that I will term as 'hybrids'. Social entrepreneurs who have started NGOs or charities that rely primarily on government funding or grants or outside donations or contributions are not included in the interview population as the skills necessary to run these types of ventures may be quite different from those skills needed to run a market-focused, revenue generating enterprise (Austin, Stevenson, & Wei-Skillern, 2006).

All individuals interviewed were members of the founding management team and had or currently have day-to-day activities in running their social enterprise. I viewed these criteria as essential requirements as the study will seek to identify gaps in resources associated with starting and running a social enterprise.

Identifying Participants.

In order to identify interview participants, I used several methods. As noted above, I targeted schools where social enterprise education is touted to students, often through the creation of business school social enterprise research centers or institutes. These centers often have websites that highlight alumni or current MBA students who have started social enterprises. Many of the top-business schools also have BPCs with social enterprise tracts. The winners of these BPCs, and often the other promising entries, are often highlighted on the schools' BPC sites. Generally, the social enterprise center and BPC websites profile the companies along with the founders. I then utilized various methods to obtain the contact info of these founders, such as LinkedIn, company

websites, or alumni databases, or by emailing the schools' social enterprise centers

directly to provide an introduction. These two sources were the primary ways to identify

interview participants since these individuals offer clear examples of people who seem to

have either attended business school in order to start a social venture or became interested

in social entrepreneurship during business school. In addition, after conducting

interviews with the participants, I asked each one for referrals to anyone else who met my

interview criteria. I did find other interview subjects this way too.

I also used my personal and professional network to identify other interview

participants. I participate in angel investing groups, BPCs, and social competitions, as

well as attend social enterprise conferences. Through these activities, I was able to

identify a few social enterprises started by top-ranked MBAs and then I targeted

individuals from these companies for interviews.

By utilizing the methods above, I created a shortlist of individuals to interview

and then contacted these individuals with a synopsis of my research and a request for my

interview. After a subject was selected and agreed to an interview, I confirmed again that

the individual met the criteria of both being an MBA graduate of one of the identified

top-ranked schools and that their social enterprise is primarily a market-based firm.

For this study, I did not believe that it was critically important to identify each

participant by name in the write-up, as this will not add to the research. I felt that

identifying participants by broad characteristics was sufficient to covey each participant's

experiences. In the summary research tables, I identified each participant by the name of their MBA program, graduation year, and a broad description of the industry and country of their social enterprise, e.g., a Columbia MBA in the food/agricultural sector in the United States. I informed each participant of this before each interview but noted that it is difficult to fully guarantee anonymity since participants in niche subject areas can sometimes be identified through deductive disclosure (Sargeant, 2012; Ravitch & Carl, 2016). The only data deemed as "identifying information" by the Institutional Review Board that I collected is Name, Employer's Name, and, at times, Phone Number and/or Email Address (IRB, 2018). I did not include this information in the write-up of my research.

Various researchers note the differing theories of the minimum number of interviews needed in a qualitative study spans from 15 (Bertaux, 1981) to 20 (Green & Thorogood, 2009) to 25 (Charmaz, 2006) to up to 50 (Ritchie, 2003). The minimum number of individuals I considered would be sufficient was 20; although I hoped to interview as many as possible bearing in mind time constraints and the response rate of the prospective interview subjects. After I reached 20 interviews, I began to see a lag in being able to connect with more individuals, but I continued to attempt to identify and contact more entrepreneurs. To check my progress, after 20 interviews, I began to monitor the subsequent interviews for the principle of data saturation (Glaser & Strauss, 1967; Francis et al., 2010, Mason, 2010). The subsequent interviews after the first 20 added to my findings, but did not reveal any truly new insights. I believed that the study had reached "the point in data collection when no new additional data are found that develop aspects of a conceptual category", so I was confident that I could end with over

30 interviews and still not miss many of the overriding themes that I was hoping to identify (Francis et al., 2010, p. 3).

Scheduling of Interviews.

Overall, I identified 89 potential subjects to be interviewed and then contacted them initially via either email or LinkedIn messaging. For the 41 individuals whom I had obtained emails for through my research, this was the initial method of contact. The emails, sent from my Penn GSE address, contained a detailed description of my project as well as the goals of the research. For those whom I did not have an email address for, I contacted through LinkedIn (everyone had what appeared to be a valid LinkedIn profile). Since a LinkedIn initial invite message is limited to only 50 words, I included a condensed description of my research in the 'Invitation to Connect' message. If a potential subjected accepted my invitation, I would then have their email address, so I subsequently followed up with the same email message to them that I initially sent to the other potential candidates via email.

I sent out invitations basically in two batches. I sent the first batch of 70 invites over the course of two weeks in early March 2018. After both Wharton and HBS held business plan competitions in mid-2018 and subsequently published the results of the winners online in May 2018, I identified another 19 potential subjects and sent out the second batch of invites by early June.

Of those participants who responded, some responded to emails and invites sometimes within hours, while others took months to respond initially or to follow-up requests to schedule actual interviews. In the end, 34 people were interviewed, 1 person declined to be interviewed citing time constraints, 4 people agreed to be interviewed but

had to cancel and subsequently never replied to follow up requests to reschedule, 5

accepted my LinkedIn invitations to connect but did not reply to further messages/emails

requesting an interview, and 45 did not reply at all to the emails or LinkedIn requests for

interviews. Of those 34 people whom I interviewed, 17 were initially contacted via

email, while the other 17 were initially contacted via LinkedIn. The interviews were

conducted over a five-month period and transcribed manually after each interview was

completed.

Methods of Data Collection

Data was collected for all three questions and I was the sole individual collecting

the data. I recorded each interview and then had each interview transcribed into word

documents for coding purposes.

Question 1.

For collection of data for Question 1, this involved a comprehensive content

analysis of wide aspects of curricula and resources at the highest-ranked MBA programs

to catalog the presence of any identified in the literature concerning training social

entrepreneurs. Utilizing the information gained in the literature review, I selected certain

characteristics to evaluate the extent of social entrepreneurship courses and resources at

each top-ranked MBA school. The data collected encompasses both MBA curricula as

well as other areas of support such as research centers, business plan competitions, and

startup incubators and/or accelerators associated either with the business school or with

the greater university community. A secondary type of data collected was the extent of traditional entrepreneurship courses and resources available as well as the same for

traditional sustainability-related topics. The data collected was primarily qualitative in

nature as it consisted of observations and excerpts from schools' websites and course

catalogs (Patton, 2002).

The categories examined are detailed more below, but the basic premise of the

analysis was to determine the extent of social entrepreneurship courses and resources at

each school. A secondary type of data collected is the extent of traditional

entrepreneurship courses and resources available as well as the same for traditional

sustainability-related topics. Whereas searching for courses, concentrations, centers,

programs, etc., some minor interpretations were required, most of the cases were fairly

clear though. Any course, concentration, center, or focus with terms such as social

enterprise or social innovation were also classified as social entrepreneurship. Courses

with entrepreneur in the title or listed under an entrepreneurship page or specialization

were classified under traditional entrepreneurship if there was no mention of a social or

sustainability aspect. Any course, concentration, center, or focus with terms such CSR;

Environmental, Social, and Governance (ESG); or Sustainability in the title or listed

under a sustainability related page, faculty subset, or specialization were combined into

the broader traditional sustainability category.

The first category examined was whether the business school offered any degrees

or certificates related to social entrepreneurship, social enterprise, social innovation, or

even sustainability related. An annotation was made if a school did have a degree in one

of those broad categories. The type of degree, e.g. standalone non-MBA Masters, dual

Masters with the MBA, or certificate supplements to the MBA, was noted too.

The second category looked at the curriculum in the main, full-time MBA program for each school. Many schools had additional executive or part-time MBA programs, but from conducting this research, it seems that most schools required all MBA students to take the same degree requirements, especially when it came to core courses, no matter in what method students are obtaining their degrees.

The first part of the curriculum analysis examined was the types of concentrations available to students. Most of the MBA programs offered some type of concentration, tract, or 'major', to their MBA students. It did vary across programs whether these concentrations were mandatory or if they showed up on the degree/transcript, but the concept of some type of specialization was present at most schools. Research was collected as the whether the MBA program in question had a specific social entrepreneurship concentration, a broader entrepreneurship concentration, and/or a sustainability concentration. All schools that offered concentrations clearly list their concentrations available prominently somewhere on their websites, so this was not an area that required much interpretation.

The second part of the curriculum analysis documented whether any social entrepreneurship, entrepreneurship, and/or a sustainability courses were included in the required core curriculum and, if so, to document the number of courses under each category. All schools required some type of course curriculum and the all schools clearly list core courses, or at least topics, so this was not an area that required much interpretation. While including social entrepreneurship courses in the core curriculum is far from what is required to thoroughly train budding social entrepreneurs, documenting the metric offers a small insight into which schools, if any, engrained social entrepreneurship in the overall MBA program.

The third part of the curriculum analysis documented whether any social entrepreneurship, traditional entrepreneurship, and/or sustainability courses were offered as part of the elective curriculum, and, if so, to record the number of courses under each category. This metric is one of the most important ones to document, as social entrepreneurs would receive a majority of their initial theory and insights into social entrepreneurship through the tailored elective curriculum. This research entailed examining the entire course catalog of each MBA program. Some degree of interpretation was required, but most schools break down their curriculum by topics, so it was often clear to see which classes fell into certain categories. I did not search the entire University-wide catalog available to students, but did include courses that students could cross-register for if they were mentioned on the MBA program websites as these courses were marketed to MBA students as part of the curriculum. The intent on this was to examine the curricula that business schools design and market to prospective students regarding social enterprise.

The next part of the analysis addressed whether the business school, and/or the greater university system, contained any social entrepreneurship, entrepreneurship, and/or sustainability related centers or research institutes, and, if not, at least had faculty research sub-divisions under these topics. The analysis first looked to see if the business school had its own social entrepreneurship center or institute, as this would be a hub for curriculum, research, and resources for the MBA students. If a center or institute was not

present in the business school, the analysis examined if there was a specific faculty sub-

department listed under social enterprise and if there was any university-wide center or

institute that offered social enterprise resources that the MBA students could utilize. The

same analysis was also conducted regarding traditional entrepreneurship and CSR centers

and institutes. All business school websites contained some link to the affiliated research

centers, and the 'About' sections of each research center clearly listed the goals and/or

subject expertise of each center, so collecting information on the stated presence of these

centers was not difficult or open to much interpretation. Later on, the interviews with the

MBA students/alumni offered the critiques of the actual depth and effectiveness of the

centers though.

The next piece of analysis examined whether the business school, or greater

university, hosted its own BPC for student entrepreneurs. If a BPC was present, it was

noted whether there was a separate category and/or prize for social enterprise related

entries. Most of the MBA websites clearly listed BPCs under references available to

students. Also, a Google search with the MBA program's name and BPC also was used

to check for the presence of BPCs.

The final piece of analysis examined whether the business school, or greater

university, ran an incubator, accelerator, or start-up lab to assist university students to

start and run entrepreneurial ventures. If an entity was present, it was noted whether

there was a separate category or tract for social enterprise related ventures.   Most of the

MBA websites clearly listed incubators or accelerators under resources available to students or as part of the centers for entrepreneurship. In addition, a Google search with the MBA program's or greater University's name and incubator and accelerator also was used to check for the presence of either entity.

Please see the appendix for the full list of data collected on each MBA program.

Questions 2 and 3.

The data for both Questions 2 and 3 was collected at the same time via semi-structured individual interviews with active social entrepreneurs who were founders or on the senior management team of a social enterprise and hold an MBA from, or were enrolled in, one of the top-rated MBA programs described in my research. The interviews were semi-structured as they included specific questions asked to each participant but also included areas for follow-up questions and free-flowing discussion (Ravitch & Carl, 2016).

Each participant was interviewed once, with topics covered in Question 2 and Question 3 contained in the interview questions. I developed a detailed interview guide with standardized questions so that I asked the same questions in the same order to each participant (Patton, 2002). The interview focused on three of the major types of interview questions: Background/Demographic Questions; Experience and Behavior Questions; and Opinion and Value Questions (Patton, 2002; Ravitch & Carl, 2016). I designed the questions as a way to evaluate the participants' perspectives on how their MBA education helped (or possibly hindered) their career as a social entrepreneur as well as to draw from their experiences as a social entrepreneur to determine how MBA programs can better meet the needs of their students interested in social enterprise. The questions addressed two major areas: Program Selection and Resources.

For Program Selection, participants were asked about their background before they enrolled in the MBA program and why they selected their program. This was designed to help to develop the narrative of participants by determining if the individual attended an MBA program with an interest in social entrepreneurship already in mind, and if they did, what skills they hoped to gain from an MBA course. This section also asked participants on if they chose their specific MBA program based on its reputation for social entrepreneurship, entrepreneurship, or other reasons, and, if they did, what resources they valued highly enough to choose to attend that program over other MBA programs. These questions were primarily part of the data collected for Research Question 2 as these topics covered the participants' views before they joined their MBA program, to include their expectations and interests in their specific programs based on information they gained from areas such as the MBA programs' marketing to prospective students.

For Resource related enquiries, the topics of the questions closely mirrored the criteria which the top-ranked MBA program were assessed against. My preliminary research showed that most of the top-ranked MBA programs do, at least nominally, offer many of the resources associated with successful social enterprise education, such as BPCs, incubators, social entrepreneurship courses, alumni network mentoring, and social enterprise or entrepreneurship centers. These questions were designed to determine if the interview participants actually used any of these resources. If they did indicate that they used them, questions were asked on the participants' perceived usefulness of the resources. If they did not use the resources, participants were asked why not. These questions also were primarily part of the data collected for Research Question 2 as they determined the participants' views of the actual usefulness of the social enterprise resources offered by their MBA programs.

After the first two topics were covered, the final stage of the interview was to ask the subject to critically evaluate how well they believed their holistic MBA experience prepared them to be a social entrepreneur. As a final question, I asked the subject to share any aspects of the intersection between social entrepreneurship and MBA programs that we may not have covered in the interview. These questions were primarily related to Research Question 3 as the themes were to generalize, based on real-world experience running a social enterprise and hindsight evaluation of their time as an MBA student, on how their MBA program, and possibly business schools as a whole, can improve the education of social entrepreneurs. Also, in relation to Research Question 3, throughout the entire interview process, participants were asked to elaborate on any ways that they felt certain resources could be improved to better train social entrepreneurs. This question was also asked as a summary follow up to ensure that the participants were able to add anything they may have omitted or realized after they had given and answer on a specific topic.

The interview protocol and questions were tested on two individuals who meet the criteria for selection. These interviews are not be included in the research. This was to serve to evaluate and refine the protocol. Once the protocol was confirmed, I will began

the interview process with the participants.

The methods of conducting the interview varied, as the participants were

geographically scattered throughout both the United States and overseas. The methods

for interviews included in-person interviews, Skype and FaceTime video calling, and via

a phone call. Not limiting the interview only to people in my geographic allowed me to

obtain data on a more diverse group of individuals with a greater breadth of experience

(Ravitch & Carl, 2016). I designed the questions to be able to be answered in a

maximum of one hour as many entrepreneurs, in my experience, are known for their

hurried schedules and time constraints. I did not want to limit participation by asking

participants for too much of their time. Each interview varied in time length, with some

as short as twenty five minutes if participants had not utilized many resources, and some

lasting over an hour; the average interview time was around forty minutes though.

Methods of Analysis

In the study, I was the only who conducted the interviews and collected the data.

Question 1.

For the data collected for Question 1, the intent was to determine the resources

available to social entrepreneurs at each MBA program and then aggregate this data for

each category for the broader population of top-rated MBA schools. Once the data was

collected, the initial analysis was a fairly straight forward summation/synthetization of

the data, e.g., eighteen of the schools sponsor BPCs and sixteen of the schools offer

specific courses on social entrepreneurship. This analysis was primarily inductive as it was used to discover patterns and themes in the data related to the relevance of resources identified in the literature as being beneficial to training social entrepreneurs. (Patton, 2002).

Questions 2 and 3.

After each interview, I organized the data into categories and analyzed the data for themes by coding the participants' responses to questions. In days when multiple interviews were conducted, I performed this step after all interviews for that day were completed. Many of the questions were posed in two parts, with the first being yes/no, and the second part asking for an elaboration on why yes or no. For the yes/no question, I simply indicated the answer in a spreadsheet and later summed the totals, e.g. fifteen social entrepreneurs found that BPCs greatly aided the development of their venture. For the elaboration questions, I coded the responses into themes and later summed and reported on these findings, e.g. of the social entrepreneurs who found that BPCs aided the development of their venture, seven believed that the mentoring from other experienced entrepreneurs was a beneficial attribute.

The coding, and creating a code set, was an iterative process. I began with deductive coding using themes that I had developed from the research and literature review and then added and refined themes and subthemes through an inductive analysis of the data (Ravitch & Carl, 2016). I began with an initial list of code themes that aligned closely with the already identified resources deemed to be valuable to social entrepreneurs, e.g. found the school's social enterprise center to be useful and relevant. As I completed more interviews, I introduced more codes for themes that I had not considered. I also refined the code on the initial interviews if I saw a pattern developing that I had missed in the first instances of coding. I also used what Maxwell (2013) describes as connecting strategies to tie coded themes together. I looked for concepts that are connected or linked to each other to attempted to analyze if certain resources or opportunities that social entrepreneurs value complement each other or jointly contribute to what the participants believed are a formative program of social enterprise instruction.

Validity Issues

There are several areas of validity that could have negatively affected my research: researcher bias, error in data code, internal validity, and selection of participants for interviews.

Researcher bias, as described by Johnson (1997), can involve researchers finding the conclusions that they already want to find and then writing their findings to confirm this. This can influence the interpretive validity of the research if the researchers do not accurately portray the intent or meaning of participants' statements. Although this is certainly a valid concern, I do not believe that this was applicable in my case. In plain terms, I am interested in the area of social enterprise education at MBA schools as an area to possibly explore further in the future in academia or the corporate sector; however, I have little or no direct involvement in the field until I started my research. I had no preconceived notions of what constitutes the best model for social enterprise education nor do I have any professional or financial interests in the topic. I believe that I can be, and was, objective and unbiased in my findings. I also tried to minimize interpretive validity by using low interference descriptors and also by including actual direct quotations when writing my research findings in order to better convey the true meaning of each participant's statements (Johnson, 1997).

I also needed to ensure that my coding of the data was consistent and accurate. I utilized the resources in Ravitch and Riggan (2017) to assist my coding process.

Internal validity concerns the degree at which I was able to justify casual relationships between factors in my study (Johnson, 1997). I believe that I was able to minimize many of these issues as my interview questions will also asked the participants to make their own connections from their life experiences in order to measure the effectiveness of their MBA education. For example, concluding that BPCs are a primary driver of success for enterprise creation simply because a majority of the participants participated in the BPCs could be drawing a false conclusion. My follow-up questions however were designed to strengthen this conclusion by asking the participants themselves to offer their opinion on how much, or little, their participation in a BPC aided their career.

The selection of my interview participants could also have led to some bias as these individuals were targeted in a precise manner and agreed to volunteer their time for this research. There is a possibility that their experiences are not representative of the general population for social entrepreneurs with MBAs. I do believe though that the population selected is quite representative of the population that I wanted to study. In the end, the participants mostly came for certain top MBA programs [Booth, Columbia, HBS, and Wharton plus Marshall, Sloan, and Kellogg close behind] with a few other programs represented by individuals. Ordinarily, this would not be consistent with a random sample, but my research is designed to target the more successful, or at least experienced, social entrepreneurs with MBAs. As the entrepreneurs whom I targeted are the most visible, via MBA program website updates, media reports, investor networks, etc., this indicates that these individuals are active in running their own social enterprises and therefore hopefully had meaningful contributions to make through their thoughts and critiques of their own experiences as an MBA.

Chapter 4: Results

Overview

Chapter 3 presented the research methodology that I used to conduct the study.

This chapter presents the results of the study. In each section, I identity themes and

subthemes and present results [direct quotations from the participants] to substantiate the

clustering and then offer an analysis of my understanding of the findings for each

subtheme. Chapter 5 offers a final set of conclusions related to each research question.

Question 1: Review of Business School Curricula and Resources offered

As indicated in Chapter 3, collection of data for Question 1 involved a

comprehensive content analysis of wide aspects of curricula and resources at the highest-

ranked MBA programs to catalog the presence of any resources identified in the literature

as beneficial to training social entrepreneurs. Below is a table with the numerical findings

of this research followed by a description of the categories.

Curricula Area	# of the 26 Schools Offering
Other degrees or certificates in sustainability or social enterprise	7
Concentrations and specializations	23
Concentration or specialization in Social Enterprise	11
Concentration or specialization in Entrepreneurship	19

Concentration or specialization in Sustainability	12
Have required core courses	26
Require Social Enterprise in the core	0
Offer Social Enterprise Electives	24

Table 4: Summary of MBA Curricula offered

Other degrees or certificates in sustainability or social enterprise.

3 business school in the top 20 offered a non-MBA degree in sustainability or social enterprise. 4 offered certificates in sustainability or social enterprises [including 1 of the schools that also offered a degree]. The remaining 14 business schools did not offer any non-MBA degrees or certificates in sustainability or social enterprise.

Concentrations and specializations.

A majority of the business schools studied offer what they deem to be majors, concentrations, focuses, minors, or specializations. This means different things at different schools; some schools offer MBAs with full specializations and some schools do not even note any specializations on the degree or transcript. Still, if offered, the MBA programs market these specialized tracks in some ways to prospective students and generally require students to take some sort of defined class schedule in order to complete these tracks.

23 of the 26 top-MBA programs in the survey advertised some sort of specialized focus tracks that students could undertake in order to gain more experience in specific subjects.

11 of the 23 top-MBA programs with subject tracks advertised some sort of specialized focus with a term or title closely linked to social enterprise or social entrepreneurship.

19 of the 23 top-MBA programs with subject tracks advertised some sort of specialized focus with a term or title closely linked to traditional entrepreneurship.

12 of the 23 top-MBA programs with subject tracks advertised some sort of specialized focus with a term or title closely linked to sustainability, corporate social responsibility, or environmental-social awareness, not including the social enterprise tracks.

Classes offered.

The next sections looked at social enterprise, sustainability, and entrepreneurship classes offered as both core and electives.

Core curricula.

All 26 of the schools surveyed appeared to offer some sort of requited core curricula.

0 schools had any specific social enterprise courses required in the core; only 2 schools required any type of specific entrepreneurship course as part of its core. 2 schools required some sort of course with a term or title closely linked to sustainability, corporate social responsibility, or environmental-social awareness as part of the core.

Electives.

24 of 26 MBA programs offered at least one course related to social enterprise or social entrepreneurship. 26 of 26 MBA programs offered at least one course related

entrepreneurship. 26 of 26 programs offered at least one type of course linked to sustainability, corporate social responsibility, or environmental-social awareness.

Examples of Social Enterprise specific classes at top-MBA programs.

The below paragraphs will detail an example of classes specifically designed for social entrepreneurs and/or starting social enterprises that are offered at top-MBA programs and will highlight the skills taught and concepts attempted to be imparted through these courses.

Wharton (2018a) offers an elective titled *MGMT812-Social Entrepreneurship.* The course is specifically designed to address social problems through a for-profit entrepreneurial lens. The course attempts to explain the process of creating a social enterprise that is profitable yet addresses a pressing social challenge. The course description stresses that social enterprises are quite different from public sector initiatives.

The University of Chicago's Booth Business School (2018) offers several social enterprise related courses. *Social Enterprise Lab 34110* covers both for-profit and non-profit social enterprises. It presents theories and tools for building social enterprises and contrasts how these can differ from traditional profit-maximizing companies. The course also offers students hands-on experiences by allowing them to consult with a local social enterprise to help this organization with a specific challenge that it faces. The *Global Social Impact Practicum 34721* is a course that sees students travelling to India to consult with social enterprises who are trying to improve the quality of life for impoverished Indians. The course attempts to teach students skills that can be transferrable if they create their own social ventures. Topics such as market assessments, impact analysis, and working in developing markets are covered. *New Social Ventures BUS34115* is a course specifically designed for students attempting to start a social enterprise and is a requirement for any student wishing to participate in the Booth hybrid BPC and incubator known as the Social New Venture Challenge. The course is designed to teach the prospective social entrepreneurs on how to craft business plans, pitch to judges/investors, and understand important concepts such as financing, managing, and growing a social startup.

The Tamer Center for Social Enterprise (2018b) at Columbia Business School offers a detailed Social Enterprise Career/Course Map for prospective social entrepreneurs. In the roadmap, there are several courses highly specific to launching social ventures. *B8559 Social Entrepreneurship: A Global Perspective* provides overviews of social entrepreneurship business models, discusses growth options for scaling social enterprises, and addresses how students can prepare to start social enterprises. *B8526 Launching Social Ventures,* as the course title indicates, attempts to provide the tools and resources to students who wish to launch social enterprise ventures. It uses case studies, visits to startup ventures, and guest speakers to address questions related to starting a venture. Students are taught how to develop a business plan and then how to pitch it to investors/judges. As a follow-up to this course, students are encouraged to take *B8527 Social Venture Incubator.* This course is intended for students with an active social venture or one that will be launched shortly. The professor and outside experts help to mentor the social entrepreneurs concerning the real-world challenges that the ventures are facing in their early stages. In the final class, the

entrepreneurs present their venture BPCs to actual impact investors and other

entrepreneurs who will assess the venture to provide advice on next steps, and, in some

cases, offer funding. Columbia Business School also offers *B8428-001: Social Impact

Real Estate,* a niche course designed for entrepreneurs who want to start social enterprise

real estate ventures.

Harvard Business School (HBS) (2018a) offers several specific courses on how to

start social enterprises. *Social Entrepreneurship and Innovation 1585* offers a theoretical

outline of the theories behind social enterprises and the differences in business models

between these enterprises and traditional firms. *Leading Social Enterprise 1505* is

designed to teach students how to develop, scale, and a lead a social enterprise. The

course aims to teach basic management and organizational skills, but with a slant that is

tailored specially towards social enterprises. The course allows for a follow-on

independent elective that sees the student further develop his/her social enterprise under

the supervision of a faculty member. HBS also offers a changing Field Course titled the

Social Innovation Lab. This course takes students into the field to study different types

of social enterprises to see how these enterprises work and to address problems facing

these enterprises. This course also allows for a follow-on independent elective that sees

the student further apply skills learned in this course to their own social venture, under

the supervision of a faculty member. HBS also offers a niche course *Public

Entrepreneurship 1623* that is designed for students who wish to start social ventures

whose clients are primarily government or other public entities, as dealing with these types of customers can be quite different than dealing with traditional private clients (Ryan, 2002). HBS (2018b) also allows second year students to undertake *Independent Projects in Social Enterprise*. Students can earn credits and cash grants to develop social enterprises. The grants even can be used for the social entrepreneurs to travel overseas if their venture is attempting to address a problem in the developing world.

Dartmouth's business school, Tuck (2018), offers numerous courses categorized in the business and ethics area, but includes one related to social enterprise in this section. *Entrepreneurship in the Social Sector* is an overview course on the rise of entrepreneurial ventures focused on improving health and wellbeing across the world. The course serves to define both for-profit and non-profit social enterprise models and organizations and then offer tools and skills that will assist an entrepreneur in launching and growing a social enterprise.

MIT Sloan (2018) offers several courses and labs designed for students wishing to develop sustainable ventures. *Strategies for Sustainable Business/Laboratory for Sustainable Business (S-Lab) 15.913* offers tools and strategies for students who are interested in the sustainability field. Both *Development Ventures 15.375* and *Effective Business Models in Frontier Markets 15.232* are specifically targeted to students who want to start social enterprises in developing countries. *Impact Ventures 15.S70* is available to fellows in social enterprise and gives practical advice and outside mentoring to these fellows on their current social ventures. *Managing Sustainable Business for People and Profits 15.662* helps social entrepreneurs to develop plans that both incorporate social and economic viability into their core operations. *Socially-Responsible*

Real Estate Development 11.S952 is a niche course designed for entrepreneurs who want to start social enterprise real estate ventures.

USC Marshall (2018) offers several classes designed for students wishing to develop various types of social enterprises. *BAEP 591: Social Entrepreneurship* is a course that provides overviews of the entrepreneurial methodologies for social enterprises and also non-profits and charities. *BAEP 567: Social Entrepreneurship: Design, Develop, and Deliver* is a course that helps social entrepreneurs develop analytical, conceptual, and practical skills needed to design, build, and grown social enterprises. *BAEP 571: Social Innovation Design* is a course designed to help early stage social entrepreneurs rapidly develop and prototype their new ventures.

NYU Stern (2018a) offers a wide array of classes under its specialization in Sustainable Business and Innovation; some of these courses are directly related to social enterprise. Courses such as the *Foundations of Social Entrepreneurship, Social Enterprise Development, Social Enterprise and Sustainable Development,* and *Social Problem-Based Entrepreneurship* arc all also included under the Entrepreneurship specialization and attempt to ground students in the basics of the field of social enterprise and give these students the tool evaluate social business models and design organizations that can solve intrinsic social problems in society. The school also offers a few niche courses related to specific domains in social enterprise. *Social Entrepreneurship in Sustainable Food Business* looks at entrepreneurship in the food supply chain that drives healthy eating outcomes and promotes positive public health outcomes. *Law and Business Social Enterprise* is joint with NYU Law School and offers a legal view of social enterprise creation.

Stanford Graduate School of Business (2017), although appearing to offer many more social innovation courses aimed to non-profit initiatives, does offer a few courses on for-profit or hybrid social enterprises. *STRAMGT 325. Starting and Growing a Social Venture* incorporates social aspects into traditional entrepreneurship topics related to starting ventures. The course is taught from the point of view of the founder and touches on the differences between social ventures and traditional entrepreneurial startups. *STRAMGT 328. Startup Garage: Social Ventures Funding Readiness* is specially designed for MBA students who are currently working on their own social ventures. The course addresses topics specific to social ventures and helps founders emerge from the course with business models. Founders are given one-on-one mentoring from faculty and outside mentors. The course is designed to prepare founders and their ventures for post-graduate funding opportunities such as fellowships or incubators or accelerators. *MGTECON 383. Measuring Impact in Practice* is a course designed to teach students how to measure impact in social enterprises and could be helpful for founders to design strategies around and measure the outcomes of the social impact of their ventures.

Specialized Centers.

15 of the 26 business schools advertised some type of center or institute with a specific focus on social entrepreneurship; 5 other business schools without social enterprise centers did indicate that the greater university housed a social enterprise center. 23 of 26 business schools advertised specific entrepreneurship centers or institutes, while the 3 without them had an entrepreneurship center run by the greater university. 11 of the

26 business schools had a center or institute linked to sustainability, corporate social responsibility, or environmental-social awareness; of the 15 without, 13 of those universities had a   center or institute linked to sustainability, corporate social responsibility, or environmental-social awareness housed outside of the business school.

Examples of Social Enterprise Centers at top-MBA programs.

Columbia Business School houses the Tamer Center for Social Enterprise (2018a). Columbia Business School did have some sort of program related to public and non-profit management since 1981 and then expanded this to specifically cover social enterprise in 2000. Tamer was established in 2015 to unify all social enterprise activities at the business school. The center runs a fund for social ventures, has a loan assistance program, expanded a social enterprise fellowship program, assists with classes and workshops, and funds social ventures in the greater Columbia Startup Lab, among other activities.

Booth Business School houses the Rustandy Center for Social Sector Innovation (2018). Rustandy offers fellowships and other programs that fund social enterprises, supports research around how the social sector operates, connects current students with Booth alumni, and manages the social enterprise curriculum courses and workshops.

The MIT Legatum Center (2018), while not run directly run out of the Sloan business school, is specifically targeted to student social entrepreneurs working on venture in the developing world and promoted heavily at Sloan as a resource for its MBAs. The center offers a fellowship programs, provides funding, travel stipends, access to mentors and other MIT resources, and specially tailored assistance to student social entrepreneurs with early stage ventures. The center also runs international activities and social conferences as well as produces research and other case studies related to social enterprise.

Duke Fuqua (2018a) houses The Center for the Advancement of Social Entrepreneurship [CASE]. CASE, founded in 2002, is in charge of the curriculum associated with Fuqa's MBA concentration in Social Entrepreneurship. CASE also organizes programs that brink together researchers, students, alumni, and other practitioners in the social enterprise space.

BPCs.

12 of the 26 business schools hosted their own BPCs, with at least 9 of those 12 competitions advertising some sort of assistance, category, or special prize for social ventures. Of the 14 business schools without their own BPC, 13 of their universities sponsored university-wide BPCs that MBA students could enter, with at least 6 of those 13 competitions advertising some sort of assistance, category, or special prize for social ventures. Only 1 business school – university combo, Tuck and Dartmouth, does not appear to be currently running a BPC between the two of them.

Examples of Social Enterprise related MBA BPCs.

Berkeley's Hass School of Business created The Global Social Venture Competition (GSVC) (2018) in 1999 to specifically address the growth of social enterprises. To be eligible, the venture must be a financially sustainable enterprise younger than 2 years old. Each team must have at least one founder who is a current student or recent graduate. The competition awards over $80,000 in prize money per year. Haas now partners with leading non-US MBA programs and certain corporate partners to run the competition. 2018 saw 550 applicants from over 65 countries.

Booth's Social New Venture Challenge (SNVC) (2018) is a hybrid BPC with a required semester-long class that complements the SNVC process. Each team must have at least one founder who is a current student with a 10% equity stake in the venture. Participants must have a plausible plan for a financially sustainable social venture to participate. The SNVC provides mentoring and other resources to the teams, as well as a chance to win a share of $100,000 in prize money.

HBS's BPC is called the New Ventures Competition (NVC) (2018). The competition has a business track that is open to all types of traditional startups as well as to social enterprises. The NVC also has a separate social enterprise track. Harvard graduate students are eligible to apply and receive feedback throughout the pitch process, to include mentorship and workshop hours. The social enterprise track offers a $100,000 prize pool, which is equal to the prize pool of the normal business track.

Columbia Business School's Tamer Fund for Social Ventures (2018c) is open to all Columbia affiliated social and environmental ventures. The fund is structured to seed grants for early stage social ventures. Participants participate in a BPC with pitches to professors, students, and an Investment Board of senior faculty, advisors, and investors in the social enterprise space. Winning teams receive up to $25,000 in funding and access to the resources offered by the Tamer Center and to incubator space associated with Columbia.

NYU Stern (2018b) offers the Social Venture Competition, and has been doing so for over eleven years. The competition offers a total of $50,000 prize money each year as well as pro bono services, and technical assistance to the ten best Stern-affiliated social enterprise startups based on an evaluation of their business plans and pitches.

MIT Sloan does not have a specific BPC at the business school, but the school assists with resources for the greater MIT $100K (2018) competition. This competition lasts an entire year and is actually broken down into three separate phases: Pitch, Accelerate, and Launch. Student entrepreneurs may enter one, two, or all three of the phases. Pitch is a medium in which students can quickly vet early stage startup ideas with judges. They must develop compact but detailed preliminary business plans. There are a few cash prizes of a few thousand dollars each for several winning teams. Launch is described as the comprehensive BPC part of the entire competition and is and iterative process of three rounds. Full business plans are required from semi-finalist teams. The teams receive funding and mentorship once they reach the semi-finals. There is not a specific track in the competition for social enterprise, but the website indicates that several social enterprises have made it the semi-finals and finals and have won cash prizes.

Incubators and Accelerators.

18 of the 26 business schools offered some sort of vehicle that met the earlier-presented definition of an incubator or accelerator; 4 of these 18 also indicated clearly that there is specific funding or training available for social enterprises. Of the 8 business schools without their own incubator or accelerator, 7 of their universities sponsored university-wide incubators or accelerators that MBA students could enter, with at least 2

of those 7 vehicles advertising some sort of assistance, category, or special prize for

social ventures. Only 1 business school – university combo, again Tuck and Dartmouth,

does not appear to be currently running an incubator or accelerator between the two of

them. This may be the case because the Dartmouth Entrepreneurial Center recently

announced a reorganization into a new center after receiving a large charitable gift and

will soon be back to offering both a BPC and an incubator or accelerator (Dartmouth

Office of Communications, 2018).

Examples of Social Enterprise related MBA Incubators/Accelerators.

Research for this paper indicates that most of the top MBA programs have some

sort of incubator or accelerator available to their students, whether they are run directly

by the business school or associated with the traditional university. As noted above, there

does not appear to be many incubators or accelerators designed specifically for social

enterprises, but most of the incubators and accelerators do accept social enterprises

deemed economically viable.

Columbia Business School's Tamer Center for Social Enterprise's (2018c) is one

of the few incubators designed specifically for social enterprises. The Tamer Center

provides funding to ventures selected and also offers office space in the Columbia Startup

Lab, referrals to a Columbia-wide network of social enterprise academics and

professionals, pro-bono legal services provided by Columbia Law School's Community

Enterprise Clinic, pro-bono consulting with various Columbia-associated social and

traditional entrepreneurship groups, office hour and mentorship access to executives in

residence at Columbia, access to other related events and workshops, assistance with websites and social media creation, introductions to venture capital professional who may

be seeing to invest funds in social enterprises, and other perks.

The Polsky Incubator (2018) at the University of Chicago is associated with

Booth Business School and focuses on traditional entrepreneurship and innovation. The

incubator offers basically the same perks to their companies as does the Tamer Center

described above. As later research will show, several of the Booth social entrepreneurs

that I interviewed were accepted with their social venture into the Polsky incubator

program.

MIT also offers a specific social enterprise ecosystem through several different

centers and partnerships. While the business school, Sloan, does not specifically run

these ventures, it has input and many MBA students participate for class credit. As

mentioned before, The MIT Legatum Center (2018) is specifically targeted to student

social entrepreneurs working on venture in the developing world. The center offers a

year-long fellowship program that serves much like an incubator, providing funding,

travel stipends, access to mentors and other MIT resources, and specially tailored

assistance to student social entrepreneurs with early stage ventures. In addition, the D-

Lab (2018) is an organization designed to incubate nascent MIT startups with a focus on

social enterprise in the developing world. The D-Lab offers students access to a

workshop where students can access resources to build and refine their companies. The

MIT delta v (2018) is another accelerator at the university, this one focusing on

traditional entrepreneurship. The accelerator is full-time during the summer months and

takes place both in Cambridge and New York. There is not a track for social enterprise, but delta v is open to for-profit social enterprises. Participating ventures receive office space, mentoring, stipends, and possible equity funding. The site lists several social enterprise-type ventures as having successfully completed the accelerator over the past few years.

Duke Fuqua's (2018b) offers the CASE Launchpad Prize, which functions like a BPC that transforms into an incubator/accelerator for the winners. Current Fuqua MBA students apply to the competition by submitting a detailed business plan and then go through an interview process with judges. The winners then receive $10,000 each in funding and one-on-one coaching from a CASE senior fellow in order to help grow their ventures. Duke also hosts the university-wide Duke Startup Challenge (2018) that also has a social enterprise track with several different prizes for ventures that address issues such as clean energy, again, and promoting ethical values. This competition is also like a hybrid BPC that transforms into an accelerator for the winners. Students submit detailed BPCs to start and go through two rounds of assessments. A select group of teams are then chosen to enter the summer incubator program where they receive a small amount of funding ($5,000 each). Next the remaining teams compete once again with updated business plans and progress reports. Here the teams are competing for a $50,000 grand prize as well as for other specialty awards, often tied to sustainability or social good. Winners of the startup challenge often come from Fuqua.

The HBS Rock Accelerator (2018) is run out the HBS's traditional entrepreneurship hub, the Rock Center. It offers basically the same services as mentioned above at Tamer and Polsky. Although the center does not have a social enterprise specific track, it is open to all financially viable enterprises and includes on its website several social enterprises on its list of successfully funded startups that it has incubated. The Rock Accelerator only accepts HBS related ventures, but participants are also encouraged to enter their ventures into the school-wide Harvard Innovation Labs (2018a) Venture Incubation Program (VIP). This is another program that offers many of the same services as the organizations mentioned above. In addition, the VIP is closely aligned with Harvard Innovation Labs (2018b) President's Innovation Challenge. This initiative is designed to inspire all Harvard-wide entrepreneurs to address pressing social challenges and offers over $300,000 in funding to winning ventures. There is a specific social impact track and also a track designed for health or life sciences, often an area where other social enterprises focus.

Wharton (2018b) offers the VIP-C incubator that is open to all students interested in starting ventures. It is designed to be a community, connecting like-minded students and alumni entrepreneurs and assist them with founding and scaling their enterprises. The most advanced ventures are accepted into VIP-X, an accelerator program that offers a more formalized structure and access to individual advising, seed funding, workshops, and resources such those mentioned at the institutions above. VIP-C and VIP-X do not have specific social enterprise tracks, but do list on their website a number of social enterprises that have been successfully funded.

Questions 2 and 3: Interview Analysis

As indicated in Chapter Three, collection of data for Questions 2 and 3 involved thematic analysis of semi-structured interviews with social entrepreneurs how had MBA from top-rated business schools.   The below sections detail information about how the interviews were conducted, the demographics of the participants, and a thematic framework of their responses.

Background Demographics of Participants

Below is a breakdown of the participants by a few major categories. The full demographic worksheet, along with each participants' answers to the yes/no interview questions is located in Appendix 7.

Participant #	Sex	School	Grad Year	For Profit or Hybrid?	Company Sector	Primary Country of Firm's HQ	Primary Target of Firm's Product or Services
1	M	Harvard Business School	2017	For Profit	Employment Technology	USA	USA
2	M	Harvard Business School	2018	For Profit	Medical/Healthcare	USA	Worldwide
3	M	Columbia Business School	2013	For Profit	Medical/Healthcare	USA	Global EM
4	M	UCLA - Anderson	2017	For Profit	Food/Agriculture	USA	USA
5	M	Columbia Business School	2016	Hybrid	Food/Agriculture	USA	Global EM
6	F	Chicago - Booth	2017	For Profit	Data/Technology	USA	USA
7	F	USC - Marshall	2018	For Profit	Food/Agriculture	USA	Africa
8	M	Chicago - Booth	2017	Hybrid	Political Engagement	USA	USA
9	M	Chicago - Booth	2017	Hybrid	Financial Services	USA	USA
10	M	NYU - Stern	2016	For Profit	Food/Agriculture	Colombia	Colombia
11	M	Columbia Business School	2017	For Profit	Food/Agriculture	India	India
12	F	USC - Marshall	2017	For Profit	Restaurant Dining	USA	USA

13	F	Northwestern - Kellogg	2015	For Profit	Financial Services	USA	USA
14	F	Chicago - Booth	2016	For Profit	Education Technology	USA	USA
15	M	NYU - Stern	2012	For Profit	Medical/Healthcare	USA	Global EM
16	M	Columbia Business School	2012	For Profit	Education Technology	USA	USA
17	F	MIT - Sloan	2019	For Profit	Data/Technology	Ghana	Africa
18	M	USC - Marshall	2014	For Profit	Apparel (Retail)	USA	USA
19	M	UPenn - Wharton	2014	For Profit	Financial Services	Indonesia	Indonesia
20	F	Cornell - Johnson	2012	For Profit	Apparel (Retail)	USA	Worldwide
21	F	Northwestern - Kellogg	2015	For Profit	Financial Services	USA	USA
22	F	UPenn - Wharton	2017	For Profit	Sanitation	India	Global EM
23	F	UPenn - Wharton	2016	For Profit	Medical/Healthcare	India	Worldwide
24	F	Northwestern - Kellogg	2017	For Profit	Food/Agriculture	India	India
25	F	UPenn - Wharton	2014	For Profit	Financial Services	Indonesia	Indonesia
26	M	Duke - Fuqua	2017	Hybrid	Political Engagement	USA	USA
27	M	MIT - Sloan	2015	Hybrid	Food/Agriculture	Pakistan	Pakistan
28	F	MIT - Sloan	2014	For Profit	Employment Technology	USA	USA
29	F	Chicago - Booth	2017	For Profit	Data/Technology	USA	USA
30	M	UPenn - Wharton	2017	For Profit	Medical/Healthcare	USA	USA
31	F	Harvard Business School	2019	For Profit	Employment Technology	USA	Global EM
32	M	Harvard Business School	2018	For Profit	Employment Technology	USA	USA
33	M	Harvard Business School	2018	For Profit	Sanitation	USA	USA
34	M	UPenn - Wharton	2017	Hybrid	Education Technology	USA	USA

Table 5: High-level participant demographics

Gender.

19 men (56%) and 15 women (44%) were interviewed. Bloomberg cites the share of women overall in MBA programs at 38% (Leiber, 2018). Below is the full count and breakdown by graduation year.

Graduation Year	F	M	Grand Total
2012	1	2	3
2013		1	1
2014	2	2	4
2015	2	1	3
2016	2	2	4
2017	5	8	13
2018	1	3	4
2019	2		2
Grand Total	15	19	34

Table 6: Participant demographics by graduation year and gender

School and Graduation Years Breakdown.

There were 11 different MBA programs represented by the interview participants. I also had sent invitations to multiple students and alumni from 4 other schools (Babson, Haas, Stanford, and Yale), but none of those alumni or students responded.

28 of the 34 participants were MBA graduates, while the other 6 were current MBA students at the time of the interview, with 4 of those 6 subsequently graduating

shortly after the interviews in May/June 2018. Below is the full count and breakdown by graduation year.

School	2012	2013	2014	2015	2016	2017	2018	2019	Total
Chicago - Booth					1	4			5
Columbia Business School	1	1			1	1			4
Cornell - Johnson	1								1
Duke - Fuqua						1			1
Harvard Business School						1	3	1	5
MIT - Sloan			1	1				1	3
Northwestern - Kellogg				2		1			3
NYU - Stern	1				1				2
UCLA - Anderson						1			1
Upenn - Wharton			2		1	3			6
USC - Marshall			1			1	1		3
Grand Total	**3**	**1**	**4**	**3**	**4**	**13**	**4**	**2**	**34**

Table 7: Participant demographics by school and graduation year

Purely for-profit vs. Hybrid Breakdowns.

Of the 34 interview participants, 28 described their enterprise as a for-profit
enterprise, while 6 considered their enterprise to be a hybrid non-profit based entity that
still is funded primarily through revenue.

Geographic Breakdowns.

For the country of headquarters for firms, i.e., where the firm and the founder is
primarily based out of, there were 6 different countries represented by the interview
participants, with 25 of the 34 founders being based in the United States. Below is the
full count and breakdown by country and whether the firm was a solely for-profit venture
or a hybrid social enterprise.

Country of HQ	For Profit	Hybrid	Grand Total
Colombia	1		1
Ghana	1		1
India	4		4
Indonesia	2		2
Pakistan		1	1
USA	20	5	25
Grand Total	28	6	34

Table 8: Participant demographics by school and For Profit vs. Hybrid ventures

For the country/region where the firms state that they primarily focused on selling
their products and/or services, there were 8 different answers represented by the

interview participants, with 18 listing the United States as their sole market, 5 stating that their market was across all global emerging markets, 3 targeting consumers worldwide, 2 focusing on Africa as a continent, and the rest contained to specific non-US countries for now. Below is the full count and breakdown by country and whether the firm was a solely for-profit venture or a hybrid social enterprise.

Company Sector Breakdown.

There were 10 different broad primary company sectors represented by the interview participants. The sectors listed as primary, often were taken from each company's own descriptions of their business models and represented the sector where a majority of their goods/services or customers were concentrated. For example, a company with a digital app marketed to emerging market farmers would be classified in the Food/Agriculture sector and not simply the Data/Technology sector since the firm's revenues depended on its clients' agricultural production. Below is the full count and breakdown by sector and whether the firm was a solely for-profit venture or a hybrid social enterprise. Overall, there were 30 different companies represented as I interviewed a set of 2 co-founders from 4 separate companies.

Sector	#
Apparel (Retail)	2
Data/Technology	3
Education Technology	3

Employment Technology	4
Financial Services	5
Food/Agriculture	7
Medical/Healthcare	5
Political Engagement	2
Restaurant Dining	1
Sanitation	2
Grand Total	**34**

Table 9: Participant demographics by company sector

Coding of Interview Data into Themes and Subthemes

Before I began coding the individual interviews, I created a broad list of themes based on my initial research questions, findings from the literature review, and thematic framework found in the interview questions. The framework was broken down into 3 major theme categories, each corresponding to a phase of the participants' MBA experience. Theme 1: *Motivations and Program Selection* was centered on the participants' education journeys, or why they initially wanted to attend an MBA program and what led them to select their specific MBA program. Theme 2: *Reflections on the Usefulness Social Enterprise Curricula and Resources* involved the participants' experiences during their MBA degree, examining what resources related to social enterprise they utilized and what they thought of these resources. Theme 3: *Thoughts on Improving Social Enterprise Training in MBA Programs and Final Reflections on the*

MBA Experience involved the participants' thoughts on how social enterprise resources and curricula could be further improved in MBA programs, based on their MBA experiences and their experiences running social enterprises.

I used an iterative coding process to facilitate in the analysis of the data (Maxwell, 2013). I created my initial code set based on the themes listed in the paragraph above and then refined these codes to create more specific codes within this code set (Ravitch and Carl, 2016). After each interview, I had the audio transcribed into a document and I examined the responses and then refined and added subthemes based on each participant's responses. After all interviews were completed, I utilized NVivo 12 software to organize my themes and subthemes and then group direct quotes under each subtheme. In addition to assigning these themes and subthemes, I also manually tabulated the responses to the Yes/No questions, e.g. 'Did you take any social enterprise courses?' in each interview and recorded these in a spreadsheet.

The sections below present the subthemes that I developed through coding, then list applicable direct quotations by participants that I assigned to each code. As mentioned earlier, I tried to minimize interpretive validity by using low interference descriptors and also by including actual direct quotations when writing my research findings in order to better convey the true meaning of each participant's statements (Johnson, 1997). After each set of quotes for a code, I indicated my summary understanding of each subtheme. Please note that the sum of all responses under a subtheme do not always exactly equal the total number of 34 participants. Some total may be less than 34, as some people may not have provided a clear answer to each question, a question may not have been applicable to a participant's experience, while

other total may be greater than 34 as participant game answers at times that covered

multiple subthemes. After each of the three major themes, I presented a summary of

integrating conclusions across the subthemes within the larger theme.

Theme 1: Motivations and Program Selection

Motivations and Reasons for obtaining an MBA.

The first few questions focused on why the participant decided to go to business

school in the first place and the skills that they thought they would obtain from the MBA

program.

Below is a chart of the subthemes and the number of participant references to each topic.

As noted above, the totals may be less than or greater than 34 based on if the participants

directly answered the questions and the responses that they gave. Not all responses

indicated in the reference table below are represented in the quotes sections below,

especially if the response was a simply Yes/No answer without much context.

Subtheme	References
1. Motivations & Program Selection	34
1.1 Wanted to start a social enterprise	28
Already had a started social enterprise or at least had the idea for their specific social enterprise.	22
Fully realized during the MBA program that they wanted to start a social enterprise.	6
1.2 Expectations from an MBA that would aid in starting a social enterprise.	28

Subtheme	References
Gain better understanding of skills and fundamentals for running a business.	15
Gain relationships and mentorship and/or access to networks.	15
Business school provides time and resources to develop a venture while in school.	8
Needed the credentials or credibility that come with an MBA.	6
Understand more about entrepreneurship principles.	3
1.3 Reasons for picking their specific school.	21
Chosen based on overall reputation of the school (best MBA program they could get into).	6
Chosen primarily based on location.	7
Perceived impression of the Social Enterprise program/curriculum was a major deciding factor.	8

Table 10: Theme 1 Subtheme reference counts

Wanted to start a social enterprise.

Of the 34 individuals interviewed, 28 responded that they either had started a social enterprise or had a desire to start a social enterprise, or some socially-minded organization, before coming to business school. Examples of some of the more detailed responses under each category are below.

Already had a started social enterprise or at least had the specific intention to start a social enterprise.

Participant 7 (F, USC): "I knew beforehand. I came up with the concept for it in my under-grad entrepreneurship class at [redacted] University. So, I always had the idea at the back of my mind, but when I was applying for my MBA program, I knew that I wanted to go back to school to get access and get resources to help me reinvigorate the idea."

Participant 10 (M, NYU): "That was like the main motivation for doing the MBA, since I applied I knew I wanted to come back to Columbia to start my own business and I knew it was like a socially oriented business, because like that's where the opportunities are in emerging markets, so that was a given from the get go."

Participant 11 (M, Columbia): "I had already started a social enterprise before I joined."

Participant 14 (F, Chicago Booth): "I knew I wanted to start some kind of social company and business during the application process; I guess the process of applying is kind of what helped me narrow down what that was, but I knew I wanted to […] The reason I was going to school was to start something and change careers."

Participant 17 (F, MIT Sloan): "I already knew, so I had started it before school and then had intentions, we were developing a new product within […] the one that I started before school uses a business model, but we are non-profit, but we had been developing a product that we wanted to spin off into a for-profit enterprise, so I knew coming to school I wanted to strengthen the non-profit, but also figure out how to found a for-profit technology company."

Participant 18 (M, USC): "I had started it beforehand and I kind of used business [...] like I always wanted to go to business school, even prior to starting the venture and I thought like okay I'll go to business school and maybe learn some things that will help me grow this venture and maybe avoid some pitfalls and stuff."

Participant 20 (F, Cornell): "Yeah, I think I applied with my vision being I wanted to start my own social enterprise. [...] I definitely had a sense that I wanted to do something along those lines."

Participant 22 (F, Wharton): "I knew I wanted to start a social enterprise."

Participant 24 (F, Kellogg): "I didn't know 100% but I did have an idea before joining Kellogg. So, I think I joined business school in August or September, 2015, and we started the company around May. But it wasn't registered. It wasn't a company it was nothing like that. It was just an idea which I knew I wanted to work on but I didn't know where it would go during business school. So, I was, I would say, like 70% sure, but then it became more positive a few months into business school."

Participant 29 (F, Chicago Booth): "I already had the idea for the company that [my cofounder] and I co-founded going into business school and had even taken a few steps to start researching it before I was in business school. But I wasn't sure if it was sort of a good enough idea to actually kind of go all in and build the company and not pursue other career opportunities, and so I knew I wanted to dig into it more in business schools and sort of test the idea, workshop it, get feedback, and I did that."

Participant 34 (M, Wharton): "I'd taken a first crack at it when I was in undergrad, and I liked it and I had the idea and the framework and so I actually came in, it was part of my application. And it was something I kind of intended to do from the day I got there."

Some of these individuals indicate that their main motivations for going to school were to gain skills to better improve their current social enterprise or to launch a social enterprise for which they have a specific idea. They had either begun the process of founding and growing a social enterprise, or had a tangible idea for a venture in their head. Others did not know exactly what organization they wanted to start, but had the ideas to start some type of social enterprise. What many of these participants had in common though is that they felt that the best way to further their goal of starting and/or furthering their social enterprise was to obtain and MBA. Analysis of later questions shows what these individuals hoped to gain from an MBA in order to start or grow their social enterprise.

Had thoughts to a starting some type of an organization, but fully realized during the MBA program that they wanted to start a social enterprise.

Participant 1 (M, HBS): "I knew I wanted to be an entrepreneur, for sure and I believe then like a socially-minded person. I would say, yes, most likely. I didn't know exactly if it was going to be a social enterprise, a B Corp, but I had an idea that I wanted to do something good for the world."

Participant 15 (M, NYU): "So, I think in the back of my mind I had an idea at some point I'd like to do something to start an organization but I never thought I'd start it right out of business school."

Participant 19 (M, Wharton): "I think I came in with the goal of starting a company that had some sort of impact. I wouldn't say I was signing on to be a social entrepreneur or even now I'm not sure I qualify. I think, depending on your definition, I might or might not qualify as a social entrepreneur, but I definitely wanted to be an entrepreneur that was working on something that would impact"

Participant 21 (F, Kellogg): "I had it in the back of my mind that it would be a dream of mine. I didn't have a specific idea or plan, but it's always something I wanted to do."

Participant 23 (F, Wharton): "I knew that I wanted to start my own company. I did not know that I would do a social enterprise […] So, during my time, I would say my second year is when I took some classes and designed my business plan. That is when it hit me, okay, this is what I'm going to do when I graduate."

Participant 25 (F, Wharton): "Even as I was coming in, I was already interested in sort of, doing something in the intersection of business and development."

A theme amongst these individuals is that many seem to have had an interest in starting some type of organization, whether it may have been a traditional start-up, a non-profit, or something else, and that their business school experience steered them towards social enterprise. Some indicate their interest in being an entrepreneur first and subsequently integrating social concepts into their thinking in order to become the founders or the social enterprises that they are today. These individuals, like those in the subtheme above, believed that an MBA program provided the best skills and resources needed to start some type of entrepreneurial or non-profit enterprise.

Expectations from an MBA that would aid in starting a social enterprise.

The individuals above who indicated that they came to business school with either an already functioning social enterprise, or at least an idea or desire to start a social enterprise, were then asked what they thought, or hoped, that they would gain from going to business school for an MBA that would help them further their goal of starting a social enterprise. Below are the main themes from their answers. The reasons given are not mutually-exclusive, so some participants indicated more than one leading reason for attending an MBA program.

Gain better understanding of skills and fundamentals for running a business.

15 Participants indicated that they felt that an MBA would give them the necessary skills and fundamentals associated with starting and running a business.

Participant 1 (M, HBS): "Generally, I think wanted to develop as a leader, as a manager, understand strategy, understand ecosystem type work."

Participant 2 (M, HBS): "Just a more well-rounded skill set. I was a trader for five years beforehand so I have a lot of hardcore finance experience, but the softer stuff, the leadership, the [….] I mean I didn't really do a balance sheet too much cause I was dealing with currency so I wanted more well-rounded business education that would give me the confidence to be able to run a company on my own."

Participant 10 (M, NYU): "I still thought that I lacked the business skills that I needed for a startup and my background is in engineering and electronic engineering and my previous work before the MBA was in consulting which was a little bit in business but still it was very much geared towards tech, so I lacked some of the skills that I knew a business degree would give me."

Participant 11 (M, Columbia): Reference 1: "I was looking for was an education in entrepreneurship, so then social entrepreneurship would pay. So I wanted to go to a school which would have that focus as well, so that I could build up my skills, specific skills too." Reference 2: "I had spent about six years before that in social enterprise before I joined my MBA… so what I was looking to, is to step back and take my operational knowledge and add on a layer of theory and structure to it."

Participant 13 (F, Kellogg): "I was hoping to get experience in the world of finance. That's something I was totally blind to. I didn't have any experience prior to Kellogg. Not even accounting. Nothing. I also thought that I would get experience in like nonprofit boards, and board seats, like just boards in general, board governance. I thought that that would be a really useful skillset. Marketing in general. Just sort of creating campaigns and marketing tools I thought also would be a key piece."

Participant 15 (M, NYU): "I was not uncomfortable with numbers, but I also couldn't look at a balance sheet or income statement and kind of immediately get it… I was kind of interested in the whole spectrum of just getting a base layer of confidence in a variety of kind of business skills and management also, I think was a big piece for sure. Thinking about how the business professionals and how does the business world think about the best practices and management."

Participant 16 (M, Columbia): "I felt like I didn't know anything about running a business… I felt like business school would be a place to learn all the things that I didn't learn as an undergrad that would actually help me run a business."

Participant 17 (F, MIT Sloan): "The first part of it is the technical skills, so I was leading an organization, I had a private sector business background as well as a government non-profit background, so I'd worked for government and NGO and private sector before going to school. With the CEO of this organization which was growing, the only one with really professional international work experience, so all eyes were on me for every business function; for operation, for finance, for merging, for everything and I felt that I was pushing the limits of what I knew and wanted to increase my capacity technically."

Participant 20 (F, Cornell): "I had, up until then, not taken any business course whatsoever, apart from a series of economics courses in undergrad which were much more focused on modeling for a very high-level, theoretical economics as opposed to practical, applied economics. So, yeah, I felt like I just needed a set of skills of how to run a business. What were the different types of qualities that I would need?"

Participant 23 (F, Wharton): "I knew I needed business skills, even for social enterprises it's so important to have an understanding for the product market space, how you scale your organization, how you get like-minded individuals together and hire them and motivate employees and it was very clear to me that the kind of skillsets I had to require, I could only get at a Business School."

Participant 25 (F, Wharton): "So business school, and particularly Wharton, seemed like the right place to be, to learn kind of the hardcore financial skills."

Participant 26 (M, Duke): "I'd been sort of running my own business, but half-assedly. Kind of making things up as I went along. And I wanted some training and best practices behind that."

Participant 29 (F, Chicago Booth): "I wanted my career to be about developing innovative business models that made a dent in social problems. I kind of wanted to learn just the basics of any kind of business model first and then apply that to social businesses."

Participant 30 (M, Wharton): "Number two is just being able to be more proficient in speaking the language of business so venture, ROI, and all that… And sure that's technically stuff you could learn on the job and everything, but I wanted to get a formal education in that."

Participant 31 (F, HBS): "Understanding how markets work, so how my personal project compared to an existing system. What intensives I could use to make it work."

A main theme present in this area is that, for many participants, they had experience in social enterprise or non-profit areas already, but felt that they did not have the 'hard' business or leadership/management skills necessary to actually start and/or sustain a market-focused business. These participants realized that, like the theories presented earlier, social entrepreneurs requires a strong grasp of traditional business and entrepreneurship skills and concepts in order to be successful. Many felt as though they had the requisite social enterprise skills but lacked the business skills to found and grow a company. Some cite financial training and others were looking to obtain more management, marketing, or operations skills. This is consistent with the research presented in the literature review that indicates that successful social enterprises are run similar to normal for-profit enterprises and thus requires their founders and leaders to have similar business skills.

Gain relationships and mentorship and/or access to networks and resources.

15 Participants believed that an MBA program would give them access to networks, relationships, resources, or mentors that they would not be able to get elsewhere.

Participant 3 (M, Columbia): "I guess I probably also figured the network would be important."

Participant 7 (F, USC): "I was hoping to get very similar things to what I had in my under-grad experience, which was just hopefully great connections with different professors. And then, of course, any sort of business competitions that might be on campus, or even off campus, that you had to be a student to be applicable to apply for. And then, any mentoring, or any other guidance that might come from just, even an academic environment."

Participant 11 (M, Columbia): "The third part was just very specific development of the business model that I wanted to build into my own social enterprise, so I wanted mentorship from the professors or alumni, or the program that they do in business school so that we could look at aspects of product implementing in a business model."

Participant 12 (F, USC): "I expected mentorship and a bit of networking relationships. I really wanted a co-founder. I mean, I was looking for a co-founder."

Participant 14 (F, Chicago Booth): Reference 1: "It would just give me access to resources, network, and I thought it would be a better way than just going out there by myself and doing it." Reference 2: "You network in with people and all of a sudden your thing just takes off. You make all these connections. Oh, you need money? You got this guy here or you need this, you've got this other guy here."

Participant 17 (F, MIT Sloan): Reference 1: "I think, too, I wanted a network of people who were interested in emerging markets, who were interested in social impact." Reference 2: "I think MBAs are kind of the best business accelerators because you get access to leaders in your field at a place like MIT you get access to a lot of money to experiment with your idea and that could mean that you have entrepreneurs."

Participant 18 (M, USC): "You network with people and all of a sudden your thing just takes off. You make all these connections. Oh, you need money? You got this guy here, or you need this, you've got this other guy here."

Participant 19 (M, Wharton): "I think the network aspect, as well. Gaining that network."

Participant 21 (F, Kellogg): "One was that I a network. I wanted to be among similarly minded folks. I knew I could get hard skills that I might need anywhere, but I wanted to be around people who were similarly minded particularly because if I did want to start something, I was hoping it would be a place I could meet potential partners, which is what exactly happened. Being in a community where I knew a lot of other people were coming to that program because they had social entrepreneurship or social innovation interests was really important to me."

Participant 22 (F, Wharton): "I also thought, through the MBA, I would get good mentorship, working with a professor."

Participant 24 (F, Kellogg): "The objective of applying to business school in the first place was to kind of incubate that idea, get a network, maybe get some co-founders, get some investors, and then re-launch the business post-business school."

Participant 27 (M, MIT Sloan): Reference 1: "I come from Pakistan, so one of the key things missing in my portfolio or my resume was the access to an international network. So one of the key things that I was keen to build on was a network which could give me access to people all over the world." Reference 2: "It made lot of sense to try and come here and get access to resources. And when I say resources, I mean people, I mean access to professors, access to technology, all that kind of stuff."

Participant 28 (F, MIT Sloan): "I thought the network was going to be one of the most important things I can gain. It was something having started in a previous social enterprise before that I been feeling had as strong a network for this work."

Participant 30 (M, Wharton): "Two things, it was the relationships and the network that you get out of it. Well actually three things I think so, the relationships and the network so, and they've already paid off like ten-folds. By the people, mentors, advisors, connections, those sorts of things. I met my co-founder of the social enterprise I'm doing now at business school so, so the networks and the connections is number one."

Participant 32 (M, HBS): "Be part of the Harvard community that I would have access to professors at the other schools, and that obviously in the Boston area that in included, the way that I found out MIT professors and even a lot of the professors at Northeastern put out a lot of research in the area that I'm working in."

In this area, participants commented that access to a diverse network of people, to include mentors, who could help them with their business plans and to build their businesses was very important.   Participants talked about the strong brands or networks at certain business schools and felt that these would be very valuable both while in business school and afterwards as an alumnus. Participants also valued the networks and contacts offered by the larger university communities, in some cases, especially when their ventures touched on areas not totally related to business, such as health or technology. This is tied to the research presented earlier that cites the importance of mentors and other resources. In addition to access to mentors, it seems that participants also valued the access to other like-minded students as these people could be good sounding-boards for business ideas as well as potential partners and co-founders in a new business.

Business school provides time and resources to develop a venture while in school.

8 participants felt that the 2 years in business school would provide them with time, resources, and structure needed to start a successful enterprise.

Participant 4 (M, UCLA): "Time. I needed time… It probably sounds like a nontraditional answer, in the sense that when I went to business school, I spent all of my time building, pivoting and iterating businesses. For me the network and the academics were all secondary because I had a specific goal."

Participant 14 (F, Chicago Booth): "I thought it was just going to be a more structured way to start something on my own…I thought it would just give me a program, or a blueprint, to follow, in terms of starting a social enterprise."

Participant 17 (F, MIT Sloan): "I found that a lot of other business schools talked about starting companies in emerging markets, but here was a community, a dedicated program, and financial resources to actually go and do that while I was in school. That was a turning point for me."

Participant 24 (F, Kellogg): "The objective was to get funds, to look for like-minded partners, co-founders, and kind of fine-tune the business model, so that we were ready for launch once I finished business school… The objective of applying to business school in the first place was to kind of incubate that idea, get a network, maybe get some co-founders, get some investors, and then re-launch the business post-business school."

Participant 25 (F, Wharton): "And that's a function of just being able to walk away from your day job, and just having that space to think about what else do you want to do with your life."

Participant 29 (F, Chicago Booth): "I already had the idea for the company that we co-founded going into business school and had even taken a few steps to start researching it before I was in business school. But I wasn't sure if it was sort of a good enough idea to actually kind of go all in and build the company and not pursue other career opportunities, and so I knew I wanted to dig into it more in business schools and sort of test the idea, workshop it, get feedback, and I did that."

Participant 32 (M, HBS): "I knew that going back to school would give me a structured window and structured schedule, with a bunch of free time where I'd be able to sort of pursue some of these experiments… I needed to have a super structured schedule for the next 18 months, and would have time to do some big experiment and then also access to people."

Participant 34 (M, Wharton): Reference 1: "I felt like I could make progress for a year or two, and it's like having an incubator where I was also building a backup plan and having alternative options if I needed them." Reference 2: "I conceivably could have just quit my job and started a startup, but I would not have been comfortable with that level of risk and I would be a head case. And I would not have nearly the amount of resources that I had."

Some of these participants valued the structure and time provided by a traditional two-year MBA program. The additional resources offered in the MBA program seems to be a key aspect of this subtheme though, as anyone could just quit their job to work on a full-time new social venture for two years, and not have to pay the several hundred thousand dollars to go to business school. These participants felt that they could quit their jobs and work on the ventures full-time, but within a structured network and program that would afford them much-needed assistance, such as access to resources. 5 of the 8 respondents in this category also cited other reasons mentioned in the prior themes for attending business school.

Needed the credentials or credibility that come with an MBA.

6 participants felt that gaining an MBA would give them credibility with investors, employees, and others in the industries in which they wished to operate.

Participant 3 (M, Columbia): "The MBA was the way to give me not only the tools that I thought that I would need, but also the credentials as well."

Participant 10 (M, NYU): "The first one is credentials, like I knew from all the master degrees, MBAs in Columbia offer a higher level of recognition, so just coming back here and having connections with the government, with the investment sector would be a lot easier with an MBA program, rather than like another Master's Degree."

Participant 17 (F, MIT Sloan): "And then the third reason, was just probably one of the most important, but the least good to say, is as a female entrepreneur trying to raise venture money, women get so little venture money that having the credentials of going to a top MBA program can really help."

Participant 19 (M, Wharton): "I think firstly would be credibility. I think if you wanted to create something that with significant impact, fundraising would always be a critical piece of that puzzle, and I think an MBA, for better or worse, does give you that credibility."

Participant 26 (M, Duke): "I think the main thing was credibility to have a career change. I was going to be making a big transition and wanted to be able to point out an inflection point in my career to allow that. And then credibility as a business person."

Participant 30 (M, Wharton): "Maybe from a more vain perspective, was having the validation and stamp of approval just from a brand perspective. Going out and raising investment money, for better or worse, whether you agree with it or not, it's easier when you have a top school's name attached to you. They just take you I think. There's one less hurdle for you to have to get over with in their mind."

While credibility is not a skill that can be taught directly at business schools, an MBA can be seen as a mark of credibility in certain cases, especially as a manager or when trying to pitch a business plan (Goffee & Nicholson, 1994; Simpson, 2000 and 2006; Cocchiara, et al., 2010). Some participants felt that an MBA from a prestigious school would offer them credibility when they were speaking to potential investors or partners. They felt that this was essential when trying to launch and grow a new social enterprise as credibility can often get you initial meetings and help investors and others overcome doubts about an entrepreneur.

Understand more about entrepreneurship principles.

3 Participants believed that business school was the best place to learn about entrepreneurship and innovation.

Participant 1 (M, HBS): "One of my goals coming to business school was to better understand the innovation economy as well, and so I didn't want to have some exposure to that side of things, to the entrepreneurship side."

Participant 11 (M, Columbia): Reference 1: "I was looking for was an education in entrepreneurship, so then social entrepreneurship would pay. So I wanted to go to a school which would have that focus as well, so that I could build up my skills, specific skills too." Reference 2: "I think one aspect was just looking at the process of entrepreneurship, and then understanding from the lens of a structure and a framework, and then putting my own enterprise into that lens and seeing how to build a bit better; so that was one."

Participant 23 (F, Wharton): "I was more interested in sort of first getting an understanding of how to build a venture and then sort of customizing my business model based on the market that it will be serving for."

Similar to the participants who wanted to gain business skills, some hope to gain entrepreneurship skills since, these participants realized that, like the theories presented earlier, social entrepreneurs requires a strong grasp of traditional entrepreneurship skills and concepts in order to be successful. Many felt as though they had the requisite knowledge of social impact but lacked the entrepreneurship skills to found and grow a company.

Reasons for picking their specific school.

Participants had different reasons for choosing their specific programs, but they generally fell into a few broad categories. Some chose their school based solely on location, as they did not want to move from where they lived due to personal reasons or preferences. Some chose the school that was ranked the best overall as an MBA program, irrespective of social enterprise. Some did consider their program's reputation for social enterprise as a primary factor. Not all participants articulated exactly why they choses their specific school.

In this category there probably are a combination of reasons why they chose that specific school though. For instance, if they said they picked their program solely based on location, a city like New York still offers probably ten or more MBA choices and

Chicago, Boston, and Los Angeles offer almost as many choices, some ranked in the top-20 . People still have the ability to pick from different schools in one location. From personal experience though, people may not give fully transparent reasons for attending a specific business school, especially if they were not able to get into their top-school for various reasons. In this question I specifically chose not to drill down too far in order to avoid putting a person on the defensive.

Chosen primarily based on location.

7 Participants indicated that they picked their program primarily based on location.

Participant 5 (M, Columbia): "For me, I only applied to Columbia. I lived in New York and I wanted to do a program in New York and so that was the basic parameters that went into it."

Participant 10 (M, NYU): "I knew I wanted to be either in San Francisco or New York, so those were the regions where I looked for business schools"

Participant 13 (F, Kellogg): "I ended only applying to Kellogg for a variety of reasons, but geographically, I needed to be in that area. I needed to be in Chicago."

Participant 15 (M, NYU): "I wanted to be in New York for personal reasons at the time."

Participant 18 (M, USC): "I'd lie if I said I did. I had already had the business going. I was in Los Angeles […] So, I decided to stay locally."

Participant 26 (M, Duke): "It was primarily location."

Participant 29 (F, Chicago Booth): "I already lived in Chicago, and so I only applied to Kellogg and Booth because I knew I was going to stay in Chicago."

Participants who picked their schools mostly based on location say that they did so due to personal reasons, the interest in living in a particular city, or the fact that they lived there already and did not want to relocate.

Chosen based on overall reputation of the school (best MBA program they could get into).

6 Participants indicated that they chose to go to what they felt was the overall best-ranked or most prestigious school that they could get into.

Participant 3 (M, Columbia): "I would say that I picked Columbia because it was an Ivy League school."

Participant 4 (M, UCLA): "No. Essentially, I applied to seven schools. I got into two, and wait listed at one. I chose between Duke and UCLA."

Participant 7 (F, USC): "I do not think I even realized that they had the social enterprise lab until after I started the program, so I think the answer would probably be no… I just knew that USC has such a great reputation and such an extensive network that even without this whole enterprise aspect thing, I knew it would be a valuable program."

Participant 30 (M, Wharton): "Honestly, I just wanted to go to the best school that I could get in to. It wasn't really their commitment to social enterprisers, it was just the best education possible."

Participant 33 (M, HBS): "Not really. I think when you apply to MBA program it's like, which one's the best, and hope you get into one, right?"

Participant 34 (M, Wharton): "I selected Wharton because it was the best school that I got into and because it was on the East Coast."

Similar to the participants who indicated earlier that they wanted to go to school for credentials or credibility, some participants valued the name-brand or perceived recognition of the school as the most important selection factor, choosing to attend the best school to which they were accepted. 3 of the 6 who chose their school based on this were in the group above who indicated that credentials were a major factor for obtaining an MBA.

Perceived impression of the Social Enterprise program/curriculum was a major deciding factor.

8 participants stated that their initial perception of their school's social enterprise program/resources was a major deciding factor in where they decided to attend.

Participant 1 (M, HBS) (M, HBS): "That was a big factor. I talked to the social enterprise initiative folks. Felt good about the focus and orientation there, both in terms of the social enterprise club but also the opportunities to do work in education, what some alumni were doing and other areas like that. I definitely felt like that would be something I could pursue if I came here."

Participant 12 (F, USC): "Marshall is the only program that has their social entrepreneurship lab that was founded by a social entrepreneur who is still the acting-director. I was really excited about this fellowship possibility because it was competitive, but that meant that it was supportive and unique. The access that a student could have by being part of this fellowship was really unmatched in any other school that I researched."

Participant 13 (F, Kellogg): "When I look back to the application process, that was something that really to me spoke about Kellogg's commitment to mission, because they had this program to teach MBA students how to be effective nonprofit leaders."

Participant 14 (F, Chicago Booth): "They also had a venture capital competition through the school, and a lot of these schools do have it, but theirs was pretty well-known at the time. And they had a separate track for social enterprises, so that was also very attractive to me. They also had a social enterprise office, just part of the entrepreneur program that was dedicated specifically to social enterprises. So that was what was attractive to me, is they seemed to have specific resources for social entrepreneurs."

Participant 17 (F, MIT Sloan): "And then the Legatum Program, which is the fellowship that I'm in was the absolute selling point for me. I found that a lot of other business schools talked about starting companies in emerging markets, but here was a community, a dedicated program, and financial resources to actually go and do that while I was in school. That was a turning point for me. I think that MIT puts its money where its mouth is."

Participant 20 (F, Cornell): "Yeah, at the time, they were one of the only programs that I knew of that covered social entrepreneurship."

Participant 21 (F, Kellogg): "I only applied to one program, in fact, which was Kellogg, specifically because of their impact investing program."

Participant 27 (M, MIT Sloan): "MIT has a lot of programs and lot of courses which focus on social enterprises, for example they have the Legatum Center, they have the Data Center, they have the Deshpande Center, and then lots of courses within MIT like the D Lab or development ventures or lots of other courses. So it made lot of sense to actually come into a school which actually had these resources that I was looking for."

These respondents seem to have done thorough research on social enterprise when applying to business school and placed a high emphasis on a strong program when selecting their school. These participants mention factors such as social enterprise resources, BPCs, community, and other related programs as being important to their decision. Interestingly though, none of the participants who selected their school based on the prior theme of overall reputation overlapped with the participants who selected their school based on its perceived reputation or resources related to social enterprise.

Theme 1 Integrating Conclusions.

Theme 1 looked to examine the backgrounds and demographics of the participants and their motivations for wanting to attend business school in relation to their involvement with social enterprises. The findings show that a strong majority of the participants (28 of 34) had either started a social enterprise or were planning on starting a social enterprise before they chose to attend their MBA program. They therefore held certain beliefs that some aspects of the MBA experience would assist then in succeeding with their social enterprise better than if they did not attend the program and instead just worked to start or grow their social enterprise on their own. Different participants placed a greater emphasis on certain aspects of the MBA program, but a few broad themes were prevalent. Many participants hoped to gain the traditional business skills often associated with MBA programs. These individuals felt that they did not have the 'hard' business or leadership/management skills necessary to actually start and/or sustain a market-focused business. These participants realized that, like the theories presented earlier, being a social entrepreneur requires a strong grasp of traditional business and entrepreneurship skills and concepts in order to be successful in founding and growing a social enterprise. Others hoped to gain similar skills associated with running traditional enterprises, as they saw social enterprises as highly related to traditional startups. This is keeping with the academic research presented in the literature reviews that finds that for-profit social enterprises as similar to traditional enterprises as both are market-focused and require business and entrepreneurial skills in order to run them successfully. Other participants chose to go to business school to obtain credentials associated with an MBA, in order to have more credibility with employees and investors. This is also related to traditional enterprise research presented earlier that shows that MBAs are signaling credentials in many for-profit enterprises. These hopeful social entrepreneurs felt that this holds true in the social enterprise space too. Also, certain participants decided to go to business school in order to obtain access to resources that they would not have if they had not gone to school. These resources included access to mentors, professors, like-minded students, research, funding, investors, and other areas. This is consistent with the research presented in the literature review regarding the beneficial resources that business schools offer to students.

Participants had varied reasons for picking their specific schools. Some said that they chose simply based on location due to personal concerns or responsibilities, but most of the group factored other considerations into their research. And even those who chose based on location often had several business schools in their area to choose from and therefore took into account secondary considerations. Others chose their program based on the perceived reputation of the school overall, not really taking into account the strengths of the social enterprise curriculum. This could be tied to the concept of credentials and acceptance by investors and employees, as those who chose based on prestige felt that they would receive certain standing in the eyes of their employees or potential investors. Some participants did choose their programs based on their perceived evaluations of the schools' social enterprise programs. These participants looked at many of the resources mentioned in the literature review, e.g. access to mentors and incubators, when they selected their programs.

Theme 2: Reflections on the Usefulness Social Enterprise Curricula and Resources

Perceived Usefulness of the Available Resources

The next set of questions, which was the bulk of the interview, asked about the various resources and activities that the participants utilized or experienced while they were at school and then asked them about their perceived usefulness of these activities and resources. Below is a chart of the subthemes and the number of participant references to each topic. As noted previously, the totals may be less than or greater than 34 based on if the participants directly answered the questions and the responses that they gave. Not all responses indicated in the reference table below are represented in the quotes sections below, especially if the response was a simply Yes/No answer without much context.

Subtheme	References
2. Reflections on the Efficacy of training and SE curricula	34
2.1. Perceived usefulness of the available Resources	34
a. Taking SE specific classes	34
Took social enterprise classes	25
Could not take all the Social Enterprise classes that they wanted to, due to scheduling limitations.	6
Did not take any Social Enterprise classes.	6
Found Social Enterprise classes relevant	24
b. Taking Traditional Entrepreneurship Specific Classes.	34
Found Entrepreneurship classes relevant	31
c. Taking CSR specific classes	34
Did not take any CSR classes	28
Reasons for not taking CSR classes, apart from not being offered.	4
d. Participating in Business Plan Competitions.	34
Participated in BPCs	28
Found BPCs to be helpful in designing and/or starting their venture, but with caveats related to social enterprise.	5
Found BPCs with a social track to be helpful in designing and/or starting their social venture.	8
Found traditional BPCs without a social enterprise track to be helpful in designing and/or starting their social venture.	12

Subtheme	References
Did not find BPCs to be helpful to social enterprise	3
e. Participating in school's incubator or accelerator	34
Participated in school's incubator or accelerator	20
Did not find participation in the incubator or accelerator helpful in designing and/or starting their social venture.	3
Did not participate in their school's incubator or accelerator program.	14
Found incubator/accelerator program to be helpful in designing and/or starting their social venture.	12
Found to be helpful, but with caveats related to social enterprise.	5
f. Use of the school's Social Enterprise center's resources.	34
Utilized the school's Social Enterprise center's resources.	28
Did not use the social enterprise center or did not find the social enterprise center to be a helpful	3
Found the social enterprise center to be a helpful	24
Found the social enterprise center to be a helpful, but with caveats related to social enterprise.	1
g. Use of the school's Traditional Entrepreneurship center's resources.	34
Used the school's Traditional Entrepreneurship center's resources.	23
Did not use the traditional entrepreneurship center.	11

Subtheme	References
Found the social enterprise center to be a helpful resource in designing and/or starting their social venture.	18
Found the traditional entrepreneurship center to be a helpful, but with caveats related to social enterprise.	5
h. Utilizing the alumni network for assistance with the social venture.	34
Utilized the alumni network for assistance with the social venture.	26
Did not utilize the alumni network at all.	8
Found the alumni network to be a helpful resource in designing and/or starting their social venture.	17
Found the alumni network to be a helpful, with some conditions.	8
i. Access to mentors	34
Had access to mentors	30
Access to mentors cultivated through other sources.	10
Direct/formal mentors assigned/provided through business school.	20
No real access to social enterprise mentors at their school.	4
2.2. Most helpful components of MBA program	34
a. Gaining knowledge, 'hard skills' & confidence	10
b. Access to broader resources & networks	8

Subtheme	References
c. Support from the Business School Community during and after the program.	11
Dedicated and supportive program staff	4
Support after graduation and staying closely 'plugged in'.	3
Support from a strong community of students.	4
d. Case studies and real life examples	6
e. Fundamentals of entrepreneurship	4
f. Funding & financial support	3

Table 11: Theme 2 Subtheme reference counts

Taking Social Enterprise Specific Classes.

25 of 34 of the participants said that they took a least one social enterprise specific class during their program, with most having taken several. In simple Yes/No responses, overall, 21 of the 25 individuals found the classes to be helpful, 3 answered yes with some conditions, and 1 did not find the classes helpful to starting and running their enterprise. Their responses on the perceived usefulness of these classes varied though and some of the participants' thoughts are detailed below.

Found Social Enterprise classes relevant to starting/running their venture.

Participant 1 (M, HBS): "There were a few classes that fit in that wheelhouse of straddling the impact and the entrepreneurship side of things. I also did an independent project related to the company I was starting, and so I worked with professor who had done a lot of research in the field, and he's now on our board of advisors. So I definitely used my time in school to be exploring that kind of stuff and in my coursework."

Participant 5 (M, Columbia): "So definitely that early stage part, very much. When it comes to pitching, when it comes to articulating your vision, when it comes to defining your strategy, yes. Very much. When it comes to some of the more tactical decisions that you need to make as a manager, I would say not so much. But then again, I feel that those are pretty well covered with the traditional business education, and there's just tweaks that you'd make in the case of a social enterprise."

Participant 6 (F, Chicago Booth): "We launched the business with that class so that was incredibly helpful, but yeah. I think that it was a good foundation on how to think about problems and how to think through, how to craft a solution that's really going to hit the pain points of that problem, particularly within the conscience of the social issue. The scaling for full innovation piece was a really good launching point for thinking through things like, if you're tackling a social issue, who are the stakeholders involved, and how might they be able to support and in some cases, even be obstacles to your position?"

Participant 10 (M, NYU): "I already knew like what was the industry that I wanted to start my business in, so the whole course was basically creating my business plan. In India, like the professor that taught the course, connected me with different people in Agriculture in India. I met VCs, I met different startups and it really helped with how I shaped and understood what I wanted to do back in Colombia."

Participant 11 (M, Columbia): "Classes were perfect with the way hands-on, building the business plan for my social enterprise which definitely helped us for expanding, you know, think about the business part more in detail."

Participant 12 (F, USC): "I took both social classes that were non-finance and then I took some finance entrepreneurship classes as well. Yes, they were definitely relevant. As you know, you get out what you put in so, so much of it is up to the student with what they are willing to do next."

Participant 13 (F, Kellogg): "The impact investing class that I took was the reason that I started [my company]. That's how I met my co-founders. That's how I met our first investor. It was just everything in launching [my company]. So that's obviously a big one. The entrepreneurial law, that's another one that I draw from quite heavily that I feel like gave me some really good instincts and technical skills and resources to look back to, especially in the earliest days of [my company] before we had funds for ongoing legal consul."

Participant 20 (F, Cornell): "I definitely learned how to approach problems and how to work through them, and approach them strategically, and how to look at it from the systematic approach. So, in that sense, yes."

Participant 21 (F, Kellogg): "The Impact Investing class was, without a doubt, the most relevant class that I took that was instrumental in me eventually starting my own social enterprise."

Participant 30 (M, Wharton): "Yeah, it was basically just a one degree separated form of the regular entrepreneurship class just with a social spin to it. Basically, that make sure that you have a mission that resonates with something the public is concerned about was the main take away."

Participant 32 (M, HBS): "I would say big picture strategy framework type stuff, yes. When it comes to how to create contracts and what your sales motion is and how to hire people, no not necessarily, but the re-imagining capitalism one for instance, was super helpful in terms of thinking about what are all the expenses of the different parties that are at this intersection and how to think about and appeal to different incentives at different times. Where can you be as the agent of change? Does it have to be at the individual level or helping level or the industry level? My short answer would be, yeah."

Participant 34 (M, Wharton): "I found that the professor who taught it one he became a personal mentor and professional advisor and then just thought the coursework was fantastic."

Participants cite the social enterprise specific classes as offering foundations in social impact and entrepreneurship, as well as access to professors and mentors that they utilized when starting their ventures. Others cited access to like-minded students in the social enterprise community. Some commented that the classes were helpful in building business plans. Some cite certain classes as the key reasons that they started their ventures or as the reasons that they gained access or introductions to key advisors or mentors for their ventures. A few participants valued the fundamentals taught in the classes even though if the instruction did not cover some highly specific topics that they were interested in.

Could not take all the Social Enterprise classes that they wanted to, due to scheduling limitations.

Participant 1 (M, HBS): "At HBS, the whole first year curriculum is determined. The elective curriculum only comes into play in the second year… I would say that there were a few that I didn't take, like for scheduling reasons. The Ed Tech class I actually didn't end up taking because it was at the same time as another course that I wanted."

Participant 6 (F, Chicago Booth): "There was one class that I wanted to take that I ended up not taking… Something like a scheduling issue."

Participant 7 (F, USC): "I guess probably my answer would be no. There were some other classes that I'd be interested in taking. I think there's one specifically related to social innovation and design that's more of a workshop based class that I just didn't have the chance to take, but I would take if I had more semesters to go for.

Participant 10 (M, NYU): "No, there were more, but really like, it wasn't the only specialization that I wanted take so it was the only one that I could fit in to the, into my core structure."

Participant 21 (F, Kellogg): "I decided to look towards some of the more traditional classes to get the specific skills I wanted to add the value because when I actually looked at the syllabi of some of the social entrepreneurship classes against some of the more traditional classes that they were benchmarked against, they seemed very similar classes except for the social component. I felt confident in what I needed to do on the social side and wanted the hard skills and so if the class was established, had one of the best professor, then was more traditional entrepreneurship, I took that instead."

Participant 29 (F, Chicago Booth): "There was one class I wanted to get into, and didn't get it. So I guess I missed one… The particular quarter that I tried to take it, I just didn't get in. You have bid points."

Of those 6 students who commented that they took some social enterprise classes, but not all that they wanted to, scheduling issues were the main reason. Scheduling could mean that the social enterprise classes were not offered that frequently or that the students had other non-social enterprise classes that they wished, or had, to take that prevented them from taking more social enterprise classes. Some felt that that other non-social enterprise classes took priority as these classes offered more of the 'hard' business skills that they needed to learn.

Did not take any Social Enterprise classes.

Six participants indicated that they did not take any social enterprise classes in business school.

Participant 2 (M, HBS) (M, HBS): "I wish that I'd taken social enterprise classes. It didn't really fit into my schedule given the stuff that I took otherwise."

Participant 3 (M, Columbia): "No. I didn't because with the Saturday program, it's basically they didn't have professors offering those courses, so I would have had to take that outside of Saturday regime which is tough with work."

Participant 4 (M, UCLA): "I actually really chose my coursework based on what classes were interesting just in general and also, how I could make sure that I spend time doing what I love instead of doing homework, to be honest. I didn't pursue any social entrepreneurship courses. I'm not sure if they were offered."

Participant 22 (F, Wharton): "[The classes] didn't fit into my schedule, if I recall, and I had to take some other requirements, and that was sort of why and there was only one that I can remember taught only in the spring and I missed it the first time, and the second time I hadn't completed my requirement courses yet. That was basically the reason."

Participant 23 (F, Wharton): "I did not. I do not recollect taking any social enterprise specific class. I was more interested in sort of first getting an understanding of how to build a venture and then sort of customizing my business model based on the market that it will be serving for. So, the sort of social angle was the second step towards professionally plashing out this idea."

Participant 28 (F, MIT Sloan): "No, not really. I didn't think they had a very robust offer in social enterprise."

Of those 6 students who did not take any social enterprise classes, some cite scheduling concerns while others felt like the traditional entrepreneurship and business classes would better prepare them in leading a social venture then social entrepreneurship classes would. Some of these individuals were there ones who already had experience in the social sector and came to business school to learn more finance, management, or traditional entrepreneurial skills. Two of the participants [3 and 28] were class of 2014 or earlier, so their schools' social enterprise offerings were more limited several years ago. Only one student [Participant 3 (M, Columbia)] felt like his school did not offer any social enterprise classes at all, but he was a Saturday executive student in a program with limited elective course offerings.

Taking Traditional Entrepreneurship Specific Classes.

All of 34 of the participants said that they took traditional entrepreneurship specific classes during their program. In simple Yes/No responses, overall, 28 indicated that these types of classes were helpful in starting their ventures as these ventures are rooted in traditional entrepreneurship business principles; 3 additional subjects indicated that the classes were helpful, with some conditions. Only 3 individuals felt that these entrepreneurship classes were not at all helpful to starting and/or running their social ventures.

Found Entrepreneurship classes relevant to starting/running their venture.

Participant 1 (M, HBS): "Our company, we're a for profit social enterprise, so we are structured as a B2B business, and so I think a lot of the principles of how do you set up and launch and build a tech company were very helpful, and I think that combined with the knowledge of the impact side of things that I had been focusing on helped me think in those principles."

Participant 2 (M, HBS): "Yeah, because when you're financing something it doesn't matter whether it's a social enterprise or whether it's just purely capitalist, you know, profits you gain enterprise. The same financial theories apply. The same funding mechanisms apply. So, the basic entrepreneurship classes are very, very helpful even just running a social enterprise. But as far as the social enterprise aspect goes, there is a kind of a push now towards the line blurring between the traditional business path and the social enterprise path."

Participant 3 (M, Columbia) (M, Columbia): "I had specifically Entrepreneurial

Finance[...] And that class was probably the most useful class of any class that I took when I was in business school or creating my social enterprises because it kind of opened up the black box on kind of how financing entrepreneurial ventures really happened and kind of how to navigate a lot of those funky things, whether it's just you know very early stage evaluation or thinking about how to evaluate opportunities and feeling comfortable with a term sheet."

Participant 7 (F, USC): "I think there were aspects of them that were relevant. I took one, specifically, that was founders' dilemma, which was all about the different phases of starting a business. From the founder's point of view, which is applicable across any industry or any type of business."

Participant 10 (M, NYU): "I did. Many. Like traditional entrepreneurship, I took venture capital, I took business plan and practicum was called, I took foundations of entrepreneurship, I took, yeah I did the whole track of entrepreneurship… But I do think like my perspective on a social business is still like, it still needs to be a business, it's not a feasible to only do it on donations or like public funding. I still wanted to have a business which was profitable."

Participant 11 (M, Columbia): "I've basically filled most of my semesters with entrepreneurship or leadership classes which aren't necessarily related in social enterprise and they helped me a lot."

Participant 12 (F, USC): "My organization is a for-profit but mission-driven organization. Any finance class that I also took, I need to understand how to create a sustainable business model and I was able to understand that process in non-social enterprise classes."

Participant 14 (F, Chicago Booth): Reference 1: "I found maybe, probably, just the entrepreneur classes more relevant in starting my venture than the social ones." Reference 2: "I think a lot of the overall entrepreneur classes that they offered at that school really were about finding purpose in your enterprise… when you have social enterprise, it was very easy to make those connections. So I feel like those were more relevant to what I was trying to do in terms of building a mission and getting my story out there and having people connect with the message."

Participant 15 (M, NYU): "What I ended up doing was taking more traditional [entrepreneurship] classes and then anytime there was a class project, we'd say, 'Hey, we can use our business that we're currently working on'."

Participant 16 (M, Columbia): "Hugely relevant. I think those were some of the best classes I took. I think as much as our venture is a social venture, it is a business, and learning from a lot of what was great about Columbia was they bring in a lot of people that have done it before and been there, and hearing from entrepreneurs how hard it is to get a business of the ground, what the real-world challenges are without making everything sound glamorous I think was a huge benefit, and then learning sort of the […] Learning the fundamentals of early stage companies, I think, was as valuable as anything that was specifically social-focused."

Participant 17 (F, MIT Sloan): "Oh, absolutely. Entrepreneurial Law, you need to protect what you're doing no matter what. Especially if you're doing a social venture where things just become more complicated, not less. So considering the legal aspects, it's highly critical. Scaling Entrepreneurial Ventures was taught by two practitioners who had scaled startups to IPO, and it was really critical operational things to think about now, so that you're not going to prevent yourself from scaling in the future… And then Dilemma's in Founding New Ventures is because most […] research says that almost 60% of new ventures fail because of issues with the founding team. So this is all about how you get co-founders, how do you recruit first employees, how do you incentivize them, what's the structure of the company that you set up, how do you make sure that everyone's driving toward the same vision for the company and so that's all stuff that's critical no matter what, if you're a social impact company, or not."

Participant 20 (F, Cornell): "I mean, running a business is, whether it's a social enterprise or an enterprise, there's still a lot of the same things that go into it. So, basically everything is relevant."

Participant 24 (F, Kellogg): "I focused more on some of the entrepreneurship courses was for me like mainstream courses on marketing, or pricing strategies for example. Because they're all relevant to a social enterprise as well, unless you're doing a standard non-profit where there's no revenue model."

Participant 25 (F, Wharton): "But to be honest, towards the end when I thought I was going to do a venture that's mission driven, what was helpful to me was the traditional entrepreneurship classes. I mean, the two classes that were most useful for me to start this venture, were most definitely the one semester entrepreneurship classes."

Participant 27 (M, MIT Sloan): "I just focused on entrepreneurship and any class that focused on entrepreneurship and social enterprises, I just chose that."

Participant 28 (F, MIT Sloan): "I think at a high level entrepreneurship is

entrepreneurship so they will all be very useful."

Participant 29 (F, Chicago Booth): "But I think what was relevant was all of the

applied stuff, so entrepreneurial selling was ultimately a class about having a sales

strategy, and that's super relevant no matter what kind of business you have."

Participant 32 (M, HBS): "Yes in the way that, I'm still in sales right? I still need

to figure out how to go to market, I still need to figure out how to deliver a product for a

client and know how to structure contracts or know how to hire a sales team. Or, think

about product development… Those entrepreneurship classes, I would say, were

definitely helpful for all types of entrepreneurship including social."

Participant 33 (M, HBS): "Yeah, tremendously, because also with social

enterprise you're sort of stuck in between two worlds a little bit because the people with

the money need to see you have a good business plan and sometimes the people that do

social impact don't understand the business side, so being in like straight

entrepreneurship class actually helped us a lot."

Consistent with research presented in the literature review that ties successful

social enterprises to traditional entrepreneurship principles, participants who found

traditional entrepreneurship classes relevant to their social enterprises often cited the

belief that entrepreneurship, although social in nature, is still entrepreneurship if you are

trying to run a for-profit, or at least market-based, company. These participants often

found traditional entrepreneurship skills to be the most applicable and most transferrable

to building and running for-profit social enterprises, since you must be financially viable if you want to succeed as a business and attract investors and financial backers. These skills include sales, legal knowledge, and just the basics of starting and running an early stage enterprise. Some participants found the traditional entrepreneurship classes even more relevant than social enterprise classes if the social enterprise classes at their schools skewed more towards non-profits or simply just measuring social impact, instead of covering more market-focused social entrepreneurship principles.

Taking Corporate Social Responsibility (CSR) Specific Classes.

28 of the 34 participants indicated that they did not take any CSR specific classes while in business school.

Did not believe that CSR Classes were offered.

Many of the 28 participants who did not take CSR classes noted that they did not believe that their school offered any CSR specific classes.

Participant 6 (F, Chicago Booth): "I don't think, to my knowledge, none of those were offered... I don't ever remember seeing classes about CSR. None whatever."

Participant 14 (F, Chicago Booth): "I did not. I don't think they offer any, to be honest with you. I don't think there's any, in fact, or anything like that, classes there."

Participant 17 (F, MIT Sloan): "I'm not sure I would take it, but I'm not sure we offer any."

Participant 22 (F, Wharton): "No. I wasn't aware of there being any to be honest."

Participant 23 (F, Wharton): "Interestingly, no. I do not even know if those classes exist to be honest, I don't have an idea."

Participant 34 (M, Wharton): "No, honestly I don't know that that's offered."

Participants 6 and 14 attended Booth. I conducted a course catalog search for the past few years and did not find any specific CSR themed courses. Participants 22, 23, and 34 attended Wharton. I conducted a similar course catalog search and did not find any specific CSR courses there either.

Reasons for not taking CSR classes, apart from not being offered.

Participant 15 (M, NYU): "No. Although, that's actually an area that I think I would have been interested to take but they were lower priority once we already had this idea."

Participant 18 (M, USC): "I feel like it's a completely different realm to be honest. I feel like it's very corporate… I honestly feel that a lot of these corporate social responsibility programs are just good marketing and putting their efforts towards something that's going to give them some sort of positive marketing."

Participant 21 (F, Kellogg): "Just none that looked interested or that I thought would add value."

Participant 25 (F, Wharton): "No, I didn't. I mean, as a joint degree student, I had only three semesters instead of four. So I had to be super judicious. So passed up on those."

Those whose programs offered CSR classes but chose not to take them, often cited that CSR, as taught in MBA programs, is not that relevant to social enterprise. These participants cited CSR as more of a part of a larger corporate strategy instead of being relevant to social enterprises. Realizing that schedules are limited, many chose to prioritize other classes over any CSR offerings. Others indicated that their time was best

suited taking a different, more relevant course, like finance and entrepreneurship

offerings.

Participating in Business Plan Competitions.

28 of the 34 participants said that took part in at least one school sponsored BPC

while in their program. Some competed only in BPCs with a social enterprise tract and

others only in traditional BPCs; some participants competed in both types of BPCs. In

simple Yes/No responses, overall, 25 indicated that these BPCs were helpful in starting

their ventures as the skills gained from BPCs were directly applicable to new venture

creation, with 6 of these participants indicating that the BPCs were helpful, with some

conditions related to social enterprise. Only 3 individuals felt that their participation in

the BPCs were not at all helpful to starting and/or running their social ventures.

Found BPCs with a social track to be helpful in designing and/or starting their

social venture.

Participant 1 (M, HBS): "I participated in the new venture competition both years

in the social enterprise track, and the idea for my company actually came out of a

hackathon that was sponsored by the school's social enterprise conference my first year.

It was like an education hackathon. That's when we came up with the initial idea, ended

up getting great feedback there and then I took that idea to the new venture competition

my first year and so continued working on it for the year and a half after that."

Participant 10 (M, NYU): "It really helped that since they had a social path we

had mentors that were involved in the space and even the panels and the judges, came from the social impact space and it helped out a lot with just even the questions that they had for us. It's very different than a standard startup Q&A, then a social impact Q&A, for example [...] Like a standard judge would not care about like the social impact of leaving people behind but she did see that there still was a trade up in bringing efficiency to a very informal industry."

Participant 13 (F, Kellogg): "It's been four years now, and just the other day I pulled out their application and was looking back at how we responded to certain questions to get inspiration for something that we're doing now."

Participant 15 (M, NYU): Reference 1: "Yes, exactly. And so, we won $15,000 right at the end, right when we graduated and that support was for sure crucial to us saying, 'Okay, this could be a viable business thing. We have some money that we can basically pay ourselves and fund things while we look for more money essentially.'" Reference 2: "So, we were fortunate to win that. Actually, that was the first one we won. So, that was, I think, five thousand dollars. And so that was the first thing that we thought, 'Oh, people are interested in this idea. Maybe this could become a viable thing.'"

Participant 21 (F, Kellogg): "One of them was an impact investing competition where you design a privately financeable investment concept. That's the one that eventually, we did win that competition and decided to start the business based on it."

Participant 25 (F, Wharton): "I participated in the business planning competition. And actually the year I participated, 2014, was the first year they had a social impact prize. So, we actually won that, oddly. I don't know, that's a little bit funny.

And I still don't quite know what the judging was; well, I mean, I know what the judging

criteria is. I don't know what's happened to it since. But yes, so that was definitely

useful.

Participant 29 (F, Chicago Booth): "We knew were launching the business, and

we've done a ton of work on the business model already, and so those were less helpful

in improving the business and more for us just about kind of just funding for the

business."

Participant 33 (M, HBS): "Yes. I think last year when we didn't win the Harvard

innovation challenge it was because we hadn't thought enough about measuring our

impact, and this year we put a lot more time into that, and the judges asked a lot about it

so it was clear that that was their focus. I did feel like when we asked the resources were

there to get some help."

Students who participated in BPCs under the social enterprise tracks often found

that, when available, the specialized assistance geared to social enterprises was relevant

and helpful to their ventures. This assistance included social enterprise-specific mentors

and judges who could answer questions about pitfalls in that space. Some cited the

dedicated prize money for social enterprises as another factor that was of much assistance

to their ventures.

Found traditional BPCs without a social enterprise track to be helpful in

designing and/or starting their social venture.

Participant 2 (M, HBS): "I actually won the competition this year, the business

track this year. And mine obviously is a social enterprise, but there's also a social enterprise track, which I wasn't in that one. I was in the business track and I still won. So, that line has been blurring over the years where people do seem to be valuing the social side as an additional benefit than just the financial projections that you provide of your last slide."

Participant 5 (M, Columbia): "Absolutely, absolutely. I think a lot of it comes down to pattern recognition. So seeing other people pitch, listening, looking at the basis of a company and determining whether you think it is viable, the propositions they have."

Participant 11 (M, Columbia): "I won each, every one of those all four of those so you know we had the support from all four of those so in that sense, I don't think they discouraged against social enterprise at all in that sense. But I do think that there is a focus as a business school there's focus on the business model much more than the impact and that might harm social enterprises. Social enterprise is a spectrum so I think we always had it, we're having a strong focus on the business model too but there are some social enterprises which are in the middle between being a business and being a complete charity."

Participant 16 (M, Columbia): Reference 1: "I mean, I think in general, they were all great, because at that time, what we needed was practice getting in front of people and being grilled on what we were trying to do. I think you get different things out of the social ones, and I think the generic ones taught us what it was like to go up to random investors and say, 'As a social venture, people are there going to connect you what you want, and they're going to want to help you, but they also are going to try to poke holes in your business model and try to convince you that you're not going to make any money as a social venture.' I think on the social side, people want to tell you you're going to succeed, but it was also really helpful to see how we compared to other ventures." Reference 2: "I think the pitch competitions were really a great way to be ready for the real world… You have to really be able to prove to someone that, despite your age, they can trust you. And I think the pitch competitions did a lot to prepare you for the volley of questions you're going to be answered both by investors and by potential customers."

Participant 17 (F, MIT Sloan): "I almost prefer when they don't have a social impact category because the prize money is always less than the real prize, and I feel like once the judges kind of cop out and give you a social impact prize, and so it ends up shuffling you away from being able to be taken as seriously as some of the traditional enterprises."

Participant 30 (M, Wharton): Reference 1: "I think that goes back to the two degree separation of social enterprise to regular for profits and a social enterprise needs to be as sustaining and equipped for growth and return on investment as the other type of business, so in terms of being on equal footing, they certainly were if they had the business model to support it." Reference 2: "Oh yeah, a bunch. We had to that's how we funded the company for the first year and a half, for nothing else, the exposure, and then the money of course. We won $140,000 in non-diluted funds for our company."

Participant 31 (F, HBS): "So the company would not exist if were not for the [BPC] prize… We made it to the finals, and by that time, we had raised money and had become a real project, but none of this would have started and we wouldn't have continued if we were not also continuing on that competition."

Participant 32 (M, HBS): "Yes. In the sense that participating in the business competition, this is just really helpful when forcing function to get all your thoughts on paper and to structure everything just because your product, your market and everything is always evolving."

Participant 33 (M, HBS): "I think the business ones our more effective. I think actually the best thing is the more at bats the better. I think every time we went into a competition or pitch we would bump into a question we hadn't heard before and then have to spend a month figuring it out."

Participant 34 (M, Wharton): "I did, and the two of the top three winners, two of them were social businesses."

Students who participated in BPCs under the traditional entrepreneurship tracks often found the experience helpful to their ventures in the same way that the students found traditional entrepreneurship classes helpful, since the participants felt that traditional entrepreneurship principles are applicable to for-profit social ventures. Funding was a major positive factor, especially since the traditional BPCs often have higher prize money than the social ones. Participants cites BPCs as the way that they funded their companies in the initial stages. Some cite that they were able to win the BPCs since their social enterprise still proved to be financially viable. These participants felt that if their venture could be seen as financially sustainable, then the social aspect would be a selling point to help them differentiate from the other BPC entries, thus why they decided to enter the traditional BPC instead of a social enterprise track one. Others cited that experiences gained in the BPCs, such as learning how to pitch and talk to for-profit investors, as crucial to developing their business plans and company structures.

Found BPCs to be helpful in designing and/or starting their venture, but with caveats related to social enterprise.

Participant 4 (M, UCLA): "They were helpful in just iterating the basic fundamentals of building a business like pitching, selling, developing your business plan, understanding your consumer. They were helpful in that context. In terms of social, no. I think there's a lot of issues like, what are the metrics that you're measuring and a little bit of confusion about that and the industry overall. I think that a lot of these competitions didn't really hit on that."

Participant 6 (F, Chicago Booth): "Yeah. It's definitely a good fit because I said before, we are a social enterprise businesses. I'm not sure through in a couple of ways, and the prize money is lower, which I think is pretty typical for the industry."

Participant 7 (F, USC): "For sure, I think any chance that you get to pitch your idea, refine it, and get feedback from a panel of unbiased uninformed judges, it's always helpful. The first year, I definitely felt some frustration, though, in terms of being compared apples to apples with just a pure revenue generating business. It's definitely a little bit of both. Overall, it's always so helpful to go through that process regardless of if it's for social enterprises or not."

Participant 9 (M, Chicago Booth): "So, to the extent that you are running a socially-minded for-profit venture, I think you are well served. To the extent that you are running a non-profit, which has fundamentally different considerations, because, obviously it's still from a fundraising model, you are never really aiming at profitability. You're only aiming at increasing your donor base to fund your programmatic activities. I don't think the material was suited to that, whatsoever."

Participant 12 (F, USC): "I think they [judges] did understand it [social impact component of the product] as having a fundamental part of your business model be something about doing something good for the world, but I don't know if they saw it as enough of a value-add that it was worth investing in because of that component."

Participant 14 (F, Chicago Booth): "To be honest, I felt like it was mostly for people really established businesses already, so I don't feel like it was really for people trying to build a business. I think it was more if you already had a business, how to refine it, and get it to market. I don't think it was really […] It was for people, I guess, that were already pretty advanced and far along in the process."

Some participants found that BPCs were generally helpful, but there were some issues associated with their treatment of social enterprises. At least 6 participants cited traditional BPC judges not fully understanding how to measure social enterprise benefits. This was more acute for those running hybrid social enterprises where profits were sometimes secondary to impacts. Participants cited that this area is where it was hardest to compete against traditional enterprises as many of the judges, especially in BPCs without social enterprise tracks, prioritized revenue and profits above all other factions. In the previous section, it was noted that some participants preferred to enter traditional BPCs over social track ones due to the difference in prize money. Some of the participants who did enter social enterprise BPCs stated their displeasure that these BPCs generally offer lower prize money than traditional BPCs.

Participating in their school's Incubator/Accelerator.

20 of the 34 participants said that they took part in at least one of their school's incubator or accelerator program. In simple Yes/No responses, overall, 12 indicated that this experience was helpful in starting their ventures; 5 additional subjects indicated that the experiences were helpful, with some conditions. Only 3 individuals felt that their participation in the incubator or accelerator programs were not at all helpful to starting and/or running their social ventures.

Found incubator/accelerator program to be helpful in designing and/or starting their social venture.

Participant 1 (M, HBS): "Basically the way it works is, if you're part of the venture incubation, you're assigned a staff mentor based on the type of business you are, and so they have mentors for healthcare, tech, social impact, I think retail. So there's a specific cohort of social enterprise startups within the VIP core, so we had a staff member assigned to us and had relevant content for that subset of companies as well… Being in the I-Lab was great. It was very helpful. I would say, I think social impact is kind of a wide brush, so you get Ed-tech, you get workforce, you get human rights, all sort of things. I think there's a wide range of businesses that you're interfacing and interacting with, but it's super helpful to be in that environment around other mission-driven people."

Participant 2 (M, HBS): "So what was particularly helpful about these accelerators and incubators is they put structure on what you're trying to do. Because if you're just trying to start something from zero the ability to build it is opaque if you've never done it before. So this puts deadlines on certain things, it gives you kind of a generic structure that you have to build the deck upon. It gives you basic data that you would need to acquire from potential customers and really starts to explain your thinking around a workable model. Which really helped a lot, because otherwise I wouldn't even have known where to start really."

Participant 4 (M, UCLA): "The fellowship offered a $15,000.00 grant over the summer. I think maybe 30 people applied and then four or five received a fellowship. It was $15,000.00 to pursue an entrepreneurial venture over the summer in lieu of a traditional internship, and I received that, and with those $15,000.00 I went to Africa and started building the venture."

Participant 26 (M, Duke): "Yeah, absolutely. It [social enterprise assistance] was the deciding factor between starting it and not starting it."

Participant 30 (M, Wharton): "Yeah, 100%. The funding is always going to be a big point, especially as a fledgling start up, but just in terms of the resources, the access to mentors, advice, free legal resource, all that sort of stuff was also huge."

Participant 32 (M, HBS): "Yeah. Not only those advisors are available and can do a little bit of coaching but more than anything I'd say, it's a dedicated space where you're not allowed to do class work. People aren't reading cases at the I-Lab. You only get other entrepreneurs that are serious about their stuff and you are surrounded by people going through but you can commiserate with a lot of people. When you need to make your first proposal to a customer, you can knock on the door of the person next to you and they can share resources or people have war stories that they can share."

Of the participants who found the incubator or accelerator programs to be helpful, there were several themes. Funding was a key attribute rated highly. This funding was often the reason that students could take the risk to start a venture as they could thus focus 100% on their venture while in school instead of having to worry about making an income elsewhere in order to support themselves. The resources associated with the programs such as workspace and access to mentors were also valued. Others found that the shared space offered access to other founders at the accelerators; this was helpful as it exposed the participants to diverse ideas and types of ventures.

Found incubator/accelerator program to be helpful in designing and/or starting their social venture, but with caveats related to social enterprise.

Participant 10 (M, NYU): "So it was just like trying to work from afar. It was challenging. It is still like they helped with the, like, the initial steps that we took towards coming back to Columbia and setting up the business in itself, but it could've been a lot better."

Participant 15 (M, NYU): "They have been very, very generous and supportive in connecting us with people and advisors and potential funders. But in terms of specific social impact assistance, no."

Participant 17 (F, MIT Sloan): "I'm in their program. I work out of our entrepreneurship center like four days a week, but it's like less explicitly a program. I haven't done the accelerators over the summer and over school breaks. I haven't done

any of that because when I have that much time off, I go to Africa to be in market. It's

like it doesn't really work for me. Even though I know people get a lot of value out of the

program."

Participant 31 (F, HBS): "Yeah. There were some mentors and they were really

helpful so they worked with people on when we could go to and they were great. But one

thing I might say is that they mentors we had on the I-lab, I worked with two, they were

much more generalist and also what we really needed was someone who really

understood tech in our case."

Participant 33 (M, HBS): "I would say I was a little underwhelmed by the

program staff, just because they were not entrepreneurs themselves, so often their advice

was a little off… The entrepreneurs and residents were good. The entrepreneurs and

residents and professors were good, sometimes the program staff around these incubators

aren't the best."

Some participants found the overall incubator/accelerator experience helpful, but

noted some issues related to social enterprise resources. These issues included lack of

mentors or other resources specific to social enterprise. Others who were attempting to

start social enterprises overseas considered some of the resources offered to be helpful

but found issue with being able to fully participate in the program while working on their

venture abroad.

Did not participate in their school's incubator or accelerator program.

Participant 3 (M, Columbia): "I had fostered an opportunity to go pretty big pretty quickly and then left my finance job after that was looking pretty solid. So by the time that we were actually ready to kind of go live, we have already had a very high level of contents that we were going to get this $9 million grant commitment, so it's just like leap frog into that whole experience."

Participant 5 (M, Columbia): "I would have but were very fortunate in that we were able to get free office space resources, so I'd planned to but we didn't end up needing to."

Participant 7 (F, USC): "The accelerators and incubators were very tech focused, or I didn't get a lot of consumer goods focus, so it didn't seem like, I didn't feel that my company would be the right fit for what they were looking for… It just didn't seem like it would be the right fit for me."

Participant 12 (F, USC): "Yeah. I just couldn't make. The office hours. I didn't apply but I don't know if I would have been accepted because of my schedule."

Participant 13 (F, Kellogg): "Our business model is so unique, and that we work primarily with municipal governments, and that typically these are not tailored towards that type of client, that it wouldn't be the best use of our time and vacation time from our day jobs at that point in time. And since we've made the same choice on a couple other occasions for the same reason. For the reason of that the incubator isn't targeted to a firm like [ours]."

Participant 21 (F, Kellogg): "Our idea is very unique, our business model. Any sort of traditional incubator that is more traditional tech focused. A lot of incubators are kind of tech focused. And because our idea isn't pure tech, it doesn't always fit in to a lot of those spaces. And that's something that we've actually struggled with in trying to fit ourselves into these boxes of incubators and pitch competitions. A lot of them, and even some of the social entrepreneurship ones, still want this tech bent and if we don't fit in, it's kind of hard to see how you can take advantage of those resources."

Participant 24 (F, Kellogg): "I was looking to get more people and it was hard to get people interested in an idea that's halfway across the world, while other people were so focused on the other side of the world. So, I think in that sense, what people go to these incubators for is finding more people to work with them and find a curriculum that's more aligned to their long term goals. And whether those didn't really align with my goals with the company, so it didn't seem like the most relevant thing."

Participant 28 (F, MIT Sloan): "I didn't. I don't think I fit their description of a corporation; I didn't seem like a high yielding, high gross, traditional business and I think that was for people who were selecting teams."

Those participants who did not enter their venture into the accelerator or incubator programs had different reasons for doing so. The majority of the respondents indicated that they did not participate because they felt that their business type of model would not be a good fit for the programs as their social enterprise model was not overly tech-focused or did not fit the clean description of a traditional enterprise. Some felt that their venture scaled quite quickly, so they believed that their time was better focused on other efforts to grow the business. Others found similar resources offered by the programs outside of business school.

Use of the school's Social Enterprise center's resources.

28 of the 34 participants said that used resources, or took part in activities, offered by their school's social enterprise center. In simple Yes/No responses, overall, 24 indicated that this experience was helpful in starting their ventures; 1 additional subject indicated that the experiences were helpful, with some conditions. Only 3 individuals felt that the resources or activities offered by the social enterprise center were not at all helpful to starting and/or running their social ventures. In certain schools, the BPCs or the incubators/accelerators are run directly out of the social enterprise center. In these cases, the participants were asked if they used any additional resources associated with the social enterprise center if they participated in either, or both, the BPC and the incubator/accelerator.

Found the social enterprise center to be a helpful resource in designing and/or starting their social venture.

Participant 1 (M, HBS): "I would say the social enterprise initiative does a lot of programming around making sure that there's support for social enterprise within the HBS community. They help organize the social enterprise conference every year, which is cohosted by HBS and HKS. They run the new venture competition social enterprise track, but they also provide fellowships for students pursuing social enterprise ideas in the summer. So they supplement funding for you if you're working on or working at a social enterprise, so they make it more financially feasible. They also have a community of alumni who are mentors and advisors to people working on social enterprise, so they do a lot to facilitate that sort of sense of community on campus, and they work very closely with the student-led social enterprise club."

Participant 2 (M, HBS): "The social enterprise initiative, they gave me a stipend over the summer. It's a, like social enterprise summer fellowship. So they gave me some money so I was able to work on this full time as opposed to getting a traditional consulting internship or private equity or investment banking, which seems to be what everyone does... I probably would've done it regardless just because I believed in the technology so much, however it would've made the decision a lot harder and I'm fortunate that I could have managed without it. But there are a lot of people who just absolutely need, need that stipend in order to pay their rent or eat. So it does make the decision a lot easier for a lot of people."

Participant 7 (F, USC): "I was a fellow in the program my second year. We had a small cohort of people that we met with regularly, and then they also gave us a small stipend for conferences and workshops. I also received a scholarship from them for international study for last summer. So, yes, I've definitely been able to tap into some resources there...It's awesome that they're kind of creating this community of people with like-minded interests where if you're just in the business school, a lot of people who are interested in consulting or financier or whatnot, where as in the social enterprise, there's a lot of people with shared interest. So, I definitely found some really good friends and people to bounce off ideas and get inspiration from. So, it's a great community to have."

Participant 8 (M, Chicago Booth): "I received a fellowship for recent graduates which is social impact specific. It came with a little bit, I guess you could call that an incubator. It came with the ability to continue to use the exchange as a co-working space, and some funding, and sort of on demand coaching even though I was a graduate."

Participant 11 (M, Columbia): Reference 1: "I applied for the Tamer Fund for Social Ventures so that helped my startup to get some seed funding." Reference 2:

"They bring in a lot of speakers, they do something called a spark workshops which is great for getting feedback on your idea. They also do the staff in the Tamer Center is very helpful if you want any one on one help and connections. So I got a lot of connections to alumni, through the Tamer Center.

Participant 12 (F, USC): "I was a Fellow. I was a Fellow with [my co-founder]. We were in the same cohort and because of that I had access to the staff, the director of course. I had relationship-building model with my Fellow cohorts and guidance I guess."

Participant 14 (F, Chicago Booth): "I have a fellowship right now that I heard about through them…I would say it was very resource-heavy in the sense of making use of resources and other things that are not theirs but are relatable to what you're doing and could help you. They had legal resources, they had connected me with somebody in the law school on my first business contract, et cetera…I will say that was one thing that they did very well, and I don't think I would have been able to access the amount of resources I was able to without them."

Participant 16 (M, Columbia): "I've taken advantage of their loan assistance program. We've received a Tamer grant. [The director] who runs the Center, is just one of the biggest cheerleaders for any Columbia social enterprise that she thinks is doing good work, and just knowing her and being in her sphere has led to great connections. I think in general, a lot of the informal work the Tamer Center does to connect people is huge."

Participant 17 (F, MIT Sloan): "I'm very involved in the Legatum Center, I've been a fellow there for two years. So they, the main programming is their fellowship, which is the class that we get together once a week to work on our ventures… And I think too the staff there is very, very helpful. They're the people I know I can go to on campus if I need an advocate and they'll do anything for me…so is super helpful in chances of connecting to investors or partners or getting funding for an idea. Yeah, they're definitely incredibly, incredibly helpful."

Participant 21 (F, Kellogg): Reference 1: "It was super valued because that's where I met both of my now co-founders, through that career track. So we took a day and visited socially impactful businesses around the city met with, a lot of them were Kellogg alums, different folks to talk about potential careers in social and environmental impact. A lot of speakers, a lot of networking." Reference 2: "One of the awards that we won was exclusively for social enterprise, so we got a $70,000 award upon graduation to actually go towards launching our business. And they also had another award that was for continuing students to work on an account over the summer in between years. So those were both really great resources."

Participant 24 (F, Kellogg): "Yes, the other resource that I didn't talk about is this funding that they have for traveling and working on your business and your idea -

like a social impact idea during school, so it's called The Project Impact funding, which I

used like five, six times over the two years of business school to travel to India. So that

was a great resource that I sort of had."

Participant 27 (M, MIT Sloan): "They helped out in terms of the business plan, in

terms of accessing social impact funds, and of accessing information about developing

countries. So they were better equipped from that point of view."

Participant 28 (F, MIT Sloan): "I was a fellow and I took advantage of some of

their seed grants to kind of try and test what I was trying to do in the US and other

markets, which was important. I think long term I did want to expand in Latin America.

So, I got a couple of travel grants to go to Brazil and research their education workforce

system and pony up interest for potential investors. So that was really useful for me."

Participant 29 (F, Chicago Booth): "My co-founder was awarded a scholarship,

so we actually got some additional funding directly from the Rustandy Center on top of

the Social New Venture Challenge funding. I went to some of the talks and events."

Participant 33 (M, HBS): "The funding was definitely helpful, yes."

As indicated above, a majority of participants used and valued the social

enterprise centers at their schools. As with the BPCs and incubators/accelerators, the

access to funding was cited the most as being extremely helpful. Funding allowed

participants to pay off tuition, pay for living expenses, or pay for startup costs incurred by

their ventures. Others noted the access to mentors and outside speakers offered by these

institutions as being beneficial as many of these mentors were able to provide social

enterprise specific advice. Networking was also valued highly as the centers often created a community of like-minded individuals who could share ideas. Some noted that they were able to meet co-founders and investors at events hosted by these centers.

> ***Found the social enterprise center to be a helpful resource in designing and/or starting their social venture, but with caveats related to social enterprise.***

Participant 26 (M, Duke): "A little bit less helpful to the enterprise itself and more helpful to me having the confidence to pursue something."

Participant 27 (M, MIT Sloan): "We got a lot of support from the Legatum Center… They do have people from developing countries, but then that is- everyone can become a part of it, so it's not an elective or, it's not a choice of everyone. It's basically through an admissions process that you need to be a part of it. And 90 percent of the people who get into the Legatum Center don't go in there with the intention of starting a social enterprise. They get in because it helps them get a discount on their fee. Which they really need to fix."

These two individuals found the centers not to be keenly focused on social enterprise, but still able to offer some types of support. Others though at Participant 27's school [MIT] did offer high praise to that school's center [Legatum], although the center is more focused on traditional entrepreneurship than social entrepreneurship. Participant 26 (M, Duke) was the only alumni of his school to participate in the study.

> ***Did not use the social enterprise center or did not find the social enterprise center to be a helpful resource in designing and/or starting their social venture.***

Participant 5 (M, Columbia): "I think it was mainly because I was in a fairly unique situation where we had a clear idea of what we wanted to do. We had the financial backing already. I had the basics of a team. So we were just much more focused on getting out and doing it. I felt the resources there were really good, and had I been doing this for the first time, I would've wanted to take advantage of them. There wasn't anything lacking, it just wasn't needed."

Participant 6 (F, Chicago Booth): "I wasn't totally clear on what services they offered to a student outside of specific classes, and they certainly did not offer any kind of career service, specific to people in social enterprise. So, no is the short answer."

Participant 18 (M, USC): "Not really. For my business, it's kind of unique because we deal with school as our primary target. We do the things outside of school for 90% of it, so it was like there was really no connections or hook ups that people were able to get me."

Participant 19 (M, Wharton): "I think at the time I was just focusing on my business. I didn't actually take part in many extra curriculars, beyond the lot of classes that did dual degree program, and working on my business, I didn't have much time left over to get involved in anything else."

Participant 23 (F, Wharton): "I did not. I wish I would have… Partly because I did not know about it early enough. I think by the time I started working on my right term it was already fourth semester and then at that point in time I was just looking to get more practical experience. But I think, I also did not because I did not know any of my peers who were part of that. So, there was no sort of word of mouth information that I was getting about the benefits of that."

Participant 30 (M, Wharton): "No, I think it's just a question of time and resources and there were a million things you could have done and taken advantage of so you can't do all of them."

For those who did not use the social enterprise center or used it sparingly because they did not find it helpful, there were several reasons for this. Some, like in the case of not using the accelerators, felt that their ventures were far enough along already and thus prioritized their time seeking other resources outside of school. Some felt that their businesses were too unique, often more of a hybrid model, that were better served by other resources offered by the great university community. 2 of the participants who did not use their school's social enterprise centers were 2014 graduates and 2 others were 2016 graduates, so the social enterprise centers may not have offered as many resources then as they do today.

Use of the school's Traditional Entrepreneurship center's resources.

23 of the 34 participants said that they used resources, or took part in activities, offered by their school's traditional entrepreneurship center. In simple Yes/No responses, overall, 18 indicated that this experience was helpful in starting their ventures; the 5 additional subjects indicated that the experiences were helpful, with some conditions. 0 individuals felt that the resources or activities offered by the traditional entrepreneurship centers were not at all helpful to starting and/or running their social ventures. In certain schools, the BPCs or the incubators/accelerators are run directly out of the entrepreneurship center. In these cases, the participants were asked if they used

any additional resources associated with the entrepreneurship center if they participated in either, or both, the BPC and the incubator/accelerator.

Found the traditional entrepreneurship center to be a helpful resource in designing and/or starting their social venture.

Participant 10 (M, NYU): "Yeah, I spent all my time there… I felt that I needed to make as many connections as possible. I wanted people both from the Berkeley lab and the center for sustainable business to get to know about me. I felt like that would improve my odds of like eventually getting grants or help."

Participant 11 (M, Columbia): "They also ran a lot of talks which was great for me to do and they also run something called immersion programs which are classes where you go and interact with the extended New York City entrepreneurship ecosystem. So, that was very helpful for me more to get to know people in the city and go to know events in the city where you can interact with other entrepreneurs so that was simple."

Participant 13 (F, Kellogg): Reference 1: "We used some law resources from the referral to the law clinic I guess from the entrepreneurial center. We used a lot of the materials that they provide in terms of business planning templates and stuff like that. Yeah. A lot of events that they organized or co-organized about like stuff that I didn't really have kind of an experience with before about like the start of HR culture, HR stuff, and culture setting, and things like that. So sort of on the operational, legal, and HR sides in particular, their resources were really, really helpful." Reference 2: "We did get a number of small Kellogg grants early on to cover the cost of specific projects like, "Hey, we need a website. Let's hire a web developer," and Kellogg gave us a grant to do that. And I think we did two or three of those for early stage company projects."

Participant 14 (F, Chicago Booth): "I found them helpful, overall. I don't think they were necessarily towards social enterprise, but building a business, they were helpful. A couple things: One thing they did was they gave me grants to pay people, insurance and also business school students, during the summers, so they had those kind of resources, which, I guess, it could be helpful to anybody if you're starting off."

Participant 16 (M, Columbia): "Yes, definitely. I mean, they had a ton of resources. Things like a probe on the entrepreneurial sounding board. We could just go speak to experienced entrepreneurs. We'd get advice. We pitched their Lang fund. We did a summer program for entrepreneurs, which is actually how I met our co-founder who was the educator who got me involved in this."

Participant 21 (F, Kellogg): "I just wanted to get the full breadth of the tools I needed to have at my disposal to try to build a successful company and a lot of the entrepreneurship stuff, they're just more established and more focused than with the social entrepreneurship, there's just so much… so I wanted to be able to get all of that, so that's why I tried to get exposure to both the traditional entrepreneurship stuff but also the social enterprise stuff."

Participant 26 (M, Duke): "Yeah, absolutely. The Duke Innovational Entrepreneurship Initiative. They have many events. Speaker series, networking events, I went to quite a few of those over the course of two years… They were a lot more on the nuts and bolts. Less sort of the corporate high level that the MBA offers and more about do I need a lawyer? And how to trademark a name. And things like that that are particularly hands on useful."

Participant 28 (F, MIT Sloan): "I think as a foundation to build a business they were incredibly helpful."

Participant 30 (M, Wharton): "And then in terms of access to the entrepreneurial center was great because it provided access in an affective door to the rest of Penn. Obviously you could just go to any other school, but the fact that it was with the entrepreneurial center other students from other schools whether they be design, engineering, medical school, if they were in the entrepreneurial center they were coming to those events, you knew that they were at least interested in doing something in entrepreneurship so it provided a network of likeminded people."

Participant 32 (M, HBS): "We did a Rock summer fellowship. We got a grant that basically covered out living expenses and we worked on our venture last summer… 100 percent, yeah. It de-risks the process. I probably would have worked on the venture anyway, meaning the money itself did not make the decision for me but it certainly helps. For a lot of people that's sort of an individual decision, but it definitely takes some of the risk out and the fact that the school encourages it and heavily promotes it too. I think Rock Center promotes leadership fellowships so I know a lot of folks that just graduate and have one year fellowships with the hospitals or with kids' schools or other large family foundations. The school does a good job of promoting and making sure you're aware of opportunities."

As indicated above, a majority of participants used and valued the

entrepreneurship centers at their schools. Similar to the participants who valued

traditional entrepreneurship classes, many valued the traditional entrepreneurship center

resources since these were applicable to any for-profit venture, social or not.

Participants indicated that the resources offered by these centers, such as mentorship and

legal help with ventures was highly valued. Some found the traditional entrepreneurship

centers to be more developed than the social enterprise centers in terms of resources. A

few participants also mentioned the access to funding as another valuable resource.

Some participants found these traditional entrepreneurship centers to be helpful overall,

but not specially related to social enterprise. Still, these participants valued the resources

offered as they indicated that all new enterprises, including social enterprises, face many

of the same challenges.

Did not use the traditional entrepreneurship center.

Participant 3 (M, Columbia): "I was thinking about that this morning actually. I

should probably go track down the folks there and access those resources."

Participant 4 (M, UCLA): "I don't believe so. What I kind of did was, I identified

which professors and researchers I wanted to speak to, and I just directly reached out."

Participant 9 (M, Chicago Booth): "They're really geared toward the mindset of,

'How do we get VC money?' which is just not a consideration when you're a [hybrid]."

Participant 19 (M, Wharton): "I feel like those resources are there for helping you

develop ideas, though when it actually comes to execution. Especially because, I think it was more because the business I was working on was in the overseas market. So not as relevant to maybe the resources that were at there."

Participant 31 (F, HBS): "I think at some point it got all so overwhelming because one thing that I found was that there are so many competitions and pitches and then it takes time from actually working on your company so I felt that the Rock Center required even more commitment and because I was struggling with the same issues and that made me doubt is it myself and if I wanted to build my enterprise, if I was an entrepreneur or not. I didn't feel like I was ready to engage with the Rock Center because I felt that it was, in a way, more professional or another reason. I don't know if that's perception or if that's really how it is, but yeah I ended up modifying, not engaging."

For those who did not use traditional entrepreneurship center, there were several reasons for this. Some, like in the case of not using the social enterprise centers, felt that their ventures were far enough along already and thus prioritized their time seeing other resources outside of school. Some felt that their businesses were too much of a social model to benefit from traditional entrepreneurship resources, although these individuals were quite few.

Utilizing the alumni network for assistance with the social venture.

26 of the 34 participants said that they utilized their alumni network to try to gain assistance with their ventures. In simple Yes/No responses, overall, 17 indicated that this experience was helpful to their ventures; 8 additional subjects indicated that the experiences were helpful, with some conditions. 1 individual felt that the alumni network had not been at all helpful to starting and/or running their social ventures.

Found the alumni network to be a helpful resource in designing and/or starting

their social venture.

Participant 1 (M, HBS): "Everything from business plan advice to the advisors to potential investors to potential customers. It's certainly has been very helpful in trying to get this thing off the ground."

Participant 5 (M, Columbia): "Recruiting. A lot of recruiting. We've had a number of staff that have come from Columbia, We've had some volunteers, others. Again, a lot of the reason I go to events now is to be on the lookout for people that are interested."

Participant 6 (F, Chicago Booth): "We have actually spoken with alumni, a company that won Social Venture Challenge a couple years before us, has been incredibly helpful for us and has spoken with us multiple times about just simple business questions and our investors and things like that. So we did leverage our network in that way."

Participant 11 (M, Columbia): Reference 1: "In terms of alumni there are a couple of them who we are in touch with on sort of a regular basis. Others, a lot of them, were helpful in getting us contacts through people that we wanted to get in touch with." Reference 2: "About 50 to 60 alumni who were my course of my MBA who were working either working in Social Enterprise or interested in Social Enterprise. So, a large part of them are part of our advisory board and have been in touch. I've been using it mainly for advisory and guidance."

Participant 13 (F, Kellogg): "A number of our investors are alumni of Kellogg or somehow affiliated with Kellogg. So especially the early ones, the ones most willing to take risk. So that has been really good."

Participant 15 (M, NYU): "Yes. In India, we have some of our closest friends in India are NYU alums that we have access through the network. Yes, we have…it's for sure been helpful."

Participant 16 (M, Columbia): "And lots of alumni who know people in the education space, who know people that run schools, have been very forthcoming with introductions and helping me set up meetings. Connecting us with potential investors. Both the Lang Center and the Tamer Center do a fair amount of informal networking when they know that there's someone in the network that you should meet, they make those connections. Their formal events are great networking opportunities."

Participant 21 (F, Kellogg): "We've leveraged a lot of contacts. Being based in Chicago, there's a lot of Kellogg folk who are still here and who are active in the impact space, so they're easily accessible. We have one investor that came through the Kellogg network, so it's definitely been of value."

Participant 23 (F, Wharton): Reference 1: "Absolutely. Hands down. That's the most, I would say, significant help that I've received from Wharton." Reference 2: "So, for me, the thing, the training, the exposure that I got from Business School actually came from some alumni that I reached out to through our alumni network who I spoke with. I think one the great things about this program was that because there are so many alumni outside of the U.S. as well, giving that I was interested more in doing something for middle-income countries, I just got a wonderful opportunity to speak with a few folks that were already in these countries running social enterprises and sort of get an understanding of the ground level challenges that they were facing. That was really helpful."

Participant 29 (F, Chicago Booth): "Our first two investors, we met through Booth. One is an alum, and one connected to Booth alum, so that was huge. Like not only initial funding, but they were the very first investors, so they took on the most risk. There's actually a new group called the Chicago Booth Angels that does investing. I was able to go pitch to a group, the group alumni are doing due diligence on the company now, so we may get additional investors through that group. And other Booth alums have also just given us kind of like introductions to potential investors and potential partners. Me and [my cofounder] both have been asked to speak on panels like related to university events that have continued to kind of boost the public profile of the company. Yeah, I mean it's just helped us in a lot ways."

Participant 30 (M, Wharton): "Yeah, 100%, that was probably at least half the reason I went to Wharton… From advisors, to just introduction, to advice, to investors. I mean, all the above."

Participants who used the alumni networks did so for numerous different reasons, everything from gaining mentors, finding investors, recruiting staff, utilizing others as a sounding board for ideas, and even finding co-founders and board members. Numerous participants noted throughout their conversations that they felt that the social enterprise community was quite tight-knit as people were often working towards altruistic goals and that the alumni community specifically associated with social enterprise, although still

small, was very supportive of current students and other alumni.

Found the alumni network to be a helpful resource in designing and/or starting

their social venture, with some conditions.

Participant 2 (M, HBS): "I have spoken to many alums, but it's been inbound so

far. But I am positive though that out bound would be much easier coming from HBS to

deal with other HBS grads. They'd be willing to help. Like I would definitely be willing

to help an HBS student as well going forward."

Participant 22 (F, Wharton): "To some extent…some that I met when I was in

India and it wasn't social enterprise specific again, this was entrepreneurship specific or

they had their own companies and we talked about. And they might have a social bend to

it… So there is a social impact bend to it but it didn't start off that way necessarily."

Participant 24 (F, Kellogg): "It's more long-term, I would say, it's not like it's

directly resulted in funding or someone coming on board, but at the same time there are a

lot of well-wishers that hopefully will come handy once we launch."

Participant 25 (F, Wharton): "My co-founder is also from Wharton, and he found

me. We graduated at separate times. But he found me through the database, right? The

Wharton database. So I think that's helpful. He wasn't necessarily looking for social

entrepreneurs. He was just kind of looking for somebody who's doing something

interesting back in Southeast Asia… Where I am, Wharton and HBS are probably the two

sort of best networks to have when it comes to business schools. And that has been

incredibly useful, just in terms of all sorts of investor meet-ups and just getting to know people in our space, and just being able to recruit. So, I would say none of it is necessarily social impact or social entrepreneurship focused, it's just a general network."

Participant 34 (M, Wharton). "I have. So I think I did quite well. My only gripe was it took a long time."

Some other participants did find the alumni network helpful, but noted that it was helpful in ways not really related to social enterprise. They valued the network, especially at large school with strong brand names (HBS, Columbia, Wharton), but found that there were not a large number of alumni in the social enterprise space, especially if the participant was operating a social enterprise in a developing country. Those operating in developing countries did seem to realize that finding alumni in their areas would be harder since their MBA program was US-based. They noted that the greater alumni network of their school or university was helpful though, even if the alumni that they found were not purely aligned to social enterprise.

Did not utilize the alumni network at all.

Participant 3 (M, Columbia): "I'm just tired, man. Ha-ha [...]Yeah. Yeah. I should probably carve out time to kind of make those connections but so yeah I could find that a useful source, but they aren't effective right now. Pick up the phone type thing."

Participant 4 (M, UCLA): "In my ventures, it's probably too early stage for me to be reaching out talking to those type of people. I have however used networking opportunities on campus to position myself to do the right type of networking."

Participant 10 (M, NYU) (M, NYU): "Most of them are not in Colombia, even though there are a lot of Colombians that went to NYU, most stay in the U.S. for a while. It's like the standard practice."

Participant 14 (F, Chicago Booth): "I have not at all, not even one time talked to anybody at the school. I still have my website access from school and I do look at those and see if there's anything that's relevant, but that's about it… It hasn't been necessary, I think. It just hasn't been necessary, so I would not even think about doing it. I just have limited time."

Participant 19 (M, Wharton): "I just haven't utilized it. I haven't had the chance to utilize it properly. I think I actually might do that going forward, but it just didn't come up yet. Again, it could be because I'm in an overseas market, I feel like either the Wharton alumni base here is a lot smaller than, let's say, the East Coast or West Coast."

Participant 28 (F, MIT Sloan): "I tried and I didn't find a lot of success. So you know some of my professors and you know people I went to school with before or after and I haven't found it was really helpful. Again, it has been other networks that have been a lot more beneficial in my enterprise."

Participant 31 (F, HBS): "I didn't. I didn't. That's on the list… Yeah, in a way, it's so overwhelming to share and talk to all the people, but I never thought of myself as an entrepreneur so I was exploring how it to be entrepreneurial while also going to the MBA."

As noted in the initial statistics, a few individuals did not utilize the alumni network at all. Some cited a lack of time as they were focusing their efforts on other areas of growing their ventures. Several of these individuals did note that they plan to utilize the network going forward though, when they have more time to devote to that effort. Only two participants indicated that they tried to use the alumni network but did not find success. One of those participants [Participant 10] was in a small overseas market.

Utilizing access to mentors for assistance with the social venture.

30 of the 34 participants said that they gained access to mentors somehow through their time at business school. In simple Yes/No responses, overall, 20 indicated that they had gained access to direct mentors through their school and the other 10 indicated that they had utilized mentor access, but through a more indirect way during their MBA program. For many participants, access to mentors came through previously mentioned sources, such as BPCs, incubators/accelerators, or the alumni network. Some of these could be considered direct access too, so the responses of the participants are somewhat subjective as to how they classify the access re: direct vs indirect. In the end though, nearly all of the participants utilized mentors during their time at business school.

Utilized mentors.

Participant 1 (M, HBS): "Yes, and so we had got mentors through a number of different sources, whether it was referrals through the social enterprise initiative or the business plan competition or professors who were interested in what we were working on, there were a lot of mentors and advisors outside of the accelerator we went through. There were the formal mentors in that program, the staff members and things like that, but we also worked pretty hard to cultivate a broader group of advisors and mentors for us."

Participant 10 (M, NYU): "Stern mentorship really helped us out by guiding us through the process and I think that's necessary."

Participant 11 (M, Columbia): "An adjunct professor helped me through the business school in mentoring my enterprise. Couple of other professors helped me with specific aspects that I was struggling with that they were experts in."

Participant 12 (F, USC): "Then it's on the students to look online, to see all the mentors. There's Fellows who are students and then there's senior Fellows who are industry professionals. Then there's admin and academic Fellows…It's on us to reach out to them, but USC provided a place where we could see who they all were."

Participant 13 (F, Kellogg): "I think a couple of phone calls that people made on our behalf to potential investors. In one case, we used a professor as an advisor board member, which was very helpful. Somebody with particular expertise in an area that we thought we needed to show more strength in."

Participant 16 (M, Columbia): "I think, to a certain extent, professors. I think beyond professors, I didn't, but I also didn't do a huge job of seeking out specifically social-focused mentors."

Participant 17 (F, MIT Sloan): "Legatum tried to do with a more formal mentorship program… I just find that when your […] formal mentorship processes don't really work for me, I want to have a more organic relationship. But there are social enterprise mentors I find in the social enterprise space, because it's so new, most mentors are sixty year olds whereas I get into a lot more peer mentorship because those are people who are in similar companies more similar to mine. And so people who are maybe three years ahead of me are much more helpful than people who have had their whole career

working for Prudential in Boston and now wants to give back."

Participant 20 (F, Cornell): "I don't know that it was necessarily framed as that,

but they definitely had people come speak who were alumni, who had started their own

social ventures, so I guess in that sense. I don't know mentoring is a tough word, because

some people formally ask someone to be their mentor, right? I wouldn't say they ever sat

us down in a room and were like, "Here, pick your mentors," you know what I mean?"

Participant 24 (F, Kellogg): "It wasn't a structured program, but then through the

center there were a bunch of mentors, like the people who were running the program, or

the administration or the administration who were running the social impact department,

all of them were like super close mentors to our business school."

Participant 25 (F, Wharton): "Yes and no. I think there are people. Part of it is on

me as well, to identify them, right? […] And so I think it was more sort of your classic

kind of alumni, who feels invested in a particular idea, and just out of the generosity of

his time, he just decided to kind of mentor me. And so I probably could've done a better

job identifying those people."

Participants cited access to mentors, both obtained through formal networks and

through less-formal methods, as being helpful to their ventures. Direct access could have

been mentors assigned specifically to students in BPCs or accelerators/incubators, or

through formal mentorship programs that students had to apply to. Indirect access could

be professors or other advisors that agreed to assist students with ventures or business

plans. Overall, mentors spanned the diverse pool of people such as professors, alumni, outside speakers, executives in residence, or administrators. Mentors provided such

benefits as advice, access to investors, help with recruiting, and board service, among

other forms of assistance.

No real access to social enterprise mentors at their school.

Participant 2 (M, HBS): "But I didn't have any from HBS. That being said, if I

had sought one out I could've had one from HBS. Like the professors are generally very

helpful and most centers do have a faculty advisor that's generally from HBS."

Participant 4 (M, UCLA): "Not really. No. As a matter of fact, when I started to

do my [company], I had to beg a professor to be my advisor just to help me out. Nobody

wanted to take that on."

Participant 19 (M, Wharton): "Not really. Although I did see a couple of faces

that I felt, I wouldn't say inspired by, but felt were good examples that I wanted it to be

some that I relate."

Participant 22 (F, Wharton): "Not necessarily specific to social enterprise…

Again, the expertise level in social enterprise, I don't want to necessarily comment on."

Participant 28 (F, MIT Sloan): "Not really. No. As a matter of fact, when I started

to do my thesis, I had to beg a professor to be my advisor just to help me out. Nobody

wanted to take that on."

Participant 33 (M, HBS): "Yeah its funny our mentors are not in the social

enterprise space. I didn't really gain access to those kinds of mentors."

For those 6 participants who felt that they did not have access to mentors, they

appeared specifically to be referring to social enterprise mentors. This is tied to the subthemes espoused by some of the participants who felt that the judges in the BPCs and other staff and experts in the accelerators and incubators often lacked experience with social enterprises, since mentors are often present in all of these areas.

Most helpful components of the MBA program

The next sections will examine the underlying themes presented by participants on their thoughts on what they valued the most from their MBA experience. These themes were present throughout the interview but reiterated during the answer in the final summary questions asking about the most helpful aspects of their MBA experiences.

Gaining Knowledge, 'hard skills', and confidence.

Participant 3 (M, Columbia): Reference 1: "It kind of opened up the black box on kind of how financing entrepreneurial ventures really happened and kind of how to navigate a lot of those funky things, whether it's just you know very early-stage evaluation or thinking about how to evaluate opportunities and feeling comfortable with a term sheet. These are all things that when it actually came time to iron out the investment and to really get our seed investors across the lines, just being able to confidently walk through all those steps and really basically invent the capital structure of the company and sound confident while doing it, and modeling out the company. All those things were essential and I don't think I would've been as confident in doing it just from a banking, kind of a yeah my banking career where." Reference 2: "But that level of confidence is the kind of knowing that I have the training of an elite business school. And no one else in the room probably knows anything that I couldn't figure out or need to be intimidated by provides a lot confidence, provides me with a lot of confidence to pursue my vision and put together a cogent financial model/business plan and bring together the logical stakeholders, advocate for how the value proposition made sense for them to bring them together to star the business."

Participant 5 (M, Columbia): "In my case, for what I do, I got a lot of benefit from the more quantitative stuff… I knew very little about that, and even though you don't go very deep at business school, it was very, very important to me to give me enough confidence to manage the data scientists, as well."

Participant 8 (M, Chicago Booth): "So, I would say like the institutional knowledge of what has succeeded, and what has not was probably the most helpful part rather than saying "Oh, they really helped me to set up my legal structure," or something like that. I would say it was really just experience. Advice based, and the experience or the institution's experience."

Participant 10 (M, NYU): "Most helpful I would say, like I think the hard skills that I needed which are like I mentioned before, were I use them every day, stuff that I didn't know before school, that's on the positive side."

Participant 16 (M, Columbia): "Being able to talk the talk and walk the walk on a variety of fronts just makes me a more confident business leader."

Participant 23 (F, Wharton): "And, of course, you know, the confidence to take a plunge."

Participant 24 (F, Kellogg): "It did give me the credibility to have those conversations and build partnerships once I moved back."

Participant 29 (F, Chicago Booth): "Probably the number one thing is like it prepared me to talk to investors, so I gained some really specific skills that I didn't have

before the MBA, like how to build a financial model, as well as some softer but important

skills like how to do well in a pitch competition, or even just like in a meeting, how to

kind of speak in the language that is expected in those settings, and I think the kind of

overall strategy education that we got, a lot of it is it's relevant, so like sales and

marketing strategy, competition, even like product strategy."

Participant 33 (M, HBS): "I think the MBA program, I think the biggest value is

giving individuals the confidence that they can run a venture, because I don't think I

came in thinking that I was an entrepreneur per-say, and I think they give you enough

cases and examples and stories of other alumni to show yourself to say yourself, "Hmm,

maybe I could do this." So that confidence, and then also some of the skills around it are

helpful."

As noted in an earlier section of Theme 1, a motivation for a number of the

participants for attending business school was to obtain business and entrepreneurial

skills and knowledge around running a firm. The 10 participants above noted that these

were the main benefits of their educational experiences, as the MBA program gave

certain individuals credibility and the confidence, as well as the skills needed, to start and

run businesses and to interact with others in their community, such as investors and

employees.

Access to broader networks and dedicated resources.

Participant 1 (M, HBS): "The access to, as I mentioned, potential advisors,

potential mentors, potential investors and angel investors, utilizing the network and being able to be introduced to folks, was really, really helpful. I think it was some element of the book learning, some element of just the community and the knowledge sharing and then some element of the network were critical in getting off the ground. And I think the time, right? Being in business school and having the flexibility to invest where I thought it made sense was also very helpful."

Participant 4 (M, UCLA): "The best thing to do is just show up at these schools and then just utilize all the resources and all the time, and then actually do it. Instead of spending two years of learning it and then trying to do it later, cause then you're kind of two years behind, and you kind of miss the learning parts like, is this the right thing for me?"

Participant 7 (F, USC): "I think definitely the alumni network and just knowing who's trying to start a company that's similar. Who can I talk to that's in the industry or has anything related to it? I get that that comes out of having conversations with different people on campus."

Participant 13 (F, Kellogg): Reference 1: "Most helpful, finding the connections… I think particularly in the field of social entrepreneurship where you need for success to have people from all sorts of backgrounds, it's less likely to happen outside of the structure of a classroom." Reference 2: "Yeah, so that would I think is really helpful, the structure of classroom's content. Especially in those courses that generally do bring people from lots of different backgrounds. That was really helpful to starting the social enterprise. It was the reason that we started it."

Participant 16 (M, Columbia): "The networking, the opportunities to pitch, the continued mentorship I have there from people on the business boat are still interested in what we do even five years out, has all been tremendous. The resources since, whether it's in sense of the Tamer fund and loan assistance, and all of that goes a long way. I think holistically, from top to bottom, it has paid, both literal financial dividends and just tons of educational dividends, and helped sort of build up my personal skills as an entrepreneur and business leader."

Participant 23 (F, Wharton): "I definitely don't think I would have done this if I didn't have an MBA. And I think if there's one word that describes why it's useful, it is networks. I think for any social venture you need access to a lot important people who can help you make introductions, they can help you because it's very, very hard to grow in this domain in general and I would think that just Wharton helped me with access to the most amazing influential mentors and that really helped me."

Participant 25 (F, Wharton): "And I think finally, the network. Just having the access to the Wharton network in general has been incredibly useful. And I suspect that would be useful regardless of what kind of venture I build."

Participant 30 (M, Wharton): "Two things, it was the relationships and the network that you get out of it. Well actually three things I think so, the relationships and the network so, and they've already paid off like ten-folds. By the people, mentors, advisors, connections, those sort of things."

Participant 31 (F, HBS): "Now I feel like I have enough tools to try it and resources that I know I can tap into and an amazing network that I can reach out to and trying is possible so the outside is not as risky as I though in the beginning. If that makes

sense."

Participant 32 (M, HBS): Reference 1: "Access to people was also a major one in

the sense that, I found my co-founder in one of my classes and we then […] When we

wanted to learn how the US military finished a program for instance, we sat down with

the veteran network at the school and they walked us through how they managed the

process for their sales, in that case." Reference 2: "I realize that's not all socially

oriented but just the depth of the bench of people was super valuable. Then, access to the

professors that were doing research in the space. Access to other social entrepreneurs that

were trying to get their venture off the ground at the same time and are graduating and

would forgo other employment opportunities in hopes of working on these ventures

which are fraught with risk."

Some participants indicated initially that they hoped their MBA program would

provide them with a larger network in order to help build their social enterprises. At the

end of their programs, 10 of the participants did in fact cite these networks, and the

resources associated with these networks, as one of the most helpful aspect of the MBA

program. Programs provided, in a concentrated space and timeframe, access and

connections to mentors, advisors, investors, workspaces, alumni, funding streams, and

like-minded entrepreneurs, among other things.

Support from the Business School Community during and after the program.

11 participants indicated that the support that they received at various stages of

the degree program, and after graduation, were some of the most helpful aspects of attending the MBA. This could be seen as very closely aligned to, or possibly even part of, the subtheme above of "access to broader networks" as the business school community is both a network within itself, but the participants used specific language when referring to community or school staffs.

Dedicated and supportive program staff.

Participant 21 (F, Kellogg): "The staff that were dedicated to social entrepreneurship and impact investing. They're really committed. They seem themselves as being early in helping to build this space. They obviously see their role in helping. They want to see us succeed because they also want to have their story about the things that their students are doing. I thought they were very accessible and very motivated to help us when we reach out. They still are. I could reach out to any of those staff members now and they would help us."

Participant 24 (F, Kellogg): Reference 1: "Kellogg in that sense was really helpful in the terms of just the funding and the faculty and the administration was extremely receptive of the needs that social enterprise had." Reference 2: "I used the professor networks, so I wrote a case on my company with one of my professors, and he also gave me a pretty decent stipend to work on the company, now, and since the case, he's connected me to a bunch of universities who are now teaching the case in their business school programs."

Participant 31 (F, HBS): "One thing that I did see is that I had professors who were super supportive so I reached out to three professors, presented them the startup, made the pitch, they gave feedback on the pitch and to one of them I talked about the keen challenges we were facing super honestly, cause in a way I though he was not as invested in the company as a mentor or coach could be he was, in a way, an external person who was there to help me as a student so I felt more comfortable to share the bad things we were happening to and they were super helpful so I really appreciated the office hours with the professors."

Participant 33 (M, HBS): "This Field X course, the professor was very helpful and he brought in investors and entrepreneurs every week who led to really important relationships. So yeah, I would say faculty at Field X and I-Lab."

In a subtheme related to networks and support, 4 of the participants noted that the level of support and assistance provided by the university professors and staff from the social enterprise centers was extremely important. They helped to facilitate access to mentors, funding, networks, and outside assistance.

Support from a strong community of students.

Participant 4 (M, UCLA): "The community was really supportive… if you're at UCLA people are like, 'Totally. That makes total sense. Why would you not do that?'"

Participant 20 (F, Cornell): "Probably that it was a strong community of people who were committed to helping each other."

Participant 21 (F, Kellogg): "The community of students. It really played out the way I hoped. By picking a school that was known for having a strong social entrepreneurship program and impact investing program that I'd meet other students who wanted the same. And that was true. That was a main reason why I didn't pick another school where I could maybe get all those hard skills and just put my social environmental bent on it because I wasn't sure I'd get that community. And Kellogg definitely had that community. The relationships that I was able to build with other students who had similar interests was super valuable for us being, for one meeting my co-founders and being able to start the company, and then having other students want to help as well. The other student that we met who we're all really supportive of us, knew who we were, would reach out with resources that was a really valuable aspect of being in that program."

Participant 25 (F, Wharton): "I definitely think that being around other people who are making career switches to being an entrepreneur made me more open to taking on that risk myself. So again, this is more a function of kind of being around people who are exploring, or have already done something similar."

Participant 31 (F, HBS): "There's a cultural thing that I feel was just a very supportive environment and this culture that failure brings learning as well so you might have to be worked out in front of until you get the right one and even the failures will even be appreciated by the market in a way."

Participant 34 (M, Wharton): "So you know you end up getting all of the Wharton students who are interested in social enterprise seriously enough to invest their academic coursework in social enterprise in one room, right? [...] That was like the most valuable, was just meeting other people who were doing this and who had different perspectives and who could shape and mold and prevent you from having to learn lessons the hard way."

6 participants noted that the support that they received from their fellow students, at both the business school and greater university, was one of the most helpful aspects of the program. Students provided the participants with access to resources, feedback, and sometimes just moral support and encouragement. This is related to the analysis of a subtheme in Theme 2 that notes the closeness of the social enterprise community on campus and the abilities for students to help each other succeeded through collaborative efforts.

Support after graduation and staying closely 'plugged in'.

Participant 1 (M, HBS): "I will say, for me, I've stayed pretty closely plugged in with the HBS community for my first year out. We were given a semester as alumni in residence at the I-Lab after graduating. We have a professor on our board of advisors, and so I stayed pretty closely tied into the community and that's been extremely helpful for a first year entrepreneur to continue having that support and community has been really, really useful. I think HBS makes it possible through this alumni in residence program. I would be curious to know if other schools have a similar set up."

Participant 13 (F, Kellogg): "And we get together once a year and talk about real life social entrepreneurship issues that we're facing, and I think to have that support network has been really cool."

Participant 24 (F, Kellogg): "And even now I'm in touch with the administration I would say every few weeks, regarding opportunities, and contacts that they want me to speak with, who they think would be of use to my business. So, I think that way, they've been really nice."

In a subtheme that closely mirrors the access to networks mentioned above, 3 participants cited that the resources and networking opportunities offered to alumni are also highly important. These social entrepreneurs are still able to draw from their business school and greater university communities and networks for support and advice after graduation. These participant's comments also reinforce the notion that the social enterprise community is small but quite supportive of each other.

Case studies and real-life examples.

Participant 7 (F, USC): "[The class] had a bunch of different cases and different guest speakers that [the professor] was able to bring in that were really helpful just to give some real life examples. Some people who were on the ground doing it. Just very honest stories of what it takes to make it."

Participant 16 (M, Columbia): Reference 1: "Different cases and different guest speakers, a lot of people that have done it before and been there, and hearing from entrepreneurs how hard it is to get a business of the ground, what the real-world challenges are without making everything sound glamorous I think was a huge benefit, and then learning the fundamentals of early stage companies, I think, was as valuable as anything that was specifically social-focused." Reference 2: "What is great about Columbia was they bring in a lot of people the entrepreneurs that have come in to talk about what they did. I think a lot of people that didn't take advantage of those programs graduated, tried to start the business, and was surprised that it was really hard. And I think the MBA can be a funny bubble, and that people come in with a certain amount of hubris sometimes. But I think I listened very carefully when people talked about the low points and how hard it was going to be, and the value of being very judicious with your expenses in the early years, because there are good days and bad days."

Participant 18 (M, USC): "It was relevant because in that field you have guest speakers come in who started businesses or failed in their business and their stories, you kind of learn from their stories. Even though those speakers don't give you all of the gory details, that you need to learn, they kind of give us a gist of general kind of things to avoid or things to look out for or to keep in mind."

Participant 23 (F, Wharton): "The way the class is structured was that they would invite speakers which would talk about their experience and talk about their journey and just getting answers from those guys and hearing about the journey. So, more sort of like experiential learning, rather than theoretical constructs on around how you build business. So, that was something I thought was very cool."

Participant 31 (F, HBS): "So it was so good to have that example in a way because I think it prepared me to know that even if we try and it doesn't work, it will be okay in the end and now they have amazing careers and everything was fine."

Participant 32 (M, HBS): "Then, access to the professors that were doing research in the space. Access to other social entrepreneurs that were trying to get their venture off the ground at the same time and are graduating and would forgo other employment opportunities in hopes of working on these ventures which are fraught with risk."

Participant 33 (M, HBS): "This Field X course, the professor was very helpful and he brought in investors and entrepreneurs every week who led to really important relationships."

7 participants also cited, through different avenues such as classes, workshops, conferences and mentoring sessions, their appreciation of hearing from current and former social and traditional entrepreneurs about real life examples of building companies, or failing while trying to build companies. The participants valued the studies of actual business cases in order to offer more than a theoretical approach to social entrepreneurship. Students appreciated that they were able to hear about the actual difficulties and challenges faced by people who once were in similar situations.

Fundamentals of entrepreneurship.

Participant 1 (M, HBS): "I think the things that were most helpful were probably the fundamentals of entrepreneurship, so just understanding what it takes to start a company and what best practices are, just a lot of exposure to a world that I had never experienced before having been in consulting and then the nonprofit world. So I thought that the core entrepreneurship wheelhouse was very helpful."

Participant 3 (M, Columbia): "It kind of opened up the black box on kind of how financing entrepreneurial ventures really happened and kind of how to navigate a lot of those funky things, whether it's just you know very early stage evaluation or thinking about how to evaluate opportunities and feeling comfortable with a term sheet."

Participant 16 (M, Columbia): "And at the end of the day, I really believe that a social venture is an entrepreneurial venture, and if you're not learning how to get your business of the ground purely as a business, and you're focusing too much on [...] I will actually say that, I think one thing that served me well was not treating it like a social venture too much, because I don't know that [...] I mean, things like the Tamer grant have been fabulous, and the loan assistance program have been fabulous, but I don't know that any of those things made the difference between us being viable and not viable, but I think the entrepreneurial training did make a difference between us being viable and not viable."

Participant 25 (F, Wharton): Reference 1: "What was helpful to me was the traditional entrepreneurship classes… not specifically social enterprise, although there are elements that are applicable. I would say." Reference 2: "I think the entrepreneurship classes were useful, in terms of having a disciplined way of tackling a particular problem. And it's applicable to social enterprise as well. A lot of the principles are very similar. So those were useful."

As noted in earlier themes around program and class selection, certain participants hoped to gain a deeper understanding of the fundamentals of entrepreneurship concerning starting their own firms. In the broader survey, all of the participants took entrepreneurship classes and all noted that the training that they gained in their program was a helpful element of the MBA. Most of the participants viewed social enterprises as similar to traditional startups, so they needed to know the fundamentals of starting a company. From the feedback above, 4 participants attributed this entrepreneurship training and fundamentals obtained in business school as crucial to starting their ventures.

Funding and financial support.

Participant 17 (F, MIT Sloan): "The money that MIT puts behind all of their entrepreneurs, social or not, I think is the only reason [my venture] is a company today.

So, besides Legatum paying for 90% of my tuition over the last two years, they also have given me $15,000 to travel to Africa to work on my venture. The MIT sandbox fund has given me $20,000, the social service center gave me a little stipend last summer so that I could research my venture so I could get an internship. I are doing my venture because I have less student loans than I would without the Legatum center, as well as they gave me money so now I naturally go into investors with a product, with customers, with months of research in our market, and that's stuff if I was not at MIT, I would not have been able to pay for it."

Participant 22 (F, Wharton): "Probably the most helpful thing for me was the fact that I was able to raise money while at Wharton and use that whatever little it was to actually go out and put up deals and answer the questions that needed answer that I couldn't do while I was in school and had a million other things going on."

Participant 24 (F, Kellogg): "Kellogg in that sense was really helpful in the terms of just the funding and the faculty and the administration was extremely receptive of the needs that social enterprise had, so I remember that when I joined Kellogg, I didn't get any scholarship, but then on graduating, apart from the $70,000 social entrepreneurship award, they also created a loan assistance program for social enterprise to pay off their loans immediately after they graduate. And it was just $40,000 but it was still a substantial amount, considering that I was going back to India. And they did give that award to like six, seven people who were joining the non-profits. So I think that was pretty cool."

Funding and scholarship funds have already been highlighted as some of the key aspects valued by participants when evaluating the efficacy of BPCs, accelerators/incubators, and the social or traditional entrepreneurship resources. 3 participants below identified funding as the most helpful part of their MBA experience since the funding often allowed the participants to focus full-time on their enterprises, travel to developing countries where their enterprises operate, avoid leaving school with large amounts of student loan debt, and expand their fledgling social enterprises.

Theme 2 Integrating Conclusions.

Theme 2 examined participants' uses of the resources offered at their business schools and then asked the participants to evaluate the usefulness of these resources in relation to starting and running their social enterprises. The subthemes were designed to tie into the literature that identified several key areas of instruction and assistance to social entrepreneurs: specialized classes, BPCs, incubators/accelerators, and specialized centers of social enterprise and traditional entrepreneurship. Overall, all of the participants utilized a varying combination of the above resources in order to assist them in starting and/or growing their social enterprise. Participants often responded that they found multiple offerings in the MBA program to be highly valuable, citing the community of resources created by their schools to be the most valuable. This was one of the most interesting findings since it shows that a blend of resources and training are most valued by the participants in this study. Individually, under each of the specific categories of resources, a majority of participants who used the resource in question found the specific resources to be useful in some way with their social venture.

Of the 25 students who took social enterprise classes, most found some merit to them. Many found merit in learning fundamentals, such as foundations in impact and

entrepreneurship or detailed instructions on how to write a business plan. Some found

the secondary effects of these classes to be most helpful, such as access to professors,

mentors, or even co-founder students that they utilized when starting their ventures. This

is tied into the subtheme espoused by the participants who felt that an MBA education

would offer the best networks and access to experts that would be needed to start

ventures. Some participants had hoped to take more social enterprise classes, but could

not do so because of scheduling constraints, often because the offering of social

enterprise classes were not as robust as other classes, thus not giving as many

opportunities to take classes that they had to forego in a certain semester. Only a few did

not take any social enterprise classes at all, any some of those participants were some of

the earlier graduates amongst the participants and they noted that their school now has a

more developed offering of social enterprise classes. Some participants did not take

many social enterprise classes since they felt that they had a strong foundation in social

enterprise but lacked training in other areas, such as management, leadership, finance, or

entrepreneurship. They therefore devoted their class time to these subjects. This is

consistent with the findings earlier of the batch of participants who had social enterprise

experience and selected to go to business school in order to gain more 'hard' business or

entrepreneurial skills.

All of the participants took at least one traditional entrepreneurship elective

course, with many taking multiple different courses. Some of the participants cited these

courses as the most useful of all of their courses, and sometimes, of their business school experience, in preparing them to start and/or lead a social venture. This was evident in

some areas where the participants felt that their social enterprise was highly market-

focused but the social enterprise classes offered at their schools were skewed towards

more non-profit or NGO focused organizations. This is consistent with the research

presented in the literature review, and with many of the participants' desires to attend

business school, that for-profit social enterprises are closely linked to traditional

entrepreneurial ventures in the skills and competencies needed to run both. Few students

took CSR classes, as not as many schools offered them, and students felt that this topic

was more relevant to large corporations rather than startup enterprises. This is consistent

with the research presented in the literature review of how social enterprise evolved out

of large corporations' CSR campaigns.

One interesting finding, or possibly lack of finding, is that, despite all of the social

or sustainability leadership models presented in the literature review, there were few, if

any direct references by participants as to learning about these in classes. There was not

a question asked directly about leadership models, so these may have been covered in the

classes that offered a broader overview of social enterprise though. Also, as noted

before, a majority of the students came into their MBA programs with some knowledge

of social enterprise already, so they possibility had studied these leadership models in the

past and therefore put more emphasis on learning 'hard skill' associated with running a

social enterprise such as finance, operations, or business plan development.

Under the BPC theme, even more students [28] participated in BPCs than took

social enterprise classes [25]. 25 of the students who participated in BPCs found the experience to be helpful in some way, with many citing funding and access to mentors as the best characteristics. There was some varying thoughts on social enterprise specific BPCs amongst the participants though. Students who participated in BPCs under the social enterprise tracks often found that the specialized assistance geared to social enterprises was relevant and helpful to their ventures. This assistance included social enterprise-specific mentors and judges who could answer questions about pitfalls in that space. For the students who participated in traditional BPCs without social enterprise tracks, some expressed wishes that there was more assistance geared to social enterprises, specifically related to the mentors and judges mentioned above. This sentiment is tied to the research in the literature review that although social enterprises are similar to traditional enterprises, there are certain differences in structures and in measuring their total returns. Some of the participants, however, felt that participating in social enterprise track BPCs hampers the venture since, if a social enterprise is really viable, it can go head-to-head with a traditional venture and win. Some of the participants actually had social ventures that won traditional BPCs. This is consistent with the research presented in the literature review that for-profit social enterprises are closely linked to traditional entrepreneurial ventures in the skills and competencies needed for both to be successful in the markets.

Participants who valued BPCs mirrored some of the research presented earlier that cited BPCs as methods of providing funds and also developing entrepreneurial skills through experiential learning, interactions with mentors and peers, and independent analysis (Cooper & McGowan, 2008; Russell et. al 2008; Goodman, 2012; Thomas et. al, 2014).

In the incubator and accelerator theme, over one-half of the participants participated in their schools' incubator or accelerator program. Nearly all of those who participated found some benefit to this exercise. Of the participants who found the incubator or accelerator programs to be helpful, there were several themes, often consistent with the research presented earlier on the benefits of incubators/accelerators (Lall et. al, 2014). Funding was rated highly by many since ventures cannot survive with funding and students find it hard to live without a way to pay their own expenses. Resources provided by the programs such as workspace and office space was rated highly. In keeping with the underlying theme of the importance of networks, participants also highly valued access to mentors and other founders at the accelerators as it exposed the participants to diverse of ventures. For those who did not participate in an accelerator or incubator, a few key reasons stood out. Those with ventures in the developing world sometimes found the incubators and accelerators to be too US focused and/or did not allow for the founders to go back and work in the country where their venture was located. Some also found the incubator or accelerator too time consuming and therefore decided not to participate.

In the realm of Social Enterprise Centers as the business schools in question, most [28] of the participants utilized the resources of the centers. A good majority [24] of those participants did value the resources offered by these centers. As with the BPCs and incubators/accelerators, the access to funding was cited the most as being extremely helpful. Keeping with other themes, access to mentors, especially with social enterprise specific experience, was seen as beneficial. Networking was also valued highly as the centers often created a community of like-minded individuals who could share ideas and meet partners and co-founders. Many of the participants also utilized their school or universities' traditional entrepreneurship centers for resources. Many of these resources were similar to those offered by the social enterprise center, but participants who felt that social enterprises were similar to traditional startups often looked to utilize as many resources as they could. Some participants cited that the traditional entrepreneurship centers had more funding to distribute and a broader selection of mentors or networking events. For those who did not use either the social or traditional entrepreneurship center, most felt that their ventures were far enough along already and thus prioritized their time seeing other resources outside of school.

The findings on the use of social and traditional entrepreneurship centers tied back to the literature associated with the useful resources offered by these centers. As noted before, Finkle et al. (2012), found that entrepreneurship centers offer student entrepreneurs assistance in several different ways with their prospective ventures to include internal benefits such as internships, student clubs, internal venture capital funding, access to entrepreneurial faculty members, technology transfers among student entrepreneurs, mentoring from successful entrepreneurs, seminars/workshops, guest speakers, and access to external venture capital funds and/or grants/seed money. The schools with the highest degree of satisfaction by participants were found to be offering many, if not all, of these resources to their students, and often alumni.

A majority [26] of the participants stated that they have used, and continue to use, the alumni network of their business school and/or university, and only one of those individuals did not find the experience useful. Of those who did not yet use the alumni network, several stated that they planned to. For those who used the alumni network, the themes were related to many other the other findings, as they found that the alumni network offered access to mentors, funding, investors, employees for the ventures, other networking opportunities, and sometimes even co-founders for ventures. Some alumni did note though that although the alumni network was helpful in some ways, they wished to have more access to alumni with social enterprise experience. This was especially true for participants whose ventures were active in the developing world, as they felt that the US-centric business schools lacked, at times, social enterprise alumni in developing world countries.

For mentorship, 30 participants noted that they gained access to mentors through business school, about 2/3 through a formal process and 1/3 through seeking them out themselves informally. Those who valued mentors did so for areas identified earlier in the literature review such as transfer of entrepreneurial experiences through an iterative learning process (Jonassen & Rohrer-Murphy, 1999; Sullivan, 2000; Edward & Muir, 2005), the development of personal entrepreneurial skills (Gimmon, 2004), offering access to resources not otherwise available to the student (Atkinson, 2001), among other areas. Mentors provided such benefits as advice, access to investors, and board service, among other things. Similar to the alumni theme, most participants found the mentors to be helpful in the advice and access that they delivered. Also similar to the alumni network, certain participants indicated that they wished that there were more social enterprise specific mentors to help with problems and questions specific to running social enterprises.

In the culmination of Theme 2, participants were asked which aspects of the MBA program that they found to be most helpful. The answers to this question closely mirrored the subthemes associated with resource usefulness already present in Theme 2. Three major subthemes seemed to be present in the participants' answers on the most useful aspects of their MBA programs: 1. Learned knowledge and skills, 2. Networks, 3. Resources. All three of these findings are tied into the concept of a holistic model of providing social enterprise education, as the learned knowledge and skills came from both traditional classes as well as from the networks and resources offered to the participants at their schools. By analyzing the data collected for Research Question 1 on resources offered by MBA programs, it shows that 20 of the 26 top programs in the study claim to offer all of the observed resources to their prospective students: social enterprise electives and either school or university related social enterprise centers, BPCs, and incubators/accelerators.

Under knowledge and skills, some participants came into business school with social enterprise experience but lacked core business or entrepreneurial fundamentals, and some were conversely situated. Participants seemed to value the theories, concepts, and skills learned in the programs as crucial to starting and running holistic ventures that were sustainable both socially and economically.

In the realm of networks, participants indicated that they believed that business schools can bring together people, and provide access to others, in ways that many other

experiences or organizations can. Networks include access to professors, mentors, other

founders, like-minded students, industry experts, investors, alumni, support staff, and

other related individuals, all of whom could possibly provide assistance to a fledgling

social enterprise.

In the area of funding, participants stated the importance of receiving funding to

either start or grow their organization or to pay for school and/or living expenses so that

they could devote their full attention to their ventures. Participants found funding to start

and grow ventures through BPCs, networks or investors, or from grants from their

centers, among other sources they encountered at business school. Participants also

received grants for living expenses or tuition reimbursements or scholarships from

various outlets at their schools also.

**Theme 3: Thoughts on improving social enterprise training in MBA programs and
final reflections on the MBA experience**

How to improve social enterprise training in business school

The next sections will examine the underlying subthemes presented by

participants on their thoughts on what they felt could be changed in MBA programs to

better address the needs of social entrepreneurs. These themes were present throughout

the interview but were reiterated in the answers to the final summary questions asking

about what the respondents wish that they could improve about their MBA experiences.

As noted previously, the totals may be less than or greater than 34 based on if the

participants directly answered the questions and the responses that they gave. Not all responses indicated in the reference table below are represented in the quotes sections below.

Subtheme	References
3. Thoughts on Improving SE Training in MBA programs	34
3.1. Need for more specialized classes & teaching around SE	30
Case Studies.	2
Explain the social enterprise concept to a wider audience.	6
Fundraising.	3
Measuring Social Impact.	4
Miscellaneous topics.	6
Soft skills or management training for social enterprises.	6
Training on addressing legal issues associated with social enterprises.	3
3.2. Improving BPCs	23
Focus less on pitch and more on long term model to measure impact.	6
Have social enterprise track or separate social enterprise BPCs.	6
Miscellaneous topics.	2
Want judges with more social enterprise related backgrounds and/or from developing countries.	9
3.3. Improving incubators, accelerators related to SE	17
More contacts or resources for working in the developing world.	7

Subtheme	References
Specific track for, or at least more tailored assistance to, social enterprises.	10
3.8 Improving the resources and programs offered by social enterprise centers or the business school in general	34
Improving access to funding resources & financial assistance	12
Building and connecting a community network around social enterprise ventures	9
More efforts on promoting students to outside investors or for recruiting.	4
Providing access to mentors with similar experience of setting up social enterprise ventures.	6
Need for the POC or centralized approach or management to the SE resources	7
Focus more on experiential learning	3
3.11 Overall satisfaction of the MBA experience	34

Table 12: Theme 3 Subtheme reference counts

Need for more specialized classes and training around social enterprise.

Certain participants noted that they would have liked to see more classes on social enterprise, both in specialized areas and on the broad topic of social enterprise itself. Below is an analysis of some of the specific topics the participants felt were lacking or needed development.

Soft skills or management training for social enterprises.

Participant 3 (M, Columbia): "One thing that I'll say that I am shocked by is that I feel like after getting a degree in management, I don't know how to manage people. Like I've never been, like I've never had a class on like here is how to be a good manager. And then I got through nine years of being in a large corporation but if you're a finance person, you're just a hired, you're basically a cowboy. You know you go out and you get your deals and you tend to your portfolio and you can have your whole career without ever actually managing people."

Participant 5 (M, Columbia): Reference 1: "Doing things like recruiting and setting up an organization. When you get to different stages, how does the organization need to switch." Reference 2: "There's something related to human resources and compensation, which I think are quite different for non-profits, and would be an area where more guidance and help could be provided. How do you get the best talent when you don't have the ability to offer equity, and things like that?"

Participant 10 (M, NYU): "I think the soft skills that an entrepreneur needs are not really developed during an MBA. Just like, one of the things that I struggle every day is that balancing act between the thousand things an entrepreneur needs to do and still try to ride that rollercoaster of ups and downs in a good way and how to create a corporate culture in a startup people like knowing how to create that culture. All of those courses, the soft skill courses were more like, were designed for corporations I felt."

Participant 13 (F, Kellogg): "I guess what I'd be looking for now would be more of a deeper dive into what do the finances of an organization that isn't on the sort of trajectory to sort of like be bought out in two years? Like more what do different growth

trajectories look like from the financial management side of the firm, and kind of

understanding that."

Participant 14 (F, Chicago Booth): Reference 1: "I would have loved to see

something on working with non-profits or working with organizations, because a lot of

social enterprises work with markets like hospitals, like school districts, like foundations;

I think it's a different market and a different way to handle those kind of relationships. So

I would have loved to see something on partnerships, there, as well." Reference 2: "I

would have loved to see something specifically on building a social enterprise, in

particular. That would have been helpful."

Participant 22 (F, Wharton): "I think, something about how to do customer

interviews would have been really great. We just barely touched on it in our

entrepreneurship class and we were given tools to do surveys and tests and math stuff, but

maybe a product or process, like a product development course, a customer development

course that focused simply, on that one piece, sort of a social enterprise and the

customers, that maybe added a realm of what typically tie in to regular businesses."

Participant 23 (F, Wharton): "I feel that they do not have an understanding of

how of what they sustain in an organization that attracts the best talent, that solves the

biggest problems, while also creating segments that may not necessarily be able to pay a

high salary with their offerings. So, I think, a course, customized around tactical

information and hacks on around how you get from 0 to 1 in this context would be very

useful."

7 participants indicated that classes dealing with the specifics of addressing different management issues or hiring challenges or how to develop relationships with customers unique to social enterprises could be beneficial. Participants indicated that certain management practices in social enterprises, such as hiring and attracting top talent, can be different from traditional enterprises since many social enterprises, although still operated as a for-profit, may not be able to offer as high of pay, perks, or upside as pure-profit enterprises. This is consistent with subthemes seen throughout that identified subtle differences between social and traditional enterprises, such as requests for more specialized training in incubators/accelerators or more specialized mentors with experience running social enterprises.

Explain the social enterprise concept to a wider audience.

Participant 12 (F, USC): "I think it would have been more helpful to have this concept [social enterprise] mentioned, brought up, conveyed somewhere in all MBA classes because this is a term that people need to know especially if they're in business school…We know what a leverage buyout is, but not enough MBA students know what a social enterprise is, what a B Corp is. I think it would be really helpful for all students to understand that this model has a place in the world and maybe an even more important place right now at this time. That would be wonderful if all teachers when they were talking about different types of business if a social enterprise, a B Corp, a Double Bottom Line company, Triple Bottom Line Company; there's lots of names for what we're doing. If it was brought up and mentioned more often so that all MBA students could have had a better well-rounded understanding of what type of business it is and then how important it is."

Participant 17 (F, MIT Sloan): "I wish there were more conversation around what is a social enterprise actually, because you get such a spectrum. I'm very much of the school of thought that if it doesn't make me a dollar of profit, its social innovation not social enterprise. So I think being a social enterprise is a competitive layer on top of being a normal enterprise in that if you don't create a business model where your social impact is reinforcing your financial impact, then you're financial impact is reinforcing your social impact, and you have trade-offs then you're not going to be successful in the long term, you're not going to scale. You're going to run into the same traps that non-profits run into when they're trying to scale."

Participant 18 (M, USC): "I feel like even nowadays I'll say social enterprise or social entrepreneurship and people have no idea what I'm even talking about. I think just educating more people on it would be a benefit."

Participant 33 (M, HBS): "[The school] could still do more to get social venture taken really seriously among the student body. I think administration sees it as valuable, and especially for marketing purposes likes it, and because gain would be teaching the students that it's a worthy endeavor."

6 participants indicated that they would like to see more classes that explain social enterprise to the general business school population. The respondents felt that the concept of social enterprise is not fully understood outside of its small community and that educating a wider audience on social enterprise could be helpful. Some of the participant indicated in their conversations that they felt that many of business school

students did not truly understand what social enterprises were. Participants believed that if more people understand social enterprise, then it will be easier for social entrepreneurs to gain more traction in the greater business community. The fact that many students do not really understand what social enterprises are may be related to the earlier course curricula analysis that found that no schools required any social enterprise courses as mandatory core courses.

Measuring Social Impact.

Participant 13 (F, Kellogg): Reference 1: "My job focuses on evaluation and how do we measure our financial, social, and environmental impacts. And I feel like that's a pretty big gap for social entrepreneurs moving forward in the MBA curriculums. It's a huge gap. And maybe some schools offer that now. Kellogg didn't at the time. I still don't think that they really do. But all of this stuff around how to run evaluations and quantify that data, especially outside of a traditional like B2C like marketing world, I guess you could argue, 'Well, I could have taken that marketing data and class.' But I would also say that it's just so different."

Participant 25 (F, Wharton): "One thing that I would love to see more, and this was again a recurring theme later on, as an investor and now as a startup person, was how to measure impact, and how to communicate it. I think, to be honest, I'm not sure anyone has figured that out, so I don't know that it can be taught, per se. But I would've loved to cover that theme a little bit more, in a more systematic way. In a more, if you will, methodological and academic way... I wish there's a more unified way of addressing some of the issues, such as frameworks for measuring impact, for monitoring etc. A lot of that is trial and error. And I just wish that I had a better grasp of that."

Participant 28 (F, MIT Sloan): "Then within that class, for example, I would have loved to learn like how to put together a logic model, how to put together a social return on investment model. These are all things that I ended up doing after I graduated and that would have been great had I, you know, used the discipline of a class."

Participant 30 (M, Wharton): "I think going back to Wharton especially, they're known as the quant school, the finance school, so if you had some way of measuring a return on the social impact aspects of things and model out exactly how you are going to make that impact, I think would be a key component so that it's not just like, oh, you move it away from being subjective, feely goody type stuff to more objective, measurements with a plan on how you would accomplish your social impact goals if that's clear."

4 participants indicated that they would like to see more teaching around how to actually measure social impact, as they felt that the measures for doing so are often not that clear. From the earlier course curricula analysis of social enterprise course syllabi, as well as from conversations with the participants, there do not appear to be many frameworks for measuring impacts that are taught in business school classes. Measuring impacts can be important metrics that certain investors and outside stakeholders value in order to evaluate a company for success and/or investment possibilities (Jackson, 2013; Epstein & Yuthas, 2017; Epstein, 2018).

Fundraising.

Participant 10 (M, NYU): "I would've liked to understand better the social investment, social impact ecosystem. I think that I managed to do that on my own and I managed to do that once I came back to Colombia. Well I started to network, then I started to figure it out but it would've been great to get that from business school."

Participant 21 (F, Kellogg): "I think structuring capital raising and how those apply to social enterprise versus a more 'traditional' start-up would have been really valuable."

Participant 24 (F, Kellogg): "I would say a bit more on the fundraising aspect. There are no classes right now. At least at Kellogg, I didn't find. There was a bunch of stuff around PE's and DC's, but like for non-profits, there wasn't much in terms of how do you approach foundations and things like that. I think that would have been important and more stuff on launching start-ups in emerging markets and things like that."

Participant 25 (F, Wharton): "What is, I think missing, is actually support when it comes to fund raising. Because, if you're going to be raising money from a different type of investor, let's say impact investors, right? I don't think business school has done a great job, preparing you to have those conversations."

Participant 29 (F, Chicago Booth): "I wish there had been more about impact investing."

Participant 30 (M, Wharton): "I think there's like a lot of resources out there available to leverage if you're in social enterprise like government funding, grant funding, free money or resources out there and there's not really a class on how to effectively go after those."

In earlier subthemes, participants indicated that raising funds and capital for social enterprises could, at times, be different than for traditional start-ups. Although social enterprises can be for-profits, investors may not see as much upside in businesses constrained by delivering a social benefit, and therefore may be more reticent to invest capital. Participants felt that they sometimes needed to target specific types of impact investors who are focused on social impact. 6 participants indicated that classes dealing with the specifics of raising funds and seed money for social enterprises could be beneficial. Early stage funding is key to many of these enterprises, so a roadmap to obtaining these funds could be quite beneficial. This theme is, in a way, tied to the above subtheme concerning measuring social impact metrics, as some of the social impact-focused investors value impact metrics highly when assessing investment decisions.

Training on addressing legal issues associated with social enterprises.

Participant 5 (M, Columbia): Reference 1: "I guess the areas that I still feel were weak in general come to legal structures… the legal mechanics are quite important. I think that's a really tricky thing, and would appreciate a bit more help around that." Reference 2: "It's probably a very narrow segment, but the idea of hybrid models, and B Corps, and the next generation of social enterprises, that's an area where I would have liked to learn more about that. And particularly some of the nitty-gritty legalities of how you structure things."

Participant 21 (F, Kellogg): "I guess more legal services. We again took advantage of some of the entrepreneurship legal services, but I think with social

enterprise there's some sort of hybrid model, like we decided to launch an affiliated non-

profit to try and take advantage of different funding streams in this space. In terms of

capitalize your business, it's just different than your traditional company and so resources

on company structuring and legal probably would have been really helpful at that time."

Participant 24 (F, Kellogg): "So if they could at least be more considerate about

the legal structure, and not be so obsessed with the 501c3 status, then I think that would

have been useful for me."

3 participants indicated that classes or training dealing with the specifics of legal

structures and initial setup for social enterprises could be beneficial. Social enterprise

legal structures are often different from traditional enterprises (Defourny, & Borzaga,

2001; Galera & Borzaga, 2009; Smith, Gonin, & Besharov, 2013). Participants indicated

that while many traditional entrepreneurship classes addressed how to setup a traditional

startup, there was little info offered regarding the legal intricacies of setting up a social

enterprise. Some participants mentioned that they were able to receive assistance in this

process through other sources, such as social enterprise centers or mentors, but that

classes would have been helpful too on this topic.

Case Studies.

Participant 25 (F, Wharton): "I wish there were more classes where we looked at

case studies."

Participant 27 (M, MIT Sloan): "So a lot of social enterprises classes were, I felt,

a little too general. And they focused too much on - even though social issues are more pronounced in developing countries - but I felt that most of the material was related to the US or Western countries. So I felt, in terms of case content, they could do a much better job."

Participant 29 (F, Chicago Booth): "I really wish there had been like just a strategy class with cases and sort of like a more traditional MBA approach but specifically focused on double bottom line businesses. I feel like there may not be enough of a body of work available for professors to build on, but I always wanted the strategy component in addition to the application component."

A number of top business schools predominately use the case method, originated many years ago at HBS, to teach students. The case method utilizes real-world examples as teaching points through the use of problem-based learning to promote the development of analytical skills. Case-based learning promotes group discussion to solve complex problems (Merseth, 1991; Bonney, 2015). 3 participants expressed the opinion that there were not enough cases about social enterprise taught in business school.

Thoughts on improving BPCs for social enterprise ventures.

Participants who participated in BPCs offered their thoughts on better designing these competitions to further assist and promote social enterprises.

Want judges with more social enterprise related backgrounds and/or from developing countries.

Participant 6 (F, Chicago Booth): "I think if you bring more of an impact industrial level crowd into it [as judges], that probably changes a little, but we just haven't gotten any of the right in bringing in impact investors to the table."

Participant 9 (M, Chicago Booth):   "[Judging] is built out of the mindset of, 'How do you build a for-profit venture? What's your business model going to look like?'. And you do customer acquisition, all these kinds of things… To the extent that you are running a non-profit, which has fundamentally different considerations […] I don't think the material was suited to that, whatsoever."

Participant 15 (M, NYU): "Having advisors that have backgrounds in this… You can never do anything about that but having the most experienced possible, social impact investors or social entrepreneurs or people that at least understand the issues. I think the kind of the more experienced people, the better and lots of times you don't have that and so, the competitions of course, because most of the time they're getting these people who are volunteering their time, are getting kind of people that are not perfectly ideal for that."

Participant 16 (M, Columbia): "I think a lot of the judges really, in a lot of competitions, have no idea of the domains they speak of."

Participant 17 (F, MIT Sloan): "I think next year their going to better prepare their judges that you can treat Africans as consumers and not just beneficiaries."

Participant 24 (F, Kellogg): "The emerging markets thing, I would still say holds, because most of the judges or people that I've met or interacted with were, with no offense, like white people who had never even really seen Indian farmers before, so just convincing them on the context was tougher. So, just having people who are more connected with the geography or the sector, I think that would be a good mix to have."

Participant 27 (M, MIT Sloan): "I think they need to get more people from developing countries. A lot of people don't understand the problems that developing countries face, and because they can't understand the problem, they can't appreciate the solutions. So, a lot of things are taken for granted, and assumes that because the US is so advanced so logic- which would be probably less advanced or creative in a developing country. So I think they need a better understanding of social issues and the problems associated with social issues in developing countries. They have a fairly good idea, not a very good idea, fairly good idea there in the US. But the moment you move outside of the US, they have no clue."

Participant 32 (M, HBS): "A lot of it is quality of judges. It's tough because you want judges that -there's a couple different dimensions to it. In terms of their industry specific, like they're actually experts in the space but it is obviously really difficult to have judges that are experts in all the things that people are applying for. What I would say is, a lot of the judges work at philanthropies or they're on the investor side. I would say the people that I have gotten the most constructive feedback are ones that have actually built something from the ground up. In a for profit sense."

Participant 33 (M, HBS): "So bringing in more folks that aren't just VCs or angel investors looking for only for-profit businesses...would be helpful."

9 participants indicated that they felt that judges in BPCs with social enterprise backgrounds and/or experiences working in developing countries would be better suited to evaluate social enterprise pitches more than judges with traditional entrepreneurship experiences. Participants believed that judges with traditional interests and experiences with solely for-profit startups did not fully understand the social enterprise model and

therefore either would overlook or discount the social enterprises' business models are could not offer specific advice on how to better improve a social enterprise business model. Conversely, judges with experiences tailored mainly to non-profits could did not have the experiences with the unique issues that social enterprises face in the market compared to traditional non-profits or philanthropies. Also, participants indicate that most judges are from developed countries and do not truly understand the problems associated with the developing world and the issues associated with operating in the developing world or the benefits that social enterprises can provide to consumers in the developing world.

Have social enterprise track or separate social enterprise BPCs.

Participant 7 (F, USC) (F, USC): Reference 1: "I don't know if there's a different scoring system or something that makes it a little bit, the playing field is not exactly comparative. Some way that maybe they can take into account if it's a social, the impact of whatever your social ventures' delivering versus the revenue model. Something for that where there's maybe a switch if you're a social venture, so it's a little bit more specific." Reference 2: "It would be great if there was a specific social innovation competition from either the enterprise lab or the business school. So, maybe if they can further evolve what they're doing with their general business plan competition. So, yeah, just more monetary resources would be great, of course."

Participant 11 (M, Columbia): "Having a social enterprise track which I've seen in a few business plan competitions, definitely helps in each area. But other ways to either have, it depends on what the mission of that business plan competition is but every business should have an impact, is what I believe, so if you have impact as a focus one of the sort of criteria for judging the enterprises specificity encourages more enterprises to apply and get plenty out of it."

Participant 12 (F, USC): "I think when you're in school it would be nice if there were separate competitions for socially good mission-driven organizations and sort of anything goes."

Participant 21 (F, Kellogg): "There can still be a question of is this just a 'non-profity' thing or is this a 'warm and fuzzy' thing, so it's not actually a real business."

Participant 22 (F, Wharton): "Maybe having a separate competition itself would send the message that they care about social impact. It kind of felt like it was just its own little, like a side thing that they care about but not that much."

Participant 24 (F, Kellogg): Reference 1: "I think, at the end, it [BPCs] may be skewed for profits." Reference 2: "I think that's tricky with any business plan competition, but it doesn't focus too much on the social enterprise aspect, but it could be something that could be thought of it."

6 participants indicated that they believe BPCs should offer separate tracks specifically for social enterprises in order for these types of originations to gain more specialized assistance, funding, and mentoring. This theme is tied into the above theme regarding a need for judges and mentors with social impact experience. Similarly, this theme recognizes that social enterprises are different from traditional startups and thus tracks in which they compete against each other for prizes and resources may be a more level playing field. This is a somewhat of a divided theme though, as some participants

indicated in their conversations that they are happy to compete against traditional start-ups since they view their social enterprises no differently from other start-ups.

Focus less on initial pitch and more on a long-term model to measure impact. Participant 1 (M, HBS): "I think a lot of times the focus of output in any business plan competition is really about, it's like a 30-page business plan and some slides, and that's what you're judged on. So I think if there were a way to access the viability or think more about the actual impact that the idea could have once it's put into practice, I think that could be helpful, but I think that's just more of the nature of a business plan competition is you want students to spend time thinking about an idea they could create in the world, and so I think that's fine and good. I think it's more just potentially having a piece of it be around the feasibility of implementation and supporting that could be valuable."

Participant 7 (F, USC): "[The judges' feedback] was basically just a number system and then there was a little box for comments that some of the judges didn't even fill out. So, I think asking the judges, or requiring the judges to give some detailed feedback on the pitch would be the most helpful thing because that's really the reason I do it. Sure, the prize money would be great, but it's more important to understand if people agree with the plan or don't agree with the plan and what their feedback is. I think a little bit more feedback from the judges would be helpful."

Participant 10 (M, NYU): "I think that what's trending is like having a longer competition, like, it nine months… Some of them were send your pitch in and if you advance, then you come you do a ten-minute pitch and that's it. And we'll let you know if you win."

Participant 24 (F, Kellogg): "But it's just the stages of start-up, whether it is non-profit or for profit, I would say it's hard to compare someone who has had traction for a few years to someone who has done nothing. And how do you judge both those on the same aspect?"

Participant 27 (M, MIT Sloan): "I mean that's what differentiates a social enterprise from a commercial enterprise. Social impact. But a lot of people aren't aware of how do you go and measure that impact?"

Participant 29 (F, Chicago Booth): "The tension is like being good at pitching your business and being good at executing your business are not exactly the same thing, and so a lot of them, pretty much all of them at the end of day are pitch competitions. You win if you give the best pitch kind of regardless of what's actually going on in your business even though obviously, improving your business can help you build a better pitch.

Participant 30 (M, Wharton): "If you had some way of measuring a return on the social impact aspects of things and model out exactly how you are going to make that impact, I think would be a key component so that it's not just like, oh, you move it away from being subjective, feely goody type stuff to more objective, measurements with a plan on how you would accomplish your social impact goals if that's clear."

Participant 34 (M, Wharton): "So actually I think that they are, it's a one-time influx of cash, and I actually think that what would be really cool is if there were milestone awards for companies who one year later or six months later are making progress, or demonstrating significant traction and progress but who haven't, you know, gotten a million dollars in funding to sustain themselves."

7 participants felt that BPCs focused too much on just pitching the idea and not enough on developing the actual long-term plan for the business. They wanted to see more emphasis on, and more awards for, putting a long-term plan into practice for social enterprises since good pitches do not always make good businesses if there is no long-term plan for the business. They also wanted to see more feedback from the judges on their thoughts about the long-term viability of the business.

Thoughts on improving incubators and accelerators in relation to social enterprise

As noted in earlier sections, many of the participants did enter their ventures into the school incubators or accelerators, and most of those who did found at least some benefits from the experiences. Participants did note that incubators and accelerators could offer resources that better suit social enterprises. Examples of requested resources and changes are below.

Specific track for, or at least more tailored assistance to, social enterprises.

Participant 1 (M, HBS): "It would just be if there was ways to increase center of knowledge or best practices, right? I think social enterprise is just generally a pretty wide brush, so thinking about maybe within that umbrella of social enterprise, what are the best practices for ED tech versus environmental sustainability, versus workforce, and what are the best practices for nonprofits versus for profits. What things are common content that should be shared across all these different organizations, because they're all mission-aligned, and then what are the things that are actually relevant to each business model or to each subset of things? I think that would have been helpful, otherwise the question of what is social enterprise can be pretty high level"

Participant 6 (F, Chicago Booth): "They didn't have specific social impact programming… my suggestion would just be if you know that you're going to have a cohort of 10 businesses and four of them qualify as social enterprise, then your curriculum should be flexible enough to incorporate some of that for the businesses, because their needs are going to be different."

Participant 11 (M, Columbia): "In the program they struggled to accommodate my needs because they were different from most of the other startups there. I think that unfortunately/fortunately for social enterprises you need to have a separate incubator."

Participant 22 (F, Wharton): "I felt a little bit isolated. I felt like I was one of very few. I felt like I was one of very few people and interested in social impact and one of very few people trying to actually run a business… Some amount of support because there are so many resources if you want a consulting job or a finance job… And I kind of wanted that kind of incentive for entrepreneurship as well. And I thought much more about social entrepreneurship because there were so few people in it if any that I can think of right now."

Participant 23 (F, Wharton): "I think they could have different program for social enterprises, they behave differently and they have different challenges. Very, very different strategies need to be employed in terms of recruiting, in terms of growing, in terms of doing types. In terms of one reason as well, so I think it makes a lot of sense to have a separate track."

Participant 27 (M, MIT Sloan): "I mean, we did not have any resource relative to social enterprises, but overall I thought that the quality of resources was pretty good."

Participant 29 (F, Chicago Booth): Reference 1: "Reference 1: There was a lot of the focus was on investors, and we were not targeting the same kinds of investors as a lot of other people in the room. It just wasn't that helpful for us to hear from venture capitalists, so having [...] To the extent you're talking about fundraising, to have that de-segmented I think is really important." Reference 2: "A lot of the speakers and mentors were not super relevant to what we were working on."

Participant 30 (M, Wharton): "Going over what you actually want to accomplish, and then being able to come up with a plan on how to do that and then how to measure the effectiveness of that. And so going over either the practices on how to do that. Bringing in other successful social impact ventures to go over how they've down that, those things I don't think were made abundantly clear."

Participant 32 (M, HBS): "There was a few people, as an example, where they had relevant experience but it was like 15 years ago."

Participant 34 (M, Wharton): "For many of these social enterprises have some elements of consumer awareness as a critical component. You know, it's either, and so you know, putting out some level of soliciting the network for help would be super helpful."

In the interviews, a many of the participants noted that the accelerators/incubators that they participated in did not have specific categories for, or much assistance geared towards, social enterprises. 10 participants did comment that social enterprises do face

some different challenges than traditional enterprises and that it would be helpful to have

a dedicated social enterprise track, or at least, specific resources dedicated to addressing

these challenges. These resources include access to mentors or investors with social

enterprise backgrounds. This theme, like the theme of whether or not BPCs should offer

social enterprise tracks, is also somewhat divided, as some participants did note that, if a

social enterprise wants to be successful, it must be run like a traditional enterprise. These

individuals favored their social enterprises participating in incubators/accelerators

alongside traditional start-ups.

More contacts or resources for working in the developing world.

Participant 10 (M, NYU): "In some ways but it could've been way more helpful.

We had an issue like when we were in New York, like we were working from there, but

our business wasn't growing… so it was just like trying to work from afar. It was

challenging. It is still like they helped with the initial steps that we took towards coming

back to Colombia and setting up the business in itself, but it could've been a lot better."

Participant 11 (M, Columbia): "But the rest of the others who are essentially

working in maybe developing countries or are looking at different kinds of investors, I

think the needs are specific."

Participant 15 (M, NYU): "I built our own networking contacts and got into that

world. But I guess interest in general, just being as close as possible to the network and to

the movers and shakers and the people who are doing this work on a daily basis, is I think

best to be able to connect in entrepreneurs."

Participant 17 (F, MIT Sloan): "I haven't done any of that because when I have that much time off, I go to Africa and be in market. It's like it doesn't really work for me. Even though I know people get a lot of value out of the program."

Participant 24 (F, Kellogg): "So I did that for a quarter, but then I dropped out of there because again, my team was in India and my geography focus was India. For me, in that sense, the community itself wasn't - I was looking to get more people and it was hard to get people interested in an idea that's halfway across the world, while other people were so focused on the other side of the world."

Participant 27 (M, MIT Sloan): "They need to find more people who have appreciation of the issues faced in developing countries. And then they also need to think where they can support people in structuring social impact measurement, which is a big part of social enterprises."

Participant 31 (F, HBS): "Another thing that I think helped other people who are in social ventures is that many of them were not in the U.S., so maybe if they had partnerships in other places. So in our case we ended up deciding for Uganda and that made it very challenging and somehow they could have used that. Having international partners."

As noted in the demographics worksheet, 8 of the 34 participants have started ventures with headquarters based in the developing world, such as India, Colombia, Ghana, Indonesia, or Kenya. Similarly to themes present when discussing networking and alumni uses, most of those participants [7 total] whose ventures were based in the developing world sometimes found that the resources offered by the incubators and accelerators were not totally suited to ventures not based on the United States. These

participants noted that the networks are not that strong and it is harder to work out of the

United States when trying to build a venture that is geographically distant.   This is

related to the theme that BPCs sometimes lack assistance or expertise related to ventures

in the developing world.

Improving the resources and programs offered by social enterprise centers or the business school in general

This next section covers a broad set of resources and activities that the

participants requested in relation to social enterprises. While it probably be the most

logical course of action to coordinate these activities under a social enterprise center, the

changes could apply to the business school overall.

Improving access to funding resources and financial assistance.

Participant 1 (M, HBS): "I think potentially having access to a community of

funders. I think one of the things could be, if you're looking to keep your venture going

after school and actually sort of actualize it, I think that would have been helpful… I

think given the difficulty of starting a social enterprise business, and the challenges that

can be associated with raising capital, I think it could be very helpful to have that same

community around."

Participant 7 (F, USC): "Just more monetary resources would be great, of course."

Participant 8 (M, Chicago Booth) (M, Chicago Booth): "There's a lot of money

in the for-profit traditional entrepreneurship alumni network, city network and all of that.

I don't know if there's anyone that convinces them to pursue social entrepreneurship projects. I guess there needs to be someone whispering in their ear that social enterprises

are probably worthy of investment as well. I don't know how much of the money cross-

pollinates."

Participant 10 (M, NYU): "Think I would go back to getting business school

students in touch with the ecosystem. It feels like social enterprise is another, like,

another weird group of people that are not all connected to the tech bubble, like they all

hype around like tech startups and I see it like, there is a good opportunity to make a

profitable business, like the same interest should go into like, helping the students

connect and have access to funds and whoever is interested in the space."

Participant 15 (M, NYU): "I think the loan assistance program was crucial…

Create a program to be able to tell students if you're interested in doing this work, we

have resources to be able to make your financial situation easier, to make that decision."

Participant 21 (F, Kellogg): "Raising capital as a social enterprise can be so

different from raising capital as a traditional venture and I wish there had been more time

spent on that."

Participant 24 (F, Kellogg): "I guess financial support needs to be more,

especially for companies that are not fully non-profit or 501c, we don't have the tax

exemption yet, and that prohibits me from getting some of the loan assistance waivers

that the university offers. So if they could at least be more considerate about the legal

structure, and not be so obsessed with the 501c3 status, then I think that would have been

useful for me."

Participant 25 (F, Wharton): "Reference 1: "What is, I think missing, is actually support when it comes to fund raising. Because, if you're going to be raising money from a different type of investor, let's say impact investors, right? I don't think business school has done a great job, preparing you to have those conversations." Reference 2: "I've often wondered about what business schools could be doing more to support people who want to go into social enterprises. I mean, funding strikes me as one."

Participant 27 (M, MIT Sloan): "The second thing I strongly feel they need to do more in terms of helping social enterprises, access the social impact funding space. They do have a couple of people but I think they need to better develop that relationship between the social impact funds and potential end."

Participant 28 (F, MIT Sloan): "Another thing would have been like the tools needed to fundraise, you know based on social enterprise because there are not the same and I felt that for traditional non-profits and for profits, you know, the landscape was clear but not for hybrids and or benefit corporations."

Participant 30 (M, Wharton): "I think there's like a lot of resources out there available to leverage if you're in social enterprise like government funding, grant funding, free money or resources out there and there's not really a class on how to effectively go after those"

Participant 33 (M, HBS): "I think more money is always useful. Bringing in more folks from foundations that you fund. Social enterprises would be great. But those folks seem to be harder to reach, like if you ever tap into those kinds of funds. To bring in a few more and have a few more available would be awesome."

As was noted in previous analysis, students who received funding for their ventures and financial assistance while in their programs often cited this as one of the most beneficial resources during their programs. As the conversations with participants showed that not all social entrepreneur students received funding or financial assistance while in school, greater access to these resources was a central theme when participants were asked about improving the MBA experience for social entrepreneurs. 12 participants asked for business schools to facilitate access to more VC or angel investors as well as for more financial/tuition assistance or scholarships. Social entrepreneurs often realize that they are taking risks starting ventures that may not pay off, but numerous participants noted that financial aid or tuition assistance at least remove some level of risk from the experience since participants will not wind up deep in debt with school loans and self-funded start-up costs if their ventures do not succeed.

Building and connecting a community network around social enterprise ventures.

Participant 3 (M, Columbia): "Maybe more social events with other entrepreneurs throughout the ecosystem here. They do try to do that though and I think that might actually be on the students who don't show up to things rather than the administration itself. But a greater focus on connecting the entrepreneurs from day one would be interesting."

Participant 7 (F, USC): "I'm thinking if there was like a directory of social entrepreneurs somewhere... So think if there was something that I'd be able to navigate where to find it."

Participant 13 (F, Kellogg): "So much of the success of the social entrepreneurship community depends on the community overall that it's a part of. And I think it's hard for the professors to take the time to really kind of make all of the connections to that local community, and so a lot of it is on the students to do so…So there's just like a little bit of a difficult geographic divide there, and I think that could cause less interaction with the community than I would have liked."

Participant 15 (M, NYU): "But I guess interest in general, just being as close as possible to the network and to the movers and shakers and the people who are doing this work on a daily basis, is I think best to be able to connect in entrepreneurs."

Participant 19 (M, Wharton): "I think one possibility would be to build a forum of some sort that alumni engage in."

Participant 23 (F, Wharton): "One feedback I would have is that we can have more offline events for alumni from around the world. Because I feel like we got access to so many resources while we were at school but once you graduate, obviously, it's hard to stay in touch, it's hard to stay in the loop as well. So, I think we can have more engagement events."

Participant 24 (F, Kellogg): "You do miss out on a lot of things that you otherwise could have kind of tapped into, like even classes, and the core professors you could have learned from, just because your focus is different. If they could build that community beforehand, that would be useful. Other than me, there was like one other person in my class of 500 people who was focused on social entrepreneurship. So just building a community beforehand and keeping us in touch with other people who have done it before, I think that would be good."

Participant 25 (F, Wharton): "I actually think it's much more about the network. I think it's about potentially having, maybe even having sort of global modular courses, or some sort of externship model, where you get to meet other social ventures that perhaps have Wharton ties, or Penn ties."

Participant 34 (M, Wharton): "I also think that probably easy thing to do is just put all the founders and alumni and founders into one email LISTSERV, right so you know if there was a LISTSERV of everyone who participated or won one of these entrepreneurship contests, that would be a pretty cool thing to have access to."

9 Participants indicated that business schools could do a better job around creating a community or network of social entrepreneurs. This includes linking the MBA social entrepreneurs to the greater social enterprise community as well as providing more assets and events for MBA alumni to interact with this community. This theme is tied to the themes that support from alumni, faculty, mentors, and the greater business school communities are seen as highly beneficial to starting and growing a social enterprise.

Need for a Point-of-Contact or centralized approach for management of the social enterprise resources in business school and the greater university.

Participant 4 (M, UCLA): "Specific to social entrepreneurship I think you would probably need a head, or center, or a person to be the POC for social entrepreneurship to start with."

Participant 10 (M, NYU): "I felt like in a way you had a lot of resources but it was up to me to go to every single one of them and try to find them and use them. And what they could do a lot better and connect all the resources in either one central location or at least a virtual location where you can like find out where the right tools are for an entrepreneur. And that would've been very helpful instead of me having to go to every center or every person available for it, for business."

Participant 11 (M, Columbia): "Business school can be a lot of startup opportunities and it's sort of tough to navigate it unless you are 100% clear on what you want to do and I probably realized that two months into the program. The first two months I was like I'm going to try and get mentorship, I'm going to try and enter a network, I'm going to try and raise funding, I'm going to do everything and I'm going to go to classes and it wasn't working out. So I think helping social entrepreneurs maybe navigate that through guidance may be a good way to help them get more out of the program than just leaving it to what they do."

Participant 13 (F, Kellogg): "I think just making that, some of that stuff, a lot more digitally available would have been nice, instead of kind of having to prompt for it and ask for it."

Participant 15 (M, NYU): "I think the administration can and the schools can step in and to make it as easy as possible for these student groups to run affectively and have knowledge of management and systems in place to be able to access alumni and previously[...] alumni who are in good positions to do good work."

Participant 24 (F, Kellogg): "The other thing I would say is the whole connection with not for me as much, but for a lot of my classmates who were launching tech startups, and all of these ad base start-ups, they were desperate for technical co-founders, and just more technical people, but it was really hard for them to connect broader Northwestern community and then kind of get those people on board. So if Kellogg itself could be some work, to do matching or facilitating interactions, so co-workers, teammates, and even opportunities like Northwestern, where there's grant money or whatever money for non-profits or social enterprises. I think Kellogg is lacking in that sense. There's not a lot of interaction with the interaction with the broader university. So, yeah, that could definitely be worked on."

Participant 32 (M, HBS): "I guess my previous point was that it's really confusing, the I-Lab and the Rock Center are two very different things and have different resources there's so many deadlines and applications different faculties advisors. There's lots of what seem like, perceived resources and it can be really confusing to the student, which is the consumer of all of these things."

7 participants indicated that they felt all of the social enterprise resources were not tied together or make easily evident to the students. While this may sound like what a social enterprise center's mission, some of the participants still felt that all of the university's resources related to social enterprise were not adequately tied together. They advocated for a central person, office, or platform that would tie all of these resources together. Unsurprisingly, 5 of these 7 participants (4,10,13 15, and 24) attended schools where the initial research on resources available to social entrepreneurs found that their schools in question did not have formal social enterprise centers or institutes.

Providing access to mentors with similar experience of setting up social enterprise ventures.

Participant 2 (M, HBS): "They have permanent residence, so people come for office hours every week where you can go and meet people who have created their own businesses and it runs the gamut of industries and of entrepreneurs, of investors, of just experts in academia who you'd want to speak to. But, there really aren't too many who come from social enterprise and I don't know if that's because they don't invite them or if that's because there just aren't as many of them… I guess what I'm trying to say is if there could be more experts on the social enterprise side that we could speak one on one, that would be helpful."

Participant 5 (M, Columbia): "I guess the one thing that would be [helpful], at some point, is having mentors that have been through the experience of setting one up. That's a big part, mentorship."

Participant 6 (F, Chicago Booth): "I think it would be helpful to have at least some level of programming where people who were interesting in social impact businesses can go hear people with experience who have been successful talk about what they're doing and learn specific."

Participant 7 (F, USC): "If they made it a little bit more clear who the mentors are that are associated with the lab on campus, that would be helpful because somebody reached out to me that was like, oh, I heard about your idea, I'd love to help you. But, I have never seen a formal list of board members or anything like that in relation to the social enterprise lab."

Participant 17 (F, MIT Sloan): "The formal mentorship processes don't really work for me, I want to have a more organic relationship. But there are social enterprise mentors I find in the social enterprise space, because it's so new, most mentors are sixty year olds whereas I get into a lot more peer mentorship because those are people who are in similar companies more similar to mine. And so people who are maybe three years ahead of me are much more helpful than people who have had their whole career working for Prudential in Boston and now wants to give back."

Participant 18 (M, USC): "I would say if there was anything that they could do, I think that having more practitioners is kind of like okay how you could build it from this by doing like bootstrapping it and here's the methodology. You could try to seek financing, you could do it from that methodology but regardless, you're going to end up running into these questions and these problems in order to grow your business."

Participant 31 (F, HBS): "They do have coaches and I went to one, but it was not very helpful and it discouraged me from going again. I would love to talk to a coach who would help me understand: where should I go from now, I feel that the MBA opened so many doors that, in a way, we expect ourselves to save some time and I honestly have so many questions on where, for me, should I go, I would have absolutely loved to have had a coach where I could have very, very honest conversation to try to identify what better fits my skills, my passions, and where can I apply them to, you know?"

The literature review, as well as information presented previously in the interviews, showed that social entrepreneurs valued access to mentors. 6 participants indicated that they would like to see programs offer more access to mentors specifically with social enterprise backgrounds and experiences, since running a social enterprise can be different from running a traditional enterprise. This theme is tied to the theme of the importance of mentors to building a successful enterprise. It is also related to participants' wishes for judges and mentors in both BPCs and incubators/accelerators to have more specific social enterprise related experience, since social enterprises contain some nuances not found in traditional startups.

More efforts on promoting students to outside investors or for recruiting.

Participant 18 (M, USC): "I think one thing the business schools could do a little bit better is push out what students are doing. Like what their students are doing and try to connect them into the communities and try to give them that upper hand… I mean they're not really putting their students out there and saying oh hey look at what our students are doing and isn't this great? You actually try to hop on board with it. There isn't any of that."

Participant 25 (F, Wharton): "Another thing that I think could be incredibly useful from my standpoint as an entrepreneur, is some sort of a recruiting slash formalized internship programs, right? I'm always on lookout. I mean, I'm on the lookout literally right now, for summer interns, MBA interns to come and help us out. So is there a way to formalize that, as a way to also give exposure to some?"

Participant 31 (F, HBS): "I think if I would summarize just in general that there are even more resources that I can tap into and what I struggle with in a way was more personal things that's the one I would like to have more support on. I wish that we had access to more technical resources. There are many people in the area with these skills and they are looking for work. It would be good to have something that links the two together."

Participant 34 (M, Wharton): "I think that one of the challenging things, and again I think of like hurdles and rewards and incentives. One of the challenging things was just making people aware of my venture and given the fantastic network of alums and everything that Penn has access to, you know if you hit a certain milestone, they will email, you know we have a monthly newsletter, we'll feature you in the newsletter or whatever it is."

4 participants indicated that they wished that the schools would better market their social entrepreneurs outside of the university. This could include advocating for these entrepreneurs in the VC or investor community or promoting social enterprises during recruiting sessions in order to attract talent to these enterprises.

Focus more on experiential learning around building a social enterprise.

Participant 11 (M, Columbia): "I think everyone is too obsessed with raising funding and everything is about funding, fundraising, funding, fundraising and not about building an enterprise, the challenge is about building an enterprise where you get resources together, people together, how do you manage leadership challenges in a social enterprise? I think those things need more focus."

Participant 17 (F, MIT Sloan): "I think more, just more support on how you pitch an emerging market to an emerged market VC. If they organized some sort of day when those VCs would come in and give feedback on like, 'Oh, you don't understand this contact' or whatever, then I think that would be helpful."

Participant 23 (F, Wharton): "I would just say, they should focus on more experiential learning and organize more advanced events, organize more conferences, workshops, talk series. That would be really helpful... Around specific topics related to challenges that you face when building a social enterprise. And then getting folks together and then maybe putting in, like having a professor, having an alumni sort of do, sort of a brainstorming session, post the workshop, drive home the key take-aways."

3 participants noted that the schools should develop comprehensive experiential learning programs, not just simple classes, focused on building a social enterprise from the ground up. This includes classes, workshops, seminars, meetings with mentors, and other resources that students could take advantage of.

Overall satisfaction of the MBA experience

The final question of the interview asked the participants, overall, if they felt that the MBA program prepared them well for starting/leading a social venture. Below is a sample of the responses.

Participant 1 (M, HBS): "I don't think I could have done this without my experience in school."

Participant 2 (M, HBS): "I definitely think that it's prepared me way more so than I would've been, than I would've been just trying to start it without having a business school education…So I think it assisted me with planning and realizing I can't do this by myself, I need somebody who's an expert in this, I need somebody who's an expert in this, and the MBA by itself isn't enough, but the MBA is necessary along with other skills."

Participant 4 (M, UCLA): "Absolutely. It's hard to think of one specific thing, but more generally I feel that it rounded out my knowledge of business and how to run an organization."

Participant 10 (M, NYU): "Yeah, like there are other things that could've been better but overall I think it was worthwhile."

Participant 11 (M, Columbia): "It definitely was helpful, I think I would say that it showed alignment with my goals, I was able to spend a lot of time in personal leadership development and a lot of those courses helped me and I've been using those lessons everyday as right now, to go from startup mode, to a scaling-up mode."

Participant 13 (F, Kellogg): "I certainly wouldn't be doing this now without it, so I guess that's a resounding yes, of course."

Participant 16 (M, Columbia): "So, I found it 100% helpful… I think holistically, from top to bottom, it has paid, both literal financial dividends and just tons of educational dividends, and helped sort of build up my personal skills as an entrepreneur and business leader."

Participant 18 (M, USC): "I would still say yes. 100%. Like if I had to choose to do it over again would I do it over again? I would because, I feel like just the general business knowledge and some of the ideas that came from sitting in class or hearing other people's ideas or that generated in my own mind are well worth it and probably saved us from going out of business or helped us grow to where we are now. I would definitely do it over again. It would be nice if it was like a fraction of the cost but, that's just the name of the game for MBA school, so."

Participant 22 (F, Wharton): "I guess, it did the best it could[...]Did it prepare me? I don't know but I don't know if anything would have if I'm being honest. It's a weird, grueling emotionally challenging process and I honestly have no idea how one would design a curriculum to do that."

Participant 23 (F, Wharton): "Absolutely. I definitely don't think I would have done this if I didn't have an MBA."

Participant 24 (F, Kellogg): "Yes, I mean, decently well, I would say."

Participant 26 (M, Duke): "I think that's a yes and no answer. I would say no the MBA itself did not, the traditional parts of the MBA. A lot of coursework that I took is very relevant for large corporations and middle management and leadership roles, and much less geared toward the risk and practical skills of starting your own venture. But at the same time I would not have done this without having gone to business school because it did provide the alumni network, the access to connections to credibility, the mentorship from the social entrepreneurship specific staff and faculty. And so that niche part of business school was incredibly helpful. The rest of it was educational and informative, but not directly useful I would say."

Participant 28 (F, MIT Sloan): "I would say it was good in preparing me to be an entrepreneur and I think what's been really helpful is using a very strong business lens to solve social problems but they didn't help me in figuring out how to apply the business lens to social problems. So I just kind of got I think a very good and well-rounded business education."

Participant 30 (M, Wharton): "Everything I wanted to get out of it, I think I've done a good job in getting out of it in terms of the network, and the education and the just the validity piece of things."

Participant 34 (M, Wharton): "So I think that overall the MBA program, I would be hard pressed to think of a different, a better way to spend that year and a half on my venture that would have resulted in a better personal outcome for me. But I conceivably could have just quit my job and started a startup, but I would not have been comfortable with that level of risk and I would be a head case. And I would not have nearly the amount of resources that I had."

While the degree of enthusiasm varied among the answers, from 'I could not have done this without an MBA' to 'it did the best it could', all of the 34 participants indicated that they valued attending their MBA program in some way. None said that they regretted taking the degree and now wished that they had taken a different path. As noted in the subthemes above, different participants found different aspects of the MBA program to be valuable, but not one person stated that they wished that they had not undertaken the MBA in retrospect.

Theme 3 Integrating Conclusions.

Theme 3 addressed participants' views of what they saw as the deficiencies of their MBA educations as related to the particulars of founding and leading a social enterprise. The earlier conclusions for Theme 2 found that all of the participants valued their MBA education and felt that they are now better positioned to lead their ventures. This does not mean though that their experiences in business school were without room for improvement. Theme 3 looks to tie together the participants' suggestions in order to better improve on social enterprise curricula and resources in MBA programs. Theme 3 closely mirrors Theme 2 in structure as participants were asked about both the usefulness of certain resources at business school and then a way to improve these resources. Theme 2 highlighted the benefits achieved from the resources and Theme 3 aims to identify any further improvements that can be made to these same resources though.

Social enterprise classes were the first subtheme of Theme 3. In Theme 2, most participants indicated that they took some social enterprise classes, and most of those who took the classes found them helpful in some ways. From participants' viewpoints though, there still is amply room for improvement in class offerings and content though.

A recurring premise related to classes is that participants asked for more specialized training regarding social enterprise since there are some differences between social ventures and traditional entrepreneurial ones. One of these areas is in relation to 'soft skills'. Certain participants felt that social enterprises, although market focused, do differ in certain ways from traditional enterprises due to the socially-focused nature of the business model. Participants noted that the social nature of the business could attract different types of employees, investors, partners, and clients than a traditional enterprise would and that they wished to see more training on how to better manager and interact with these different types of people. In a similar vein, social enterprises also can differ from traditional enterprises in legal structure and organization. Participants also felt that training on this area was lacking in certain business school classes. Also related, social enterprises sometimes raise capital from different investors and sources than traditional startups. Participants asked for more training on how to interact with these types of individuals and entities.

Another premise related to classes is that social enterprise is not that well-known of a concept outside of a relatively small community. Participants asked for more classes and training in business school not for themselves, but for the 'normal' business school students so that these students would be more aware of the social enterprise concept and could integrate this into their thinking when addressing business decisions in their varied careers after business school. Participants also indicated that there were not many established and accepted frameworks on how to measure social impact. They felt that if social enterprises could better measure their exact impacts, then they would be better able to engage people outside of the social enterprise community, thus increasing the awareness and impact of social enterprise.

In the subtheme of BPCs, most participants noted in Theme 2 that BPCs were quite helpful to their ventures but that, in Theme 3, traditional BPCs still were lacking in some ways in regard to social enterprise. The main premise is that BPCs should offer some assistance and expertise related to social enterprise. This mainly encompasses experts related to social enterprise, including expertise in developing countries, such as the judges and mentors. Although a few participants felt strongly that social enterprises should be able to stand toe-to-toe with traditional enterprises in order to be successful, most participants felt that there were some uniqueness to social enterprises that required more-specialized resources than they were currently receiving in traditional BPCs.

In the subtheme of incubators and accelerators, the findings are quite similar to those of BPCs. The main premise too is that incubators and accelerators should offer some assistance and expertise related to social enterprise, especially regarding ventures addressing, and located in, the developing world.

The research in Theme 1 found that many business schools did have social enterprise centers that were fairly well-developed, but other schools did not have these centers, or if they did, these centers were in their early stages. The next subtheme, therefore, addressed how social enterprise centers, and business schools in general, can improve their social enterprise resources. Overall, for those schools without social enterprise centers that help combine all assets across the greater university, participants asked for this to happen, i.e. establish a centralized approach for the management of the social enterprise resources across the business school and greater university, in general. One recurring ask from participants is an increase in funding for social enterprises and social entrepreneurs. This was a common thread throughout conversations as research presented earlier in this paper found that funding, in the form of seed money to the startup or scholarship money to the student founders, is one of the most important and valued resources. In mirroring the findings in Theme 2 that a vibrant social enterprise community of like-minded and diverse resources in highly beneficial to founders, participants asked for those schools without these networks to build them out, and for those schools with networks to develop them further. Also similar to subthemes in BPCs and incubators/accelerators, participants asked for schools to provide access to mentors and alumni with specific experiences in social enterprise and the developing world. Similar to a suggestion for improvement of classes, some participants also asked for the social enterprise centers to better promote social enterprise to the greater student population in order to ingrain the concept of social enterprise into the larger business community.

Chapter 5: Conclusions

This study attempted to address a specific topic, evaluating the usefulness of social enterprise education at top-MBA programs, and then build on the findings to offer suggestions for improvement of this pedagogy. Below is a brief summary of a few key findings, in relation to the 3 research questions as related to the major identified themes and subthemes presented in the research.

Question 1

Which resources associated with prominent academic theories regarding training social entrepreneurs do the top-rated MBA programs in the United States offer to their students?

Content analysis of MBA programs found that business schools attempt to offer a combination of numerous resources during school and an ongoing support network both during the program and after graduation in order to make MBA programs attractive to many prospective social entrepreneurs. Findings presented in this paper show that the benefits of an MBA program include a centralized delivery of varied types of resources deemed by research be beneficial to starting and running a social enterprise. These resources include classroom instruction in both general business concepts as well as in both social and regular entrepreneurship theories, access to professors and mentors, participation in BPCs and/or incubators/accelerators, the presence of vibrant and diverse networks related to social and traditional entrepreneurship, and funding to start organizations or pay for tuition, among others. Prospective social entrepreneurs can take advantage of these resources while in business school, and sometimes even after graduation. All programs surveyed make their networks available to alumni to utilize in certain ways.

Findings for Question 1: Business School Curricula and Resource Content Analysis.

Area Identified in Research as Beneficial to Teaching Social Enterprise	Advertised Availability at the 26 MBA programs studied
Concentrations and Specializations	• 23 programs offer concentrations or 'majors' • 11 schools offer some specialized concentration in social enterprise
Classes	• All schools have required core course • 0 schools have any specific social enterprise course in the required core • 24 schools have at least one social enterprise elective, with numerous schools offering multiple social enterprise courses
Specialized Centers	• 15 business schools advertised some type of center or institute with a specific focus on social enterprise • 5 of the other schools without social enterprise centers indicated that their MBA programs work with a social enterprise center run by the greater university
Business Plan Competitions (BPC)	• 12 schools hosted their own BPCs • 9 claimed to offer some sort of assistance, category, or special prize for social ventures
Incubators/Accelerators	• 18 schools offered some sort of vehicle that met the definition of an incubator or accelerator

	• 4 of these indicated clearly that there is specific training or funding available for social enterprises
Mentors	• 30 participants gained access to mentors somehow through their time at business school • For many participants, access to mentors came through previously mentioned sources, such as BPCs, incubators/accelerators, or the alumni network

Table 13: Findings: Business School Curricula and Resource Content Analysis

Question 2

From the perspectives of selected MBA alumni and current students involved in

the creation and management of social enterprises, what is the relationship

between the resources that top-rated MBA programs in the United States offer

and the usefulness of these resources in reality?

There are different ways to learn the fundamental of social enterprise and to start

a social enterprise. This study does not claim that the MBA program is the best way to

do so, but from the findings presented in this paper, MBA programs appear to offer

certain benefits to prospective social entrepreneurs, as every participant in the study

found value in attending the program and none expressed regret of doing so instead of

taking another path to founding a social enterprise. Participants all found value in certain

resources offered by their programs, as presented in the findings section of Chapter 3.

Numerous participants stated that they do not envision having been able to have started or

280

grown their social venture without the training and resources provide by their MBA

program.

Nearly all of the participants felt that their schools' curricula and resources could

be improved though, mainly in ways that focused more on social enterprise instruction

and on resources available that specifically target social entrepreneurs.   While some

debate still exists, a majority of the academics in the literature review and the participants

in the study believe that social enterprise, although similar in some ways, is different

enough from traditional entrepreneurship that social entrepreneurs benefit from

specialized assets, resources, and training.   Hence, the schools that offered more social

enterprise-specific training and resources were often seen as more useful to the

participants.

Findings for Question 2: Theme 1 - Motivations and Program Selection.

Sub-theme	Participant Responses

Motivations for Obtaining and MBA	• 28 of the participants had started or planned to start a social enterprise prior to business school and felt that the MBA program would give them skills to start or grown their organization
	  ◦ Majority already had a started social enterprise or at least had the specific intention to start a social enterprise
	  ◦ Some had thoughts to a starting some type of an organization, but fully realized during the MBA program that they wanted to start a social enterprise

Expectations from an MBA that would aid in starting a social enterprise	• Obtain necessary skills and fundamentals associated with starting and running a business • Access to networks, relationships, resources, or mentors that they would not be able to get elsewhere • 2 years in business school would provide them with time, resources, and structure needed to start a successful enterprise • Provide credibility with investors, employees, and others in the industries in which they wished to operate • Believed business school was the best place to learn about entrepreneurship and innovation.
Reasons for picking their specific school	• Perceived impression of the Social Enterprise program/curriculum was a major deciding factor • Chosen based on overall reputation of the school (best MBA program they could get into) • Chosen primarily based on location

Table 14: Theme 1: Motivations and Program Selection

Findings for Question 2: Theme 2 - Most Helpful Components of the MBA.

Sub-theme	Details
Gaining Knowledge, 'hard skills', and confidence	• Gaining credibility and the confidence, as well as the skills needed, to start and run businesses and to interact with others in their community, such as investors and employees.
Access to broader networks and dedicated resources	• Programs provided, in a concentrated space and timeframe, access and connections to mentors, advisors, investors, workspaces, alumni, funding streams, and like-minded entrepreneurs, among other things
Support from the Business School Community	• Closely aligned to the subtheme above of "access to broader networks" as the business

during and after the program	school community is a larger network within itself
Case studies and real-life examples	• Participants cited, through different avenues such as classes, workshops, conferences and mentoring sessions, their appreciation of hearing from current and former social and traditional entrepreneurs about real life examples of building, or failing to build, companies
Fundamentals of entrepreneurship	• Entrepreneurship training and fundamentals obtained in business school as crucial to starting their ventures
Funding and financial support	• Allowed participants to focus full-time on their enterprises, travel to developing countries where their enterprises operate, avoid leaving school with large amounts of student loan debt, and expand their fledgling social enterprises

Table 15: Most Helpful Components of the MBA

Question 3

From the perspectives of selected MBA alumni and current students involved in the creation and management of social enterprises, what are ways MBA programs in the United States best train social entrepreneurs?

A noted above, social entrepreneurs can benefit from specialized assets, resources, and training that specifically address the nuances of starting and running social enterprises. Consequently, the more of these assets, training, and resources devoted to, and specialized on, social enterprise that a business school program can offer, the better. The better that business schools can build-out these resources, they better they can train their students to be successful social entrepreneurs.

Also, an MBA program does present some challenges to social entrepreneurs who decide to pursue the degree instead of simply starting their venture without it through attempting this through different means. The two most prohibitive limitations are cost and time commitment. For time commitment, students must take classes as well as work on their venture, instead of devoting their time solely to the venture, as in a full-time job. Most participants found the benefits provided by the classes and the other resources available only to MBA students as positives that generally outweigh this time commitment requirements. Cost, however, is something not entirely offset. Without financial assistance resources, students can be forced to pay, and often take out loans for, well over six-figures in tuition and living expenses. This is a main drawback of attempting an MBA while also trying to start a social enterprise on a shoestring budget. Participants who received substantial funding often noted that this was a major component of them being able to start their social enterprise. Substantial funding resources specifically for social enterprises was not a concept that was found to be present at a majority of the business schools attended by the participants. Funding, therefore, is one of the key areas that can be addressed by all schools in order to make the MBA experience even more beneficial to prospective social entrepreneurs.

Sub-theme	Participant Responses
Need for more specialized classes and training around social enterprise	• Soft skills or management training for social enterprises • Explain the social enterprise concept to a wider audience • Measuring Social Impact • Fundraising • Training on addressing legal issues associated with social enterprises • Case Studies on Social Enterprises
Improving BPCs for social enterprise ventures	• Want judges with more social enterprise related backgrounds and/or from developing countries • Have social enterprise track or separate social enterprise BPCs • Focus less on initial pitch and more on a long-term model to measure impact
Improving incubators and accelerators in relation to social enterprise	• Specific track for, or at least more tailored assistance to, social enterprises • More contacts or resources for working in the developing world
Improving the resources and programs offered by social enterprise centers or the business school in general	• Improving access to funding resources and financial assistance • Building and connecting a community network around social enterprise ventures • Need for a Point-of-Contact or centralized approach for management of the social enterprise resources in business school and the greater university • Providing access to mentors with similar experience of setting up social enterprise ventures • More efforts on promoting students to outside investors or for recruiting

	• Focus more on experiential learning around building a social enterprise
Overall satisfaction of the MBA experience	• While the degree of enthusiasm varied among the answers, from 'I could not have done this without an MBA' to 'it did the best it could', all of the 34 participants indicated that they valued attending their MBA program in some way • As noted in the subthemes above, different participants found different aspects of the MBA program to be valuable, but not one person stated that they wished that they had not undertaken the MBA in retrospect

Table 16: Thoughts on Improving Social Enterprise Training in MBA Programs

Overall Summary Conclusions

Drawing together the above conclusions, I believe that the research can be synthesized into three main findings.

1. The top business schools do appear to be increasing their offerings in relation to social enterprise training and resources as they see an increase in students interested in these topics.

2. The student social entrepreneurs who participated in this study appear to value the entire holistic social enterprise community offered by top business schools as the most important differentiator between what MBA programs offer versus

trying to learn social enterprise and found and/or grow a social enterprise in

another way.

3. Although social enterprises share many characteristics as traditional

enterprises, social enterprises do differ enough that social entrepreneurs value

and want more training specifically related to these challenges faced by social

enterprises.

Theoretical Contribution of this Research and Implications for Future Research

This research reviewed literature and identified and analyzed frameworks

associated with sustainable development, ESD, sustainability leadership, and social

entrepreneurship. The study attempted to identify if any top-ranked MBA programs are

integrating these frameworks into their curricula designed to train social entrepreneurs; it

ultimately found that many of the top-ranked programs are in-fact actively promoting

integrated social enterprise programs at their schools and that social entrepreneurs find

value in these programs. The research found that many of the social entrepreneurs found

the most value in the holistic nature of the social entrepreneurship ecosystem that offered

multiple types of resources and opportunities for students to gain hands-on experiences

that they can apply to founding and growing their social enterprises.

Research in Theme 1 of the study found 5 high-level critical resources that MBA

programs can offer for training social entrepreneurs: Classes, Specialized Centers, BPCs,

Incubators/Accelerators, and Mentors. The research also found that the more specialized

the above resources can address social enterprise concerns and issues, the better these

resources are often valued by the social entrepreneurs. Further research in this area could look deeper into the comments made by participants in Theme 3 relating to improving the critical areas mentioned above. Participants often gave very specific recommendations for improving certain resources, e.g. more classes on the legal structure of a social enterprise or the need to facilitate access to VC investors focused specifically on social enterprise. Any of these areas could be further examined to provide more concrete and actionable plans or frameworks.

This study could have benefited from the perspective of other stakeholders associated with social enterprise. This study's field research exclusively utilized the perspectives of social entrepreneurs to formulate recommendations. If I would have had more time, resources, and capacity, I would also have included the perspectives of others involved in the social enterprise field, such as business school faculty and administrators and also investors in social enterprises.

As noted earlier, not much literature exists about how to specially design a social enterprise program at business schools. Business schools are actually attempting to do this though, so speaking to individuals involved in this process would be helpful. Business school faculty and administrators likely could provide perspectives that students cannot not, such as the feasibility of actually integrating some of the suggested changes into curricula and the limits of what a school can actually offer. Investors could provide perspectives on the strengths and weakness that they see in recent social enterprise MBAs who pitched ideas to them. These perspectives could be used to further alter curricula in order to account for these observations. Further research could cross-reference the perspectives of these stakeholders against the findings of the participants in this study.

Further research could also look as whether the recommendations of the study are applicable to less prestigious and/or less wealthy MBA programs. The research drew from a relatively homogenous pool of schools to gather participants. These schools were the ones both empirically and anecdotally ranked near the top (Wharton, Columbia, Harvard, MIT, etc.). The research was designed to only look at the top schools, and schools with a disproportionate contribution of participants seem to offer the most resources to social entrepreneurs; therefore successful social entrepreneurs were easy to identify at these schools. In this way, the uniformity of the sample may be beneficial, since the study was to look at best practices. However, all of the business schools in the study were in the list of the wealthiest schools in the US, and the business schools with the most participants all ranked in the top-ten in endowment size and endowment per student (Bonsoms, 2016). This raises the question of how much does the overall reputation of the business school and its wealth contribute to a school's ability to build a successful social enterprise program. Could schools with less money and less prestige to draw students, faculty, and mentors to a smaller, more remote campus still succeed? One might argue that this is true for any subject taught in business schools though; that the more prestigious schools have better abilities to start and grow any disciple as a result of their superior financial resources and prestige associated with their names, rankings, and histories. Could a relatively small and remote business school develop a regular finance program that rivals those offered by schools like Columbia or NYU in a financial center such as New York City, or with the long-standing prestige and research power as Wharton or Booth? Further research could examine the actual feasibility of replicating a successful social enterprise program at business schools without the money and prestige associated with the schools in the study.

Final Summary

The research examined the state of social entrepreneurship curricula at leading business school MBA programs in the United States and seeks to contribute to understandings of how sustainable development and entrepreneurial curriculum can be best integrated to enhance the training of social entrepreneurs. The research shows that theories that incorporate sustainable development principles into basic business and entrepreneurial theory do exist and that top-MBA programs are actively working to build curricula and offer resources to their students who aspire to become social entrepreneurs. Most of the social entrepreneurs interviewed for this study initially felt that business school was the best way to achieve their goals of starting or growing a social enterprise and thus chose the MBA path instead of another route to achieve their goals. All of the social entrepreneurs in this study indicated that they valued the skills learned and resources offered to them during their MBA program, with no participant regretting their decision to attend an MBA program instead of taking an alternative path into social entrepreneurship.

The study's findings synthesize and advance research around social enterprise education in business schools. It shows that certain schools have assisted in creating active social entrepreneurs by offering a holistic mix of specific resources and it offers suggestions on further improving these resources to even better suit the niche needs of social entrepreneurs. Further research should be conducted to examine the resources areas more deeply and provide more detailed recommendations for their improvements.

Further research could also incorporate the perspectives of other social enterprise

stakeholders in order to confirm the findings of this study and to increase the list of

attributes and resources necessary to create a successful social entrepreneur.